Conflict at Plevna

Conflict at Plevna
Two Accounts of the Russo-Turkish War
of 1877-78

Under The Red Crescent
Charles Ryan and John Sandes

The Third Battle of Plevna
William V. Herbert

Conflict at Plevna
Two Accounts of the Russo-Turkish War of 1877-78
Under the Red Crescent
by Charles Ryan and John Sandes
The Third Battle of Plevna
by William V. Herbert

FIRST EDITION

First published under the titles
Under the Red Crescent
and
The Third Battle of Plevna

Leonaur is an imprint of Oakpast Ltd
Copyright in this form © 2013 Oakpast Ltd

ISBN: 978-1-78282-138-0 (hardcover)
ISBN: 978-1-78282-139-7 (softcover)

http://www.leonaur.com

Publisher's Notes

The views expressed in this book are not necessarily those of the publisher.

Contents

Preface	9
From Melbourne to Sofia	11
The Preliminaries to the Russo-Turkish War	28
The Imminence of War	41
From Widdin to Plevna	58
The First Battle of Plevna	72
The Interval Between the First and Second Battles	89
The Second Battle of Plevna (July 30)	99
The Fiascos of Pelischat and Lovtcha	114
The Third Battle of Plevna	130
The Investment of Plevna	146
The Horrors of the Hospital	162
From Constantinople to Erzeroum	176
A Beleaguered City	190
The Surrender of Erzeroum	207
The End of the War	223
Conclusion	237
The Third Battle of Plevna	243

DEDICATION

This record of
The stirring adventures of my early years
I dedicate to my son Rupert.

C. S. R.

Preface

In submitting to the popular verdict this book, which aims at being a plain, straightforward account of the experiences of a young Australian in the last great battles which have been fought in Europe, I feel that a few words of explanation are necessary.

In the first place, it may be asked why I have allowed twenty years to elapse before giving these reminiscences to the world. I must answer that, as a hard-working surgeon leading a very busy life, I had but little "learned leisure" at my disposal; and I must also admit that I did not feel myself equal to the literary labour of writing a book. Indeed it might never have been written if my friend Mr. Sandes had not agreed to my suggestion that he should reproduce in a literary and publishable form the language of the armchair and the fireside, and so enable me to relate to the world at large some of the incidents which my own immediate friends, when listening over the cigars to my recollections, have been good enough to call interesting. So much for the matter of the book, and also for its manner.

In the second place, military critics as well as the general public may be inclined to wonder how it was that a young army surgeon, a mere lad in fact, should have been allowed to play such an independent part in the field operations at Plevna as is disclosed in the following pages, and should have been permitted to move about the battlefield and engage in active service, with the apparent concurrence of the general staff and of the officers commanding the different regiments. In reply, I have to explain that the Ottoman Army was not guided by the hard-and-fast regulations which no doubt would render it impossible for a junior surgeon in any other European army to act on his own volition and carry on his work as he might think best himself.

Furthermore, I may mention that through my close friendship with Prince Czetwertinski, who was the captain of Osman Pasha's bodyguard, I was always kept in touch with the progress of the military operations; and I am also proud to say that I enjoyed the confidence of Osman Pasha himself, and was on terms of the closest intimacy with that gallant and true-hearted soldier Tewfik Bey, who won the rank of *pasha* for his magnificent courage when he led the assault that drove Skobeleff from the Krishin redoubts.

These facts may explain many of the adventures narrated in this book which would be inexplicable to critics accustomed to the rigid discipline under which medical officers do their work in other European armies.

It is only right to say, in conclusion, that I consider myself singularly fortunate in my coadjutor, who, while he has brightened this narrative of my early adventures with all the resources of the practised writer, has nevertheless left the truth of every single incident absolutely unimpaired. At a time when the Eastern Question looms like a huge shadow over Europe, and when the very existence of the Turkish Empire is once more threatened, may I hope that this story of the military virtues of the Ottoman troops may not be found without real interest?

Charles S. Ryan.

Melbourne, *July*, 1897.

CHAPTER 1

From Melbourne to Sofia

People have often asked me how it was that I, an Australian, came to take a part in the defence of the Ottoman Empire, and to serve as a military surgeon under the Red Crescent, which, as everyone knows, is the Turkish equivalent of the Red Cross of the Geneva Convention. Red Cross and Red Crescent are alike the symbols of a humanitarian spirit, in which philosophers and students of ethics profess to see the small beginnings of a future age of universal peace; but as for me, I have seen how Cossacks and Circassians fight, and I cannot help regarding the future prophesied by the philosopher as an impossible dream. When one has seen a soldier of a civilized force sawing off the head of a wounded but still living enemy with the edge of his sword-bayonet, it requires an unusually optimistic nature to believe in the abolition of war and a perpetual comity of nations.

It was as the outcome of my *Wanderjahr*—the sweet old German custom which sends every young man roaming when he has completed the technical training of his future avocation—that I first smelt powder and saw the glint of the Russian bayonets. The *Wanderjahr* of the German seems to be an unconscious survival of the nomadic instinct of primitive man—a small concession, as it were, to the roving habits that took his ancestors the Huns and Visigoths to Rome. It lets a young man escape from the fixed atmosphere of "staying point," as our American friends call it in one locality, into the "*largior æther*," the wider life of travel. And here I must be excused for introducing a little bit of necessary autobiography.

I must record that, after spending three years at the Melbourne University, I went to Edinburgh to finish my medical course; and having taken my degree there, I was launched at the age of one and twenty, as an expressive colloquialism puts it, "*on my own hook.*" Thus it was that I began a period of wandering over Europe which ultimately landed me in my ambulance at Plevna in July, 1877. I need not dwell upon those early travels, except to say that the allowance which my father made me enabled me to go far and to see much. Like Odysseus of old, I could say that "many were the men whose manners I saw and whose cities I knew."

After a run round Norway and Sweden, I spent a few months in Bohemian Paris, and then went on to Bonn, where I attended the clinic of Professor Busch, and indulged in all sorts of romantic visions under the shadow of the castled crag of Drachenfels and the Sieben Gebirge. Next I made my way down to Vienna, where the sight of some Servians in their national costume gave me my first glimpse into the romance of the proud and chivalrous peoples of the Balkan States, and fired me with a desire to see Constantinople itself. During those months at Vienna I knew my "*Schöne Blaue Donau*" well, and often made excursions as far as Pressburg and Buda-Pesth, looking forward to the day when I could get an opportunity to follow the great waterway down to Rustchuk, and so into Turkish territory. But for the time being I got no chance, and travelled instead through Styria and Bavaria, finally turning southward, and finishing in Rome.

It was about this time that I met a Spanish surgeon, Senhor Garcia C——, who was connected incidentally with the events immediately leading up to my appointment as a surgeon to the Turkish troops. He was a delightful companion, but improvident in money matters; and I hope he will pardon me after this lapse of years for disclosing the fact that he made me his banker, inasmuch as it reduced me to such a low financial ebb that, had it not been for his gold watch, I am afraid I should never have seen the inside of the Grivitza redoubt. I remember that he and I put up when at Rome in a very fashionable and exclusive "pension," to which I had been introduced by a French count whom I met in Paris. I was always regarded, perhaps on account of my name, as a good Roman Catholic; and but for an unfortunate little contretemps I might have married into a princely Italian family there and then, and never had to eat dead horse on a campaign at all.

It was this way. Among the other residents in the "pension" was an old Italian marchioness, who had brought her two daughters to Rome to introduce them to his Holiness the Pope. She was kind enough to take a great interest in me; and there is no knowing what might have happened—the elder daughter was really a charming girl—if it had not been for that unlucky incident of the mutton chops. On the second Friday that I was there an elderly Scotch lady, who was a rigid Presbyterian, and took no trouble to conceal the aversion with which she regarded all Papists, ordered mutton chops in the middle of the day for her lunch. When I came in from a visit to the Vatican I was very hungry. The chops were brought in, and they smelt very good; so, as the Scotch lady was late, I forgot the consideration due to age and rigid Presbyterianism, I forgot my scruples as a supposed good Catholic, I forgot that it was Friday—and I ate them.

Next day the *marchioness* stuck me up in a corner, and asked me how I could disgrace myself by eating grilled chops on a Friday; she led me to understand that I had deceived her, and she withdrew an invitation which she had given me to visit her and renew my acquaintance with her charming daughter. Thus ended my first and last chance of a dukedom.

After a few weeks in Rome, I began to get seriously embarrassed from a financial point of view. Garcia was a charming fellow; but he was a poet, and, like all poets, he had expensive habits. He even challenged me to a duel once for laughing at some of his verses; but when I threatened to kick him, he fell on my neck and embraced me. However, my purse was not long enough to sustain the two of us, and I was sitting in a little *café* one day considering the position and glancing idly over the *Times*, when my eye fell on an advertisement announcing that the Turkish Government had vacancies for twenty military surgeons, and inviting applications. I read the advertisement again with delight, and at once determined to send in an application. Here was a chance of seeing life with a vengeance.

But my spirits fell at once. I had only a few *liras* in my pocket; and how on earth was I to get to the Turkish Embassy in London? C—— was in his usual poetic condition of impecuniosity, and I was afraid to think how much he owed me. But I could not afford to be chivalrous, or I might lose the opportunity of a lifetime; so I tackled him at once. He assured me with tears in his eyes that he had not even the price of a flask of *Chianti* in his pockets; but I was inexorable. I pointed out to him that he had a very fine gold watch,—it was really a remarkably valuable timepiece, and had come down to him as an heirloom from some haughty old Castilian *grandee*. I impressed upon him that a gold watch is a most unsuitable adornment to a penniless person, who is moreover in debt, and I indicated to him a means by which it could be converted into currency of the realm.

I think he felt it very much, poor fellow; but it was not a time for being over-scrupulous, and the heirloom of the Hidalgo of old Castile was duly deposited with the Roman equivalent for "my uncle" in a small and stuffy establishment situated in a narrow street with the suggestive name of the Via del Poppo. In return we received twenty-five *napoleons*—it was certainly an extremely handsome watch. Garcia gave me enough to take me to Neuchâtel, where I counted on receiving fresh supplies, and I let him keep the balance. So I left my Spaniard with a flask of wine before him in the city of the Cæsars, and I never saw him again. Peace be to his soul! He was intended by nature for an Irishman.

I wanted to go through to Neuchâtel; but when I got to Turin, there was a fresh difficulty to be overcome. The Po had overflowed its banks, and the railway was washed away, so that there was no possibility of continuing the journey until next morning. I had not enough money to go to a hotel, so I walked about the streets of Turin all night. Shakespeare has something to say about people who

wallow naked in December snow
By thinking on fantastic summer's heat.

And as I wandered through the cold, dark streets of Turin, I warmed myself by imagination in the sunbeams that played on the gilded pinnacles of the Seraglio and the marble towers of St. Sophia in far away Stamboul.

At Neuchâtel I found supplies awaiting me at the post office, and I hurried across to London at once, where I sought out the late Mr. J. E. Francis, of Melbourne, who was an old friend of my father, and asked his advice about going to Constantinople. "Go by all means, my dear boy," was his cheery reply; "and I will tell your father that I advised you to take the chance." I had excellent credentials from my professors in Edinburgh; and armed with a letter of introduction to Dr. Forbes, who was the doctor to the Turkish Embassy, I presented myself at the embassy, and sought an interview with Musurus Pasha, then the Turkish ambassador in London. The ambassador was engaged; but I had an audience with one of his sons, and two days afterwards I was *en route* for Constantinople, with £25 for expenses in my pocket, and an agreement with the Turkish Government to perform the duties of a military surgeon at a salary of £200 a year, paid monthly in gold.

They gave me a letter to the Seraskierat, or War Office, at Constantinople, and instructed me to report myself there for duty forthwith. Among the other nineteen selected applicants were two whom

I knew, one named Geoffrey, and a fellow named Stephenson, who had been at Edinburgh with me. Naturally I was in high spirits at my success; and when I reached Vienna and looked up all my old pals, we had a great day on the Danube on the occasion of the first regatta held there, and finished up with fireworks and other jollifications in the evening. After a couple of days at Vienna, we went through Buda-Pesth and Belgrade to Bazias, where we took steamer and voyaged down the Danube to Rustchuk.

What a magnificent trip it was! I knew the Rhine pretty well while I was at Bonn: I remembered the great stream that tumbled over the falls of Schaffhausen beyond Mainz, swept along past St. Goar and Bingen, the home of that soldier of the legion who lay dying in Algiers, down to Coblenz, where Marceau fell, and Ehrenbreitstein, the great fortress that now no longer frowns threateningly out towards France. I remembered the castles perched high on the beetling cliffs, and how strange the setting sun used to look when seen through their deserted windows. I recalled the haunted spot where the Loreley used to sing, and the towering heights of the Drachenfels, where the hills finally ceased, leaving the river to broaden out and flow more sluggishly between the low-lying banks down to Bonn and to Cologne, and thence away towards the misty flats and the grey distances of Holland.

But to my excited fancy, fired as I was by the prospect of being brought under the spell and the glamour of Islam and of serving under the Mussulman flag, the recollection of the fairy-like beauty of the Rhine faded before the dark grandeur of the river that was bearing me farther with every revolution of the paddle-wheels from European associations, and nearer to strange, new experiences among the subjects of the Shadow of God. At times we steamed through fairly open reaches, and at times through seething rapids, with the dark water swirling about the bows, and the still darker cliffs rising till they almost seemed to touch over our heads.

It was a two days' voyage down to Rustchuk; and I shall never forget my sensations when I caught my first glimpse of Turkish troops on one of the islands in the middle of the stream. Among my fellow passengers was a Mr. Jeune (later Sir Francis Jeune). He had been out in Australia as counsel in the Tichborne case, and had met my father. When he heard that I came from Australia, he took an interest in me, and I found in him a sympathetic listener as I confided my ambitions to him. Among the others on board with me were Captain the Honourable Randolph Stewart, a Queen's Messenger going down with despatches to Constantinople, and several of my professional brethren, including Dr. George Stoker, brother of Bram Stoker, Sir Henry Irving's manager, Dr. Simon Eccles, a well known London physician, and a Dr. Butler, an eccentric old fellow who had been in the Crimea. There were a number of pretty Roumanian women on board too, and altogether we had a jolly party.

At Rustchuk we took the train for Varna, the seaport on the Black Sea which was our point of embarkation for Constantinople; and here I remember old Dr. Butler lost his ticket, and the Queen's Messenger had to use all his influence to prevent an angry little Turkish stationmaster from "running him in." At last, however, we were all safely on board an Austrian Lloyd's steamer for the last stage of our journey, a short voyage of twelve hours; and I got my first insight into polygamous Turkey by discovering an aged Turk who came on board with his *harem*, a huddling little band of beauties veiled to the eyes, who were housed in a sort of canvas tent on deck, and at whose faces I made several unsuccessful attempts to get a peep.

Next morning we saw Stamboul rising out of the Bosphorus, and my dreams were at last fulfilled. Fresh, as one might say, from Melbourne, which forty years before was a camping-ground for blacks, I saw before me in this gorgeous vision of mosques and minarets, dark green cypress groves, towers of gleaming marble, and gilded pinnacles of the far Seraglio, a city of unknown antiquity. The story goes that, more than three hundred years before the Christian era, the Athenians, inspired by the burning eloquence of Demosthenes, fought to defend it against Philip of Macedon. One dark night, so the veracious historians of that period tell us, the Macedonians were on the point of carrying the city by assault, when a shining crescent appeared in the sky, disclosed the creeping forms of the enemy, and enabled the beleaguered forces to repel the attack with such vigour that the Macedonians raised the siege and retired.

Such was the origin of the crescent which figures on old Byzantine coins, and when the Osmanlis captured Constantinople they adopted it as their national device. It is a pretty story, and well—"*si non é vero é ben trovato.*" I saw before me a city which had already been besieged twenty-four times since its foundation and captured six times. Among others, Persians, Spartans, Athenians, Romans, Avars, Arabs, Russians, Crusaders, and Greeks had besieged it before it fell at last under the terrific assault of the forces of Mahomed II. in 1453. I landed at Galata, the port of Pera, which is separated from Stamboul proper by the Golden Horn, and went straight up to Misserie's Hotel, which is to Constantinople what Shepheard's Hotel is to Cairo, one of the famous hostelries of the world.

Next day we reported ourselves at the War Office. We were shown into a room where four or five old *pashas* were sitting cross-legged on divans, and we handed in our credentials. We presented our respects through the medium of an interpreter, and I was told to leave my address and hold myself in readiness for active service at once in the Servian war, which had then been going on for about six weeks.

I was no longer a civilian. I was now commissioned as a military surgeon in the service of the Sublime Porte, and engaged in a practice which included some three hundred thousand patients more or less, of whose language I was entirely ignorant, and of whose manners all previous impressions had taught me to be suspicious. It is right to say here, at the outset, that my experience of over two years among the Turks proved to me that the estimate formed of their character by other reputedly more civilized nations was entirely false and misleading.

That there was a large amount of corruption in the officialdom of Turkey at that time was no doubt true; but the real samples of national character, the men in the rank and file of the army, I found to be simple-minded, courteous, honourable, and honest in time of peace, while braver men on the battlefield than those who fought under Osman Pasha at Plevna are not to be found in Europe. The magnificent physique and robust constitution of the ordinary Turkish private soldiers I believe to be due mainly to two causes. In the first place they never touch alcohol, and in the second the traditions of Turkish social life and the rigid guardianship exercised over Turkish women have effectually kept out the scrofulous taint which has so appreciably affected the populations of other European nationalities.

Having been gazetted at once as an army surgeon with the rank of *colghassi*, or major, which entitled me, among other privileges, to draw rations for four men, I left the luxuries of Misserie's Hotel behind me, and installed myself in the barracks close to the War Office, with a determination to see as much as possible of Stamboul before we were ordered to the front.

There are few cities in the world where nightfall makes such a difference as in Stamboul. By day the surroundings of the city as well as the city itself make up a kind of earthly paradise. I climbed the tower of the Seraskierat, and gazed with astonishment at the panorama which lay before me. I saw two seas, the Black Sea and the Sea of Marmora; two straits, the Bosphorus and the Dardanelles; two gulfs, the Gulf of Ismet and the Gulf of Nicodema. At my feet lay twenty different cities, the houses of which, painted with the true Oriental love of bright colours, nestled against a background of hills clothed with patches of dark cypress and tall, spiry pines. Before me was the spot where two continents meet; and as my eye passed from the streets of Stamboul in Europe to Scutari lying yonder across the mouth of the Bosphorus in Asia, I realized how the tide of Eastern thought had swept across the waters of this narrow strait, and left its mark indelibly upon the strange people among whom I had come to take the chances of the battlefield.

I knew too that across there in Scutari was the burial-ground where the bones of those English officers and men who died in hospital after the Crimea lay buried, and I felt that with the brave dead of my own race so near me I was in good company. The old military hospital at Scutari has been turned into barracks now; but the room which Miss Florence Nightingale occupied while she was performing her mission of mercy to the wounded there is still preserved untouched, while her name is kept in affectionate remembrance by the sons of many whom she nursed back to life, or whose last hours she soothed with womanly ministering. As I looked out upon the landscape, I saw it set in the clear atmosphere of Southern Europe, so that every separate minaret stood sharply out and the marble domes of St. Sophia glistened in the bright sunlight.

All is warmth and colour, life and brightness, in Stamboul by day. By night, however, the difference is appalling. The streets were never lighted, and people were not supposed to be out after nine o'clock. If one went out at all, one went at one's own risk, and took the chance of attack by any of the thousands of stray dogs that prowl at will about the city and camp undisturbed in the streets. To one who had been accustomed to Paris and Vienna, where it is never night in this sense, where gas and arc lamps form an admirable substitute for sunlight, and where the patter of feet on the *trottoirs* and the hum of human life in the *cafés* are practically ceaseless, the sensation of wandering through these dark, deserted streets among hordes of starving curs was a strange one. By day Constantinople is modern, pulsating, alive. By night, with those dogs about, it is like one of those deserted cities of a long forgotten civilization, in which Briton Rivière shows us the panther and the tiger that have taken the place of man.

During my stay in Stamboul I often walked through the bazaars, where solemn old Turks in baggy breeches sought to swindle me with polite decorum, and where the whole atmosphere breathed of the *Arabian Nights*. One half expected to see Prince Camaralzaman come swaggering down the street, with his scimitar clanking on the pavement behind him; or Amina or Zobeide, heavily veiled, and with only her dark eyes showing through the *yashmak's* folds, slide past demurely with a sidelong glance at the stranger from the West.

The population of Constantinople do not believe in overwork; and for business purposes there are practically three Sundays in the week—namely, the Turkish Sunday, which falls on our Friday; the Jewish Sunday, which falls on Saturday; and the Christian Sunday. I went out one day to the "Sweet Waters," a favourite picnic place near the head of the Golden Horn, where the Turkish women and children enjoy their holiday under the trees, and the real Turkey lollymen drive a thriving trade in sweetmeats and sherbet. It was curious to note how the veneer of Western social routine was superimposed upon the changeless institutions of the East. I saw the ladies from the *harems* of sundry wealthy Turkish gentlemen driving out to "Sweet Waters" in the afternoon in carriages as perfectly appointed as any that roll through Hyde Park or the Bois de Boulogne in the height of the London or Paris season. Two ladies from one *harem* generally occupied one carriage; and the gigantic eunuch on the box, who was responsible for them while they were out under his charge, would use his London carriage whip without hesitation on the heads and shoulders of any young Turkish or Giaour *mashers* who attempted to make eyes at the closely guarded beauties.

I spent many a pleasant hour too in the long, narrow *caïques* that plied for hire on the waters of the Golden Horn like the *gondolas* of Venice; but I still had much to see when, after a week's stay, an official communication was handed to me informing me that I had been appointed regimental surgeon to the Kyrchehir regiment, so named from the town in Asia Minor where it had been raised. I packed my portmanteau at once, and followed the messenger, who led me to the barracks where the regiment was quartered, and where I was introduced to my new colonel. He was most polite, and invited me to have supper with him; and then it was that I had my first really Turkish meal.

I cannot truthfully say that I enjoyed it; and when my host, to mark the warmth of his hospitality, picked up a piece of chicken off his own plate in his fingers and placed it in my mouth, I must confess that I almost spoilt all my chances of a distinguished military career by an instantaneous attack of nausea. I spent the night in the barracks tossing sleeplessly on a divan, and soon after daybreak marched down with my regiment to the railway station.

The regiment, which was eight hundred strong, was officered by a colonel, two majors, eight captains, sixteen lieutenants, and a paymaster. When the process of entraining was completed, I found myself *en route* at six o'clock in the morning for a destination of which I knew nothing, and in company with a regiment of troops who were as ignorant of English as I was of Turkish. I was accommodated in a compartment with the colonel, the two majors, and the paymaster, Mehemet Ali, with whom I afterwards chummed up and lived on terms of the closest friendship. It was decidedly awkward, however, at first; for as the Turkish officers could speak neither French nor German, all communications between us had to be by signs.

The men were packed closely together, and the train crawled slowly on towards the terminus, stopping for one hour in every three. We were three days and two nights on the journey towards Tatar Bazardjik, and I had plenty of time and opportunities for forming an opinion as to the kind of men with whom my lot was cast. I found that these men, who were all conscripts, formed the second regiment which had been raised at Kyrchehir, and fine fellows they were. I could have picked fifty men from among them who were as grand specimens of physical humanity as could be found anywhere in the world. They were all well clothed in the serviceable infantry uniform, and were armed with the Martini-Peabody rifle.

We camped each night at a railway station, and I remember on the morning of the second day seeing an old *pasha* who was organizing troops locally come galloping down to inspect us. Our regiment was paraded, and the *pasha* rode down the lines scanning the men closely. Presently he spotted me, and, seeing at a glance that I was not a Turk, he addressed a question to the colonel, who evidently replied that I was their new English surgeon. The *pasha* trotted up to where I stood at attention, and addressed some incoherent query to me; but as I could not even conjecture what it was all about, I imitated the gentleman whom Tennyson speaks of, and "smiling put the question by." I thought that the old *pasha* looked hurt; but the mystery was soon cleared up by the arrival of his own private barber with razor, soap, and brush. It seemed that "sideboards" were not allowed in the Turkish Army, and the small hairy appendages which covered my youthful cheeks, and of which, to tell the truth, I was rather proud, had deeply offended the old *pasha's* trained sense of order. So I had to submit myself to the *pasha's* barber, and in a few minutes the offensive adornments were removed, and I could no longer be distinguished from any of my Turkish colleagues.

At last we reached Tatar Bazardjik at eleven o'clock at night; and as there was no accommodation at the railway station, camp-fires were lit, and the regiment bivouacked for the night. Next morning at five o'clock I was roused up, and the colonel brought up four horses, giving me to understand by signs that I was to select one for a charger. I chose a little grey stallion, a powerful animal, with a look of endurance about him. He had a heavy Turkish peaked saddle on him, a most uncomfortable thing to ride in until one gets used to it; but there was no choice in the matter, so I had to make myself as comfortable in it as I could. Then we started on the march for Sofia, and a very unpleasant march it was at first.

It was then the month of June, and the weather was intensely hot; while, to add to our discomforts, a terrific duststorm swept down on us soon after leaving the bivouac, filling eyes, noses, and ears with fine, impalpable powder, and getting down the men's throats so that they could hardly breathe. The regiment marched all day, and of course I assumed that a good many of the men would be knocked up; but at five o'clock we halted, and pitched camp for the night, having covered about twelve miles of the journey.

Soon after the tents were pitched I had my first patient to attend. They brought up a man who had all the symptoms of an ordinary fit, and I had to make up my mind at once whether it was a genuine fit or whether he was malingering to avoid duty. It seemed to be a real fit, and then again there was something suspicious about it. I knew that if I was imposed upon at the outset I should have endless trouble, so I took my resolution at once, and explained by signs to Colonel Suleiman, who was standing by, that the man was shamming. The colonel's remedy for cases of this kind was drastic, but very effective. He had the patient sent to the rear, and given a round three dozen with a stick on that part of the person which schoolmasters have found to be especially suited for the receipt of chastisement. Of course the word was quickly passed round, and I had no more cases of fits to attend to during the march.

I shared a tent with Mehemet Ali, the paymaster, who turned out to be a really good fellow. He was a little man with a very fair complexion—his mother was a Circassian—and he had twinkling steel grey eyes. He was the strongest man I ever met. I had a horse, but I still wanted a servant, so Mehemet Ali brought up four men for my inspection. I chose a man named Ahmet, an Asiatic Turk and a married man with five children. He turned out a splendid servant; but, poor fellow, he never saw his home again, and his bones lie buried with those of many of his countrymen on the banks of the Danube at Widdin.

Next morning I was given to understand that I should have to see a number of patients; however, I fortified myself with two or three Turkish phrases, and went my rounds without trepidation. My diagnosis was in each case remarkable for simplicity, and I asked few needless questions. My first remark was invariably, "*Dilli nitchika*," which means, "Put out your tongue." If the man seemed really feverish and bad, I remarked authoritatively, "*Hoiti araba*," which means, "Go to the waggon," and I allowed him to ride in the waggon instead of route-marching. If I had any doubts as to the genuineness of the indisposition, I ejaculated sharply, "*Hoiti balook*," which means, "Go to your company." Of course all the men who were really ill I made to take two paces to the rear, and when my inspection was finished I prescribed for them, and dispensed my prescriptions from the well equipped regimental medicine chest.

It took the regiment five days altogether to march to Sofia, the colonel, the two majors, the paymaster, an adjutant, and myself being the only mounted officers. At first the route lay through mountainous and very picturesque country, heavily timbered with pines, beeches, elms, and walnuts. The walnut trees seemed to grow wild throughout the country, and the nuts were in great profusion.

One night we stopped at the Bulgarian village of Ichtiman, and for the first time I saw Bulgarians at close quarters and slept in a Bulgarian house. Dirt appeared to be the national characteristic of Bulgaria, and a cheerful disregard of all sanitary rules a leading feature in the national disposition. For size and ferocity I have never seen the domestic insects of Bulgaria equalled; and in the brief armistices which occurred in the unequal combats of that horrible night, I longed for my clean and cosy quarters in the paymaster's tent again.

The Bulgarian men are tall and fair, and the samples that came under my notice wore huge bonnets of black sheepskin and baggy garments of a kind of coarse yellow frieze of their own weaving. Instead of boots they wore sandals laced to the knee in Spanish fashion, and their whole appearance was grimy and forbidding to a degree. Most of the inhabitants of the village disappeared into the surrounding hills on our arrival, and the few who remained forbore to present us with an address of welcome or to erect a triumphal arch in our honour. Sullenly and suspiciously they offered us bowls of *yuoart* to eat, a horrible sticky mess made of curdled milk, of which I partook to my subsequent sorrow.

At last we came in sight of Sofia, the capital of Bulgaria. It lay at the farther end of a great plain dotted here and there with Bulgarian villages, well watered by a river running through it, and nicely timbered like a great park. Against the dark background of the hills, to use a pretty line of Tennyson's, "*the city sparkled like a grain of salt.*" Sofia was then a place of about twenty thousand inhabitants, and the seat of government. At one time the famous Midhat Pasha was the governor of this *vilayet*.

The regiment moved in column of route along the main road through the plain towards the white houses glinting in the sunshine, every man stepping jauntily as the close of the long march drew near. But Sofia looked better at a distance than it did under our noses. At that time there was only one hotel in the place, a filthy little *cabaret* kept by a Greek, whose views with regard to beds and meals were most primitive. The railway runs right through from Stamboul to Sofia and beyond now, and French cooking has replaced the black bread and beans which formed the Spartan fare placed before his guests by that "base scion of a noble stock" who took us in and "did for us" in '76.

The first English-speaking person whom I met in Sofia was Mac-Gahan, the war correspondent for a London newspaper, and from him I learnt at last where I was and what was happening round us. We dined together, and he told me how the Servians had been beaten all along the line. I found that there were four other Turkish regiments besides my own quartered in Sofia; and among the English surgeons attached to the troops I was glad to find an old friend named Stiven, with whom I could exercise my tongue at last after my enforced silence of the previous week.

However, I was already able to speak a few words of Turkish, and the paymaster used to give me lessons regularly, pointing to the different articles in our tent and repeating the Turkish word for each until I had grasped it thoroughly. I conformed to Turkish customs of course in everything, and soon accustomed myself to my new surroundings. What strikes a new chum in Turkey very much at first is the absence of chairs. I never saw a chair there; but I soon learned to sit down to dinner on my own haunches on the ground with my brother officers.

A Turkish dinner was a curious meal. First my servant brought me a basin of water, soap, and towel, and I washed my hands, preparatory to attacking the soup with my wooden spoon. Mehemet Ali and I used to eat out of the same bowl, dipping our wooden spoons in alternately. The *pièce de résistance* was invariably *pilaf*, or boiled rice, with little bits of meat cut up in it, and sometimes scraps of chicken or turkey when we could get hold of any. The *pilaf* was eaten with the fingers; and the dexterity with which an experienced Turk would *fossick* out a tender bit of the liver, wing, or a satisfying "drumstick," from the superincumbent mass of rice reminded one strongly of a digger unearthing nuggets in a patch of rich alluvial.

It was astonishing at Sofia to notice the humane way in which the Turks treated the Bulgarians, who were to all intents and purposes a hostile people, and who never lost an opportunity of showing their hostility whenever they could do so with safety to themselves. During the whole of the time that I was in Sofia I never saw a Bulgarian ill treated; and I think it only right to emphasize this point, because, either from want of knowledge or from that tendency to take *omne ignotum pro malefico* which is so common to mankind, the other nations of Europe have contrived to affix the stigma of barbarous cruelty to the Turks in such a manner that it is difficult to remove or even to lessen the impression.

All I can say is that, as an unprejudiced observer with ample opportunities, I never saw any cruelties inflicted during a state of peace, nor any punishments dealt out to Bulgarians except in cases where they were fully deserved. The Turk when under fire does not fight with rose-water any more than the soldier of reputedly more civilized nations; but if needless barbarities were committed by both Turks and Russians when their blood was up, one has to remember the grim remark of the great Frenchman that one cannot have an omelet without breaking a few eggs.

It was in Sofia that I was called in to attend my first lady patient; and the case is worth noting as an illustration of the difference between Eastern and Western methods of diagnosis. In Turkey a practitioner does not get much to go on in forming an opinion. A wealthy old Turk in the town who had an extensive *harem* wanted advice for one of his wives, and I was asked to call and see her. I gladly accepted the opportunity, and followed my guides, a couple of eunuchs, and an interpreter to a fine house, where they took me upstairs and halted outside a thick, heavy curtain reaching from the ceiling to the floor. Inside was the *harem*, an institution which I had always had a scientific curiosity to see, and at last I felt that my ambition in this direction was to be realized.

A few low spoken words in Turkish were whispered at the edge of the curtain by a tall black-garbed eunuch, and then I heard the rustle of draperies approaching on the other side. A low toned colloquy ensued between the eunuch, who seemed to be threatening, and my interesting patient, whose accents had in them a touch of plaintive entreaty. Presently a white and beautifully moulded arm was shyly insinuated through the space between the wall and the edge of the curtain, while the eunuch bade me, through the mediumship of the interpreter, diagnose the complaint from which the fair one suffered and prescribe a remedy. The hand was small and finely formed, and above the wrist was a heavy bangle of beaten gold. I felt the pulse, which was fluttering and unsteady, and clasped the white and tremulous fingers, feeling that with such slight data to go upon any treatment that I could prescribe would not be likely to enhance my reputation. Accordingly I demanded to be admitted, in order that I might see and question the patient, whom I judged to be a Circassian or a Georgian girl certainly not more than one and twenty, and probably pretty.

A long debate ensued, in which the eunuchs, the interpreter, and myself took part; but all my arguments beat unheeded against the rocks of their Oriental stolidity, and the logic of the whole British Medical Society would not have sufficed to persuade the principal eunuch to let me see that unknown lady's tongue. With that thick curtain between us, it was a case of Pyramus and Thisbe and the wall; so I abandoned my quest after the unattainable, and lost the only chance that I—plausible Giaour though I was—ever obtained of seeing the inside of a real Turkish *harem*. Probably the lady was eventually treated by a *hakem bashi*, or Turkish physician and surgeon, many of whom are very clever in their own way, or by a *jarra bashi*, a sort of "legally qualified medical practitioner," who is recognized as a person entitled to prescribe, but whose abilities do not go much further than drawing teeth or fixing up sore feet.

From Sofia our regiment pushed on to Pirot, close to the Servian border, where we were brigaded with two other regiments of infantry and strengthened by a battery of artillery, our mission being to defend the road into Servia in case of a flank attack. We camped in the hills; and as I had little work to do, I spent most of my time shooting hares with the colonel's double-barrelled gun, and also duck, which were very plentiful. In the evenings I learned to smoke the *narghileh*, and I also improved my scanty knowledge of Turkish as best I could with the aid of Mehemet Ali.

At last we got orders to leave, and at daybreak we struck camp. The last that we saw of this pleasant resting-place was the flame of our burning camp-stables of brushwood, to which we set fire before we started on our new march.

After a stay at Ak Palanka, we were moved on to Nish, the headquarters of the Turkish army; and here I met several English surgeons, who had been despatched to the seat of war by the Red Cross Society in England. Among them was Armand Leslie, who was afterwards killed in Egypt, in the rout and massacre of Baker's poltroon levies while marching from Trinkitat towards Tokar; and a couple of others, Litton Forbes and Dr. S——, whom I got to know very well. At this time Nish formed the base of our army, and the wounded were brought back to us from Alexinatz, where the fighting was going on. The first sight of those poor fellows, gashed with sabre and bayonet, torn with shell, and riddled with rifle-bullets, made me realize the actuality of the conflict in which I was there to assist.

Life in camp was irksome enough; but I found a difficulty in getting out of it, for while one of our majors, Edhim Effendi, was a jolly, good-humoured fellow, who was not above a glass of liquor when he could get it, the other, Izzet Effendi, was a dry, fanatical Turk, who spent most of his time at his prayers, and always looked upon me as an *infidel*. Izzet Effendi refused to allow me to go into the town; but I appealed to the colonel, and, having secured his permission, I took up my quarters in Nish with S—— and Litton Forbes. Then I was drafted to look after the general hospital, and I left the regiment altogether.

There were about twenty of us in all on the surgical staff, and the hospital arrangements were excellent. It was here that I performed my first big operation, the patient being a Turkish infantryman who was brought in from Alexinatz with his knee shattered by a shell. He refused to take chloroform, and I took his leg off above the knee without any anæsthetic. He never said a word, and went on smoking a cigarette all the time.

When the captain came round with his notebook afterwards to take down the name, age, and regiment of each wounded man, my patient answered all the questions quietly and unconcernedly while I was stitching up the flap of skin over the stump. It was a marvellous exhibition of fortitude, and a striking illustration of the mettle of the men whom I was soon to see charging with such splendid courage upon the bayonets of the Russians.

CHAPTER 2

The Preliminaries to the Russo-Turkish War

At Nish I first met a young soldier whose remarkable personality and singularly adventurous life could not fail to attract attention, and with whom I formed a close personal friendship, which was only ended by his death barely a year ago, (as at time of first publication). Prince Czetwertinski, whom I first saw mounted on a magnificent black charger in the main street of Nish, belonged to one of the oldest families in Russian Poland, and was himself the head of the family. His mother had been living at Lemberg in Galicia, and the young prince had been educated in France, and afterwards at a military school in Prague, with the object of entering the Austrian army.

At the last moment, however, the Russian Government intervened, deeming it unwise to allow a Polish prince, who, though a Russian subject, was as hostile at heart to Russia as were all his countrymen, to accept an Austrian commission. The official world of St. Petersburg set its face against Czetwertinski, and refused to furnish him with the necessary papers; so that when the Servian war broke out he gladly seized the chance of taking service against the Russians, the traditional foes of his Polish house, proud still, although its glories had been sadly tarnished.

Young Czetwertinski was well received at the court of the Emperor of Austria, and was admitted to the intimacy of Prince Metternich; but there were grave difficulties in the way of the military career upon which he had set his heart. At last, however, through the kind offices of General Klapka, the well known Hungarian general, who was on friendly terms with the Turkish Government, the young prince secured an entrance to military life, and was appointed, not to a commission, but to the grade of private in a Turkish cavalry regiment, in which capacity he had at first to perform the most menial offices. When Alexinatz was taken in October, 1876, it was Czetwertinski who brought the news to Nish; and for his conduct in the engagement he received a captaincy, and also the decoration of the fifth order of the Medjidie. He was a magnificent rider, and his victory over a vicious black stallion that no one in the regiment could sit was a good passport to the affections of the Turks, who dearly love fine horsemanship.

I met him afterwards at Widdin, and got to know him intimately. At that time he was captain of a guard of eighty troopers attached to the person of Osman Pasha; and the colonel of his regiment, a man named Mustapha Bey, was himself a Pole, who had fled to Turkey as a boy, entered the Turkish service, and become a Mohammedan. Czetwertinski fell ill at Plevna of dysentery, and passed through my hands, afterwards coming to live with me in the Bulgarian house where I was quartered, and bringing his servant Faizi with him. As the young cavalry officer was attached to the person of Osman Pasha, I was kept *au courant* with all that was going on; and it was through him that I was enabled chiefly to know and admire the courage, the honour, the high military ability, and the pure patriotism of the great chief under whom we both served.

Czetwertinski fought with signal bravery in all the engagements that took place at Plevna, and on one occasion had his horse killed under him at Pelischat—the famous black stallion that none but he could ride.

He was afterwards selected for his knowledge of French to act as *parlementaire*, and visited the Russian headquarters in that capacity with Tewfik Pasha. Before I left Plevna, Czetwertinski was sick and wounded; so I sent him down invalided to Constantinople together with Victor Lauri, a German artist, who had chummed in with us on the field. Had Czetwertinski been left behind at Plevna, he would infallibly have been shot by the Russians for a deserter, as Skobeleff himself, who met him at a dinner party after the war was over, assured him.

I said goodbye to Prince Czetwertinski, or, as he used to call himself, Mehemet Bey, at Constantinople, and lost sight of him, as I thought, forever; but years afterwards—it was in 1884—I found a note at my house in Melbourne saying that Mehemet Bey would call back in half an hour. I waited to see him, and then he told me his story.

It seemed that he owned some villages near Odessa; but when they were confiscated by the Russian Government upon the termination of the war, he went to live with his mother at Lemberg in Galicia. However, after the exciting scenes amongst which he had lived, the dreary life of the provincial Galician capital was intolerable to him, especially as the small revenue still left to the family was miserably inadequate to support the position of a prince. Accordingly Czetwertinski, who was always an inveterate gambler, scraped together about £3,000 and made for Monte Carlo, with the hope of breaking the bank and restoring his fallen fortunes. In three days at the tables he had lost all but £25; and knowing that I was somewhere in Australia, he went over to London, and took a steerage passage in an emigrant vessel bound for Brisbane.

His fellow passengers were such a rough lot that he would not associate with them, and consequently he learned not a word of English during the voyage, eventually landing at Brisbane with one solitary shilling in his pocket. He walked the streets of Brisbane for the first night, nearly starving, and towards morning heard a man speaking a few words of French to another. Czetwertinski went up to him, and found that the man was really a Frenchman—he turned out afterwards to be an escaped communard from New Caledonia—and that he owned a small ten-ton cutter, with which he plied up the coast, carrying provisions to the northern squatters and planters. Czetwertinski took a billet as deck hand to the escaped convict trader, working for his tucker alone; but during his three months' service on board he amassed capital in a sense, for he learned English. His next step was from the deck of the cutter to the schoolroom of a station, where he secured an engagement as tutor in a squatter's family, who little guessed that the quiet Mr. Jules who explained the irregular French verbs to them with exemplary patience was Prince Czetwertinski, the dashing light cavalryman who made his mark at the taking of Alexinatz a few years before.

Meanwhile his mother in distant Lemberg was searching Europe high and low for her missing son, and at last she confided the story of his disappearance to the Jesuits, by whom he had been brought up as a child. Setting the machinery of their vast religious organization to work, the Jesuit fathers in Galicia sent inquiries flying through the ramifications of their order in all quarters of the globe, and at last their brethren in Sydney discovered the wanderer, and placed him once more in communication with his family. They also offered him a post as master in a Jesuit college near Parramatta, and it was during a holiday from his duties there that he came down to Melbourne to see me. His mother longed for him to go home again, and sent him out money, imploring him to return to Europe, which he did soon after I saw him. I had letters from him afterwards, in which he told me that he had resumed his title of prince, and was living in Rome with his uncle, who was a cardinal. He had a special audience with his Holiness the Pope, who took a warm interest in him.

With revenues depleted by continual confiscations, Czetwertinski found himself unable for long to support the social position which he was called upon to fill in Europe, and he accordingly returned to Australia, and for three years held a post as master at St. Xavier's College, near Melbourne. I heard that he was a good teacher, but very harsh with the boys. When he left the school, I got him a post as tutor to the son of a friend of mine at a good salary; but when he had been there a week, there was a race meeting at Flemington, and he got a holiday to come down to town. Now Czetwertinski, though a magnificent rider, knew nothing about racing; but he tackled the ring with the same gay audacity as the tables at Monte Carlo, and with £7 in his pocket commenced a plunge in cash betting. His luck was in this time, and he backed winner after winner, leaving off at the end of the day £300 to the good.

Two days afterwards I heard from him that he had thrown up his billet, and was leaving that night for Sydney, *en route* for Bagdad or Havana! I surmised that he would find his way back to Europe, and eventually marry an American heiress with £20,000 a year, with whom his mother had arranged a *mariage de convenance* for him, with a promise that £500,000 should be settled upon him on the day of the wedding. As a matter of fact, however, he got no farther than Batavia, where he opened school, which was a failure. He worked his way back to Cooktown, and thence in a state of starvation to Sydney. On one occasion a butcher's wife, who wanted to engage a tutor, came across him in a registry office, and explained to him that it was usual for people in her country to wear collars. The poor wandering prince had no collar, so he lost the billet.

However, he eventually made his way down to Wagga, where he opened a school, which turned out very successfully. He was doing splendidly, and meditating another trip home, when he caught a chill, and died in a week of pneumonia. A Wagga man brought me down poor Czetwertinski's final goodbye, saying that he thought of me to the last. So died as noble, brave, and high-spirited a soldier as ever drew the sword.

Nish, which is close to the Servian border, is one of the most flourishing towns in Bulgaria, and it was at that time fortified by several large forts and earthworks. Many of the houses were extremely handsome, and the villa in which we were quartered was a beautiful residence. A fine Bulgarian church and several Turkish mosques lent stateliness and dignity to the little city that nestles in the valley of the River Moravia. In the evening, as we sat over our cigarettes after dinner, there was a quiet restfulness in the beauty of the landscape that had a special charm; and when my comrades asked me to sing, I would give them that sweet old song, "Sweet Vale of Avoca, how calm could I rest," altering it to local circumstances by substituting "Moravia" for "Avoca."

Routine comes to mould a man's daily life in the Balkans as well as in London or Paris, and before many days had passed we had settled down to very regular habits. After breakfast at eight o'clock, a walk of half a mile took us to the general hospital, where we had a couple of hundred wounded men under treatment; and after going our rounds, and conferring with the head of the hospital about any matters demanding immediate attention, we were practically free by one o'clock for the rest of the day. One day a week was set apart for operations; but on the other days we used to go out riding in the hills and to the surrounding Bulgarian villages, with an occasional coursing match—for hares were very plentiful—by way of keeping our sporting proclivities properly exercised.

A very favourite trip was a ride of seven miles out to a famous hot mineral spring, where the water, strongly impregnated with sulphur and chalybeates, gushes out of the living rock in a stream over a foot in diameter at a temperature of 120° Fahr., and falls into a natural basin, largely resorted to by the residents as a bath. Close to this bath, as the afternoon wore on, the deep-bosomed, dark-eyed Bulgarian women would bring the clothing of their households to wash, as Nausicaa and her maidens used to do long ago in the fabled land of Phæacia, where Odysseus, shipwrecked on his homeward voyage from Ilium, was saved from the sea. The Bulgarians, like their cousins-german the Servians and Roumanians, are fond of bright colours, particularly the women.

Darwin throws the cold light of science on the important subject of feminine attire, when he points out that the gorgeous plumage of certain birds has been developed by them as a special sex attraction to secure for them the notice of a mate. With birds and animals, however, it is almost invariably the male who decks himself out in the most brilliant colouring, hoping thereby to make himself the cynosure of all the eyes of the females; but in the human species, by a curious piece of satire, Nature seems to encourage the female to adopt this gentle art.

At any rate the Bulgarian women were adepts at it; and in spite of their Finnish type of features, many of them looked positively pretty as they stooped over the pool in their short, white kirtles of homespun frieze and loose-sleeved scarlet bodices, making a bright note of colour in the picture. And as they dipped their garments in the steaming washtub of Nature's own brewing, these rustic *blanchisseuses de fin* would sing the plaintive folk-songs of their country in the smooth Slavonian tongue, which had come to them in the old migratory days, during their long residence on the Volga, before the Avars swooped down upon them and drove them across the Danube to the country under the shadow of the Balkans, where they have remained ever since.

In the Bulgarian folk-songs, with their plaintive semitones and their melodies sliding away invariably into the mournful minor, one seemed to hear the echoes of the history of the people who have degenerated from the warlike race that crossed the Danube under their great chief Zabergan in the sixth century to the feeble and lethargic tillers of the soil, who have grown up under their long subjection to the great Byzantine Empire with its seat of government at Constantinople, and afterwards to the despotic Turkish power which superseded it.

As the evening drew in we would race our horses back across country to Nish, haunted by the recollections of those plaintive Bulgarian airs and of the low, rich voices of the dark-eyed singers. The Turk, though an excellent fellow in many respects, has peculiar notions in the matter of voice production, and to hear a group of them all singing in unison through their noses as they squatted on the ground round a camp-fire was an experience to which one had to get accustomed before one could thoroughly enjoy it. It was a pleasant variety to exchange the nasal tenor squeak of the Turkish Tommy Atkins for the soft *contralto* of a Bulgarian *blanchisseuse*.

One of the principal sights of Nish is a squarely built brick tower covered over with plaster, in which are set three thousand Servian skulls. This ghastly trophy, which is about fifty years old, celebrates a long forgotten victory. The heads were stuck there freshly shorn from the shoulders of the Servians, and the whole grim monument reminds one of those *sámadhs*, or cenotaphs of heads, of which Kipling gives such a vivid description in one of his "Departmental Ditties."

Our party was joined at Nish by a son of the Duke of Cambridge, Colonel FitzGeorge, and a Captain James, who had come over with him from Widdin. I bought a capital grey pony from James for £8, and I always fancy that he imagined I had got at him over the bargain. However, *caveat emptor* is an admirable maxim in horse-dealing; and the law presumably imagines the vendor capable of looking after himself, as no maxim has been framed for his guidance. At any rate the grey pony stood me in good stead; and in our nightly race home from the mineral spring, or the particular Bulgarian village which we happened to be patronizing with a visit, I generally finished in the first three. It was a flat race of course, for you can walk from one end of the country to the other without meeting a fence of any kind.

At night after dinner the entire British medical staff at Nish, supported by FitzGeorge and James, were in the habit of discussing the Eastern Question in all its bearings, not from the outside point of view of the unprejudiced observer, but with the keenness of people who felt that they had a close personal interest in the solution of the problem. There were not wanting alarmists, who took the cheerful view that, if disaster overtook the Turkish arms, the exasperated Turks would turn their swords against the Giaours in their own ranks, and we should all get our throats cut for our pains.

One of the speakers who invariably ranged himself on the side of the minority in these discussions, and whose chief delight it was to be the Ishmael of debate with his hand against every man and every man's hand against him, was an extraordinary man named Foley, who quarrelled violently with every one of us except, I think, myself. Afterwards, just before the Russian war broke out, the poor fellow met a tragic end. He was quartered near Sistova in a Bulgarian house on the bank of the Danube, and it was found one morning that he had disappeared. His fate was a mystery which was never cleared up; and whether he drowned himself in the Danube, or was knocked on the head by some wandering Circassians, we were never able to find out.

Another of my comrades at Nish was Ralph Leslie, a Canadian, who has had a fairly adventurous career, and was afterwards with Stanley on the Congo. He was a nice young fellow; but he used to read *Gil Blas* to me in French when I was in bed at night and required all my energies to circumvent the strategy of the Bulgarian insects.

An incident occurred one afternoon which came near terminating seriously for some of us, and it forms a good illustration of the dangers which the travelling Briton incurs as often as not through his own pig-headedness. S—— and I, with three or four more of the medical staff, were walking down the main street in plain clothes after lunch, when we noticed half a dozen Turkish soldiers engaged in cleaning the street. They were scooping up the liquid mud in great shovels, and throwing it into a cart drawn up near the footpath. A good share of every shovelful of mud came down on the footway, and as we approached S—— shouted to them in English to "knock off" whilst we went past. They either did not or would not understand, and before we had gone three steps farther my companion's Bond Street tweed suit received a liberal baptism of black mud from the shovel wielded by a dour old Turk, the ugliest of the party. S—— lost his temper, and sent in a heavy left-hander, which caught the old fellow on the point of the jaw, and landed him kicking on his back in the middle of the road.

The whole gang at once raised a yell, and rushed us with their shovels, while we had to rely upon our fists alone for our defence. Matters were beginning to look very ugly indeed, when a Turkish lieutenant who knew us rushed up, and drawing his sword interposed himself between ourselves and our assailants, who retired in disorder under a vigorous volley of Turkish maledictions. It was a close thing for us all the same, and the adventurous career which I had marked out before me came perilously near to being abruptly terminated by an inglorious end at the hands of an infuriated scavenger.

But this same S——, capable man as he was at his profession and good-hearted fellow to boot, had an unhappy knack of getting into difficulties, and his death resulted eventually as an indirect consequence of a mysterious quarrel which he had with a Turkish major under circumstances which I recollect with great distinctness. While we were at Nish, one of the British surgeons attached to the general hospital, Howard Keen by name, was quartered in a fine Bulgarian house, which he shared with a Turkish major, whose name it is not necessary to mention. S—— and I went up to spend the evening with them; and as it was a bitterly cold night with snow on the ground outside, Keen advised me to stop with him, and camp in his half of the house, which I did. At about twelve o'clock I wrapped myself in my heavy military overcoat lined with wolf-skin, and lay down to sleep on the floor in front of the fire in Keen's room, while Keen also went to sleep on his camp-bed. We left S—— and the Turkish major drinking *raki* together in the major's room at the other side of the house.

As the fire was burning low I woke with a start to find the Bulgarian owner of the house standing over me in a state of violent agitation, gesticulating wildly and repeating again and again some words of the meaning of which I had not the faintest notion. He was holding in his hand a revolver which belonged to S——. I guessed at once that something was wrong; and fearing that S—— had got the worse for liquor and insulted the Bulgarian's wife, I woke Keen, who ran out in his shirt and trousers to the other side of the house. I followed him almost immediately, and he yelled out to me to come to the major's quarters at once. I rushed in, and found the major in a state of tremendous excitement, chewing his big black moustache and hurriedly buckling on his sword. Guessing that S—— had got into trouble again, I sang out to him to clear out; but as I did so the door opened, and in he walked as white as a sheet. The major drew his revolver, and fired at S—— point-blank, but the bullet missed its mark; and before he could pull the trigger again, Keen and I had closed with him, and for about two minutes the inside of that Bulgarian's sitting-room was about the hottest corner I have ever been in.

The Turk was a big, powerful fellow, and he was mad with *raki*; while Keen and I were both tough, and in pretty good form. Over and over on the floor we rolled, the Turk trying to throttle us, while we hung to him like a couple of bull-terriers, and gradually wore him out. At last we had him fairly beaten, and, grabbing his revolver, we blew out the light and fled, taking S—— with us, and locking the door behind us. S—— staggered off to his own quarters; but when the morning came, he was found lying in the snow outside his own door, and the exposure brought on an attack of inflammation of the lungs, from which he eventually died. In the morning we tried in vain to find out the cause of the quarrel; but neither S—— nor the major would tell us. I think the Bulgarian knew, but he kept his own counsel.

One night in Nish I met a very remarkable Turkish officer named Ahmet Bey, who was introduced to me as a man who had killed seven Servians with his own sword during the final attack upon Alexinatz. I never in my life saw a man with such a magnificent physique. He was very handsome, splendidly proportioned, and of astounding physical strength. A few days before I met him he had been the hero of a feat about which all the troops in Nish were still talking. It seemed that Abdul Kerim Pasha, the commander-in-chief, while inspecting the troops one morning, casually expressed a wish that he could capture a Servian prisoner from the Servian lines. Ahmet Bey, who overheard the remark, rode up, and, saluting, asked to be permitted to get the commander a prisoner.

Abdul Kerim wonderingly gave the required permission, and Ahmet Bey without another word wheeled his charger, dashed the spurs into his flanks, and galloped off in front of the astonished detachment straight for the nearest Servian outpost. As he approached the Servian lines half a dozen rifles cracked, for the Servian vedettes opened fire upon him, hoping to drop him on the wing. But Ahmet Bey galloped on unharmed, having deliberately marked down one sentry for his prey. The sentry emptied his rifle at the audacious horseman in vain, and too late started to run. Ahmet Bey swooped down on him like a sparrow-hawk upon a landrail, and bending down grasped the man by the collar in an iron grip and flung him without an effort across the saddle in front of him. Then he galloped back again, bending over his horse's neck as the bullets whistled over his head, and delivered his bewildered prisoner to the Turkish commander amid the delighted shouts of the whole detachment.

The hero of this extraordinary feat was afterwards attached to the staff of Mehemet Ali Pasha, in command of the Army of the Lom. With the same army corps was Baker Pasha, the famous Colonel Baker, who was accounted one of the finest cavalry leaders in Europe; and Baker Pasha, who should be a good judge of soldierly qualities, has left it on record that Ahmet Bey was the *beau-id*eal of a soldier. Baker Pasha has given it as his written opinion that he never met the equal of this Turkish officer in instinctive military knowledge. He seemed to be able to divine the movements of the enemy and forestall every change of position or modification of strategy.

The frequent defeats of the Servians seemed to indicate a speedy termination of hostilities; and had it not been for the thousands of Russian volunteers who flocked to the Servian standard and took service under the Russian General Tchernaieff, who commanded the Servian army, it was evident that the resistance of Servia must have collapsed much earlier. At last, when Servia appealed to the Powers to stop the war and an armistice was declared at the instance of Russia, a large number of Turkish troops were sent to the rear, and among them was my regiment the Kyrchehir. We were ordered to retire to Sofia, and of course I had to sever my connection with the general hospital and rejoin my regiment.

It was December. The sky was the colour of lead, and the snow lay with a dead weight upon the pine trees. The regiment started early in the morning, and when I left for the long, solitary ride to Sofia I was several hours behind my troops. As I cantered my grey pony over the frozen ground a mishap befell me at the outset, for the gallant little animal cast a shoe, and I had to stop at a Bulgarian village to get him shod. Throughout the Turkish Empire they use flat plates which cover the whole of the foot with the exception of a small round orifice in the centre, instead of the crescent-shaped horseshoes which have come down to more civilized countries from the Roman times, and I had to hunt up a farrier to do the work. I found him at last, a surly, black-bearded fellow, who gave free vent to his hatred of the Turkish troops, and flatly refused to assist me.

Out came my revolver; and as I tapped the barrel, significantly pointing first to the shoeless hoof and then to the farrier's head, he came to terms and consented. But when I remounted the grey, I found that he was dead lame. The rascally farrier, I discovered afterwards, had driven a long nail straight into the frog of the unfortunate pony's foot, and then nailed the plate on over it. Before I reached Sofia a Circassian stole my English stirrup-irons while I slept, and leading my lame pony I finished the journey on foot.

However, we were a very jolly party at Sofia, where a fresh lot of English surgeons chummed in with us, and we all resolved to celebrate Christmas in the proper English way by a splendid dinner. On Christmas Eve a special sub-committee was formed to arrange the details of a banquet which should be worthy of the occasion. We were going to have no more of the eternal *pilaf*, with its accompanying hard biscuit and gulps of hot black coffee, but a real hot joint, a turkey, a goose, a plum pudding, and plenty of wine. I went to sleep that night with my soul filled with beautiful dreams of Christmas, and peace on earth, goodwill towards Bulgarians, and of roast turkey and celery sauce. In the morning I woke, and learned with horror that the regiment was ordered to march at once to the bleak, detestable pass of Orkhanieh in the Balkans, and that we should probably get no dinner at all.

They went away without me, and as Christmas morning wore on I came to the conclusion that I had better follow them or else I might get lost. I did follow them, but I got lost all the same; and after riding until ten o'clock at night I reached a filthy Bulgarian village, and decided to camp there. The house which I selected as the most promising was about as clean as an English piggery; but I found a kind of loft where maize was stored in the cob, and there I stopped for the night. I lay on the cobs of maize which were as hard as paving-stones, and made my Christmas dinner off one of them, hardly knowing whether to curse or laugh at the irony of fate and the "happy Christmas" which my friends in England and Australia no doubt were wishing me.

Next day I overtook the regiment, and went into quarters with it for five weeks at Orkhanieh. I had plenty to do there, for the men suffered greatly from dysentery; and as they could not all be accommodated in the village, they had to live under canvas, a mode of life which was very severe at that time of the year. After a few weeks there my stock of medicines, which was never very large, began to run out, and I got permission from the colonel to ride into Sofia, a distance of thirty miles, to replenish the regimental medicine chest.

Of all my campaigning experiences none were more awful than those lonely rides from Orkhanieh to Sofia and back again. My horse went lame soon after I started, the cold was intense, and in half an hour I was overtaken by a snowstorm which nearly blinded me. All day my poor horse hobbled along on three legs, while I was afraid to dismount, knowing that if I once left the saddle I should be frozen to death on the ground. When I arrived in Sofia at ten o'clock that night, I had to be lifted off my horse and put to bed. In the morning my good horse was found dead in the stable, killed by that fearful journey. An Italian doctor, who drove into Sofia on the same day, was lifted out of the vehicle dead. Perhaps if he had ridden he might have been saved.

After a rest of two days, I had to start back for Orkhanieh with my replenished medicine chest. The prospect was not a pleasant one; but I faced it with a fresh horse and renewed confidence. Before I had gone half-way I missed the road, and going across country came to a frozen river, which I was afraid to cross, lest the ice might give way and let me and my horse through into deep water. Accordingly I rode along the bank until I came to a place where I judged from the colour of the ice that the water was shallow, and there I resolved to attempt the crossing. When I was in the middle, there was a crack like a pistol shot, the ice broke, and we fell through to the river-bed, my horse standing up to his shoulder in the icy water, which reached to my knee. I was off his back in a moment, and the poor brute, after a couple of frightened plunges, stood still shivering.

It was plain that the ice would not bear us, even if I could get myself and the horse to the surface again, so the only course open was to cut a way out. I took my two heavy stirrup-irons, fixed them on one leather, and, using this improvised implement as a hammer, broke away the ice piecemeal, and dragged myself and my horse up the bank on the opposite side. At last I reached the camp, as stiff as though I was encased in plaster of Paris, and with my clothes frozen hard to my body. It was three weeks before I properly recovered sensation in my bridle-hand.

The regiment was ordered to Widdin before I had recovered from that last ride, and on the eve of our departure I had a severe attack of dysentery, which weakened me terribly. However, they lifted me on to my horse, and at last we reached the town of Vratza, one of the most picturesque towns in Bulgaria. Here I found the Turkish regiment to which my friend Stiven was attached; and to my great joy almost the first man whom I met was Stiven, who was living in the house of a Polish apothecary. I was very weak and ill; but I accepted Stiven's invitation to dine, and he prescribed a nourishing diet with plenty of good blood-making wine. What is more, he saw that I had it; and my performances at that dinner, which was the first European meal I had eaten since leaving Sofia, made our Turkish servant open his eyes. I am afraid to think how many bottles of the wine of the country Stiven and I got through between us; but I know that, when at last I tumbled off to bed in the mosque where the regiment was quartered, I slept the deep sleep of those who have dined both wisely and too well. It was a good prescription of Stiven's, and next day I was completely restored in health.

CHAPTER 3

The Imminence of War

A march of four days brought us to Widdin, the journey being accomplished by easy stages and with a fair degree of comfort. Of course it must be remembered that there was no such thing as a commissariat department in the Turkish army. The *zaptiehs*, or mounted police, in each district received notice of our approach, and requisitioned the necessary supplies from the farmers, who received acknowledgments of government indebtedness for the amount due. We always sent forward a few *arabas* with an advance party and a number of cooks; so that when the regiment reached the camping-place for the night all the preparations were made, and a hot meal was ready for the men. We usually camped in a Bulgarian village; and if there was no other shelter for the men, we appropriated the mosque, and made up our beds in it. I have slept many a time on the paved floor of a Turkish mosque, in the very arms of Islam as it were; and I must candidly admit that my slumbers were quite as refreshing and my dreams as sweet as they have since been within sound of the cathedral bells of Christendom.

Widdin is a town of considerable commercial importance, and a strongly fortified position of great military significance, being, in fact, one of the keys of Bulgaria, for it is situated on a wedge of Bulgarian territory, having both the Servian and Roumanian frontiers almost under the muzzles of its siege-guns. When we were there the population numbered about fourteen thousand persons, of whom perhaps one-half were Bulgarians, one-third Turks, and the remainder Levantines, Greeks, Italians, Spanish Jews, and Tchiganes or Gypsies. There are a great number of Jews everywhere throughout the Turkish Empire, and they are very well treated by the Turks. It is hardly necessary to say that almost all the bankers and financial agents in the country belong to this race.

There are practically two towns in Widdin—namely, that which is within the fortifications, and that which is outside. The fortified portion faces the Danube, which forms its protection for a distance of about one mile; and it is defended besides by a high castellated wall fully twenty feet in height, which runs right round the town. Facing the Danube, when we were there, were several powerful and perfectly organized batteries, armed with at least fifty Krupp siege-guns of the most modern description. From the Danube side the town was practically impregnable. On the other side, beyond the castellated wall, was a wide and deep moat; and over this was a drawbridge, which was pulled up at six o'clock every night, so that after that hour ingress to the fortified town was impossible until the morning. Inside the fortress were the principal public buildings, including the *konak*, or town hall, the seat of administration of the Turkish governor in charge of the *vilayet*, as well as the barracks, which accommodated four thousand men, a large government mill for grinding corn, and the great granaries in which a reserve of grain was stored for victualling the town in the event of a siege.

The greater portion of the population lived outside the fortress in the different suburbs; and beyond these again was the outer line of defence, a huge wall of earth about twenty feet high, and studded at short intervals with redoubts. Outside this wall the country was low-lying and swampy, capable of being flooded from the Danube, and thus affording additional protection to the town. One result, however, of all this circumjacent water was that Widdin was one of the most unhealthy towns in the whole of Turkey. The climate was excessively damp, and we were never free from malarial fever. At one time there were no fewer than four hundred men in the hospitals with this fever.

A staple article of export from Widdin is caviar, which is obtained in enormous quantities from the roe of the sturgeon, and sent away packed in barrels on board the flat-bottomed boats that ply up the river. I have seen a sturgeon fully twelve feet long caught in the Danube. Three men were dragging it with a rope through the streets of Widdin. The town has also a great reputation for its filigree work in silver and gold, which is very beautiful.

In February, 1877, when our regiment reached Widdin, we found about thirty thousand Turkish troops in the place, mostly infantry, though there were a few batteries of field artillery and about a thousand cavalry. The Kyrchehir regiment went into quarters in the barracks inside the fortress; but of course there was not sufficient accommodation there for all the troops in the town, and a military encampment was formed a couple of miles out of the town for the bulk of the army corps.

Osman Pasha, at that time a comparatively unknown man, was then commander-in-chief of all the troops in Widdin, and Adil Pasha was the commandant in charge of the camp. Osman Pasha had already won considerable reputation by his brilliant defeat of the Servians at Zaitchar; but it was not until his subsequent successes against the Russian arms that his name was flashed through the length and breadth of Europe, and that congratulations poured in upon him from all quarters. It fell to my lot to open and read many of the letters sent to him from England, in which the writers, a large proportion of whom were ladies, expressed their admiration for his gallantry and begged the favour of his autograph. Osman Pasha lived in a large house within the fortress, and I myself was billeted in the same quarter, where I lived quite in the Turkish fashion, sitting cross-legged on the floor and eating my food with my fingers.

At this time hostilities with Servia had ceased, and a long armistice had been declared, during which the Powers were occupied in dictating terms to Turkey, which, however, she declined to accept, her determined attitude in the matter leading ultimately to the declaration of war against her by Russia. The town of Kalafat in Roumania is close to Widdin; and we could see the Roumanian troops there busily engaged in fortifying it in anticipation of hostilities breaking out, and of an attack being made on the town by the forces in Widdin at any moment. The position, therefore, was decidedly interesting, for we could actually see the Roumanians, who were nominally our vassals, building up their redoubts against us as fast as they could. It will be remembered that during the early part of the Crimean war the Turks occupied Kalafat, Osman Pasha being the commander of the forces; and that the Russians lost some twenty thousand men in a vain attempt to take it.

The time of waiting in Widdin was fairly quiet, although everyone felt that war was in the air, and that the interval of rest was only the hush that precedes the hurricane. I had plenty of work to do, for dysentery and lung troubles affected the troops severely as well as malarial fever. There were about thirty military surgeons in the town including myself, but most of them were Hungarians or Austrians; and the only other British subject among them besides myself was a man whom I shall call Dr. Black, although that was not his name.

Dr. Black was by no means a credit to his country. In fact, not to put too fine a point upon it, he was a perfect disgrace; and as every fresh scrape that he got into reflected more or less upon me, I began to get heartily sick of him. Few of the people in Widdin had ever seen an Englishman, and Dr. Black's manners and customs were not calculated to prejudice them favourably with regard to the nation in general or myself in particular. Fortunately for me there was one other Briton in the town. To use a convenient Irishism, he was a Scotsman, and he was commonly known as Jack; in fact, I never heard his surname. Jack was a high-class mechanical engineer, and he had been specially imported from Glasgow to take charge of the Government flour-mill inside the fortress. He lived there with his wife, a charming little Scotswoman, and they both spoke Turkish like natives. I had many consultations with Jack as to our common *bête noir* Dr. Black; but we had to suffer in silence for a while until the whirligig of time brought its revenges, and Dr. Black was at last turned out of Widdin.

I had met Dr. Black before in Sofia, and it was with intense disgust that I came across him again in Widdin. He was a middle-aged man, who might possibly have been of some good in his profession when he was younger; but he had spoiled his life and ruined his chances with drink. He was the most awful drunkard I have ever met. In fact, he was never sober, and in his habits he was perfectly filthy. He used to wear a long, dirty overcoat, in one pocket of which he invariably carried a bottle of the commonest and vilest rum, while in the other he carried a loaded revolver, with which he would blaze away at any one who gave him the slightest provocation. On one occasion I saw him stagger into a Bulgarian boot shop and yell out in English to the proprietor, "Give me a pair of boots, you ———!"

Of course the Bulgarian could not understand, so Black whipped out his revolver and blazed a few cartridges away among the stock in trade before the trembling cobbler could pacify him. He was perpetually firing off this weapon, and he was such a terror to the unfortunate Bulgarians in whose houses he was quartered, that he was never allowed to stay more than a week at a time in one place. At last he became such a nuisance that old Hassib Bey, a most courtly old Turkish gentleman, who was the head of the hospital, sent for me, and asked me what on earth they were to do with this compatriot of mine. I suggested that he should be quartered in the military hospital, where he would have fewer opportunities of being a nuisance, and my suggestion, which was adopted, speedily brought matters to a crisis.

One night, when Dr. Black had retired to rest in the military hospital, drunk as usual, a number of mischievous *jarra bashis*, dispensers and dressers, began to tease him by hammering at his door and making offensive remarks to him. He yelled out to them in English that if they did not desist he would bring out the inevitable revolver; but they could not tear themselves away from the fascinating sport of baiting a boozer; and suddenly, as they were gathered outside in the passage whistling, cat-calling, and shouting out uncomplimentary epithets, the door opened, and Dr. Black appeared in his night-shirt, revolver in hand. There was a frightened stampede down the passage, and as they fled Black emptied the revolver at random at his assailants.

A piercing shriek told that one of the bullets at any rate had gone home, and presently the whole hospital was in an uproar, as a little Italian dresser staggered into the house surgeon's room declaring that he was murdered. A hasty examination, however, showed that the bullet had entered a portion of the anatomy where it could do little harm, namely, the fleshy tissues adjacent to the base of the spine, and no attempt was made to extract it. Probably that little Italian dresser carries the bullet about in his back still as a souvenir of campaigning days in Widdin.

When Dr. Black put his head out of his door next morning, he found a couple of soldiers stationed there waiting to arrest him; so he retreated inside the room again, and devised a plan of escape. The window of the room looked out over a courtyard about fourteen feet below; and as there was a thick layer of snow in the yard, Black decided to escape that way. He knotted his blanket into a rope, and dropped into the yard—also into the arms of the sentry stationed below. He was brought before old Hassib Bey, who sent for me; and I sent for Jack the mill engineer to act as interpreter. Finally Hassib Bey decided that it would be no good to put Black in gaol, and to my intense delight he resolved to send him away out of Widdin altogether. He treated my discreditable compatriot most generously, for he had him placed on board one of the large river steamers which plied once a week from Widdin up as far as Belgrade, and sent him away scot-free after his escapade, and with £10 in his pocket to carry him out of Turkish territory as soon as possible. I thanked Hassib Bey for his forbearance, and to my great joy I never saw Dr. Black again.

When my regiment was sent out of the fortress to the encampment, I was detailed for hospital duty, and took up my quarters at a small fifth-rate Bulgarian hotel on the banks of the Danube. The principal diversion was to go on board the big passenger steamers, and hear the news of the outside world and what people were saying of us in England. I met a charming Frenchman on board one of them, a highly cultured and agreeable military man, named Captain Bouchon, who was going down to Rustchuk. However, I persuaded him to stop with me for a week, and his society gave me the greatest pleasure.

The first war correspondent whom I met in Widdin was a man named Fitzgerald, who came out as the representative of the London *Standard*. He was a fine fellow, and had seen service in the British army. It was the month of April when he arrived, among the first of the petrels who presaged the coming storm; and about the same time there came two battalions of Egyptian troops under Prince Hassan, the *khedive's* second son. These made a strong reinforcement for the large body of troops already in Widdin. One day Fitzgerald came to me, and said that he was going away up the river for a few days. He asked me to look after his correspondence, and to send any items of news worth telegraphing to the *Standard*. He took the boat, and went away leaving me in charge, and I have never seen him from that day to this. I took up his work, and sent several messages during the campaign which followed to the *Standard*, spending a considerable sum of money out of my own pocket upon telegraphing. Afterwards, when I got down to Constantinople and explained matters to Mr. Frank Ives Scudamore, a well known personality there, he refunded me the money.

When the Egyptian troops arrived, they naturally occasioned a good deal of stir, and they were keenly criticised by their Turkish allies. For physique and fighting qualities there could be no comparison between the two bodies of men, the Turks easily carrying off the palm. Still, the Egyptians were by no means to be despised. Their officers were highly trained and intelligent, and the equipment of the troops was new and good, far superior, in fact, to that of the Turkish soldiers. Moreover, the Egyptian force brought with it an excellent band of brass and strings, which proved a perfect god-send, as we had no band among all the Turkish forces, and the bugles were not particularly agreeable to listen to. The Egyptians afterwards behaved well in action, and many of them fought at the defence of Widdin under Izzet Pasha, who successfully beat off the repeated assaults of the Roumanians and the Servians, and preserved the town intact.

Among the many interesting men who were gathered together in Widdin during this period of waiting and watching was a singularly attractive and talented Armenian named Zara Dilber Effendi, who was a resident of the place and the chairman of the local chamber of commerce. He had been brought up in Germany, and spoke every European language with equal fluency. I became very intimate with him, and was a frequent visitor at his house, finding him thoroughly well informed and an intimate friend of Osman Pasha.

In fact, Zara Dilber Effendi and Osman Effendi, a Turkish doctor who had been educated in Paris, and who was the best surgeon that I came in contact with during the whole of the campaign, were my constant companions during my stay in Widdin, as my medical *confrères*, with the exception of two or three, had few tastes and no ideas in common with me. Dr. Kronberg and Dr. Busch, however, both capital fellows and married men, were sociable enough; and I have always attributed to the promptings of Madame Kronberg and Madame Busch a brilliant social idea which was developed by Osman Pasha immediately after the declaration of peace with Servia.

Civil and military society in the town was convulsed one day by the announcement that Osman Pasha intended to give a grand ball to celebrate the cessation of hostilities and in aid of the funds of the military hospitals. All the arrangements for the ball were left in the hands of Zara Dilber Effendi on the strength of that gentleman's intimate knowledge of the highest circles of European society; and as it was generally understood that Osman Pasha's invitations would be issued on the recommendation of Zara Dilber Effendi, the feminine world of Widdin was much fluttered. It leaked out pretty early that no one below the rank of a field officer would be invited, and we were kept on the tiptoe of excitement until the eventful night arrived.

A fine Bulgarian house with a large room was taken for the night, and for a whole week beforehand Zara Dilber Effendi was missing. People said that he made several mysterious visits into Roumanian territory, bringing back each time a small army of Roumanian servants and many suggestive cases and packages. It was rumoured that there were to be chairs at the ball, and knives and forks. People whispered of a regular set supper, with European dishes and champagne. But Zara Dilber Effendi kept his own counsel, and went on his way, wrapped in impenetrable Oriental secrecy. As for myself, having received my invitation, I bought a brand new uniform, wondering a good deal where the ladies were to come from, and how the Turks would enjoy a ball carried out according to Western ideas. My invitation bore Osman Pasha's signature, and I sent this interesting souvenir out to my father in Australia afterwards.

When I entered the ballroom on that memorable night, I was fairly staggered. The room had been beautifully decorated by the Turkish and Egyptian troops with festoons of flags and picturesque devices composed of swords, rifles, revolvers, and arms of every kind. Upon a raised *daïs*, at the end of the room, stood Osman Pasha in full-dress uniform, supported on either side by Madames Kronberg and Busch beautifully dressed. He received the guests with courtly politeness, shaking hands with each as they came up; and as the long line of brilliant uniforms sparkling with decorations, and of beautiful women dressed with exquisite taste, filed past in front of him, it was difficult to realize that one was not assisting at some great State ball in London or Paris, but at a function in a small Bulgarian frontier town lying almost under the guns of an avowedly hostile force.

A wide divan ran round the room, and on this the Turkish officers sat cross-legged, observing the proceedings with grave interest. The Turk is quite used to paying people to dance for his amusement, but he would never dream of dancing himself. I watched one dignified old Turkish colonel striving hard to maintain that decorous impassivity which a few of the ballroom exquisites of the Western world seem to have borrowed from the East; but every now and then, as some audacious young Giaour like myself glided past clasping a vision of beauty all silk and lace and pearls and flowers in his arms, I saw the old Turk's eyes open wider and wider in spite of himself. Zara Dilber Effendi had performed his share of the work well, for he had collected about sixty of the most cultured, refined, and beautiful women that I have ever seen together in a ballroom.

There were a few Bulgarian ladies of the highest class; but the majority were Spanish Jewesses from seventeen to twenty years of age, with the rich colouring, the dark hair, and liquid eyes of all their race, or stately Roumanians, statuesque in type. There was a liberal sprinkling of Levantines, Italians, Greeks, and possibly two or three Servians; but though they differed in race, they were alike in one particular, for all were beautiful and refined. These ladies, I must admit, were little short of a revelation to me, for I had only seen a few thickly veiled Turkish women in the town hitherto; but Zara Dilber Effendi was evidently a person of some note in Widdin, and the invitations had been sent out to none but the ladies of the most aristocratic families in the country.

I was the only Englishman present at that remarkable ball; and

I suppose it is not often that an Englishman finds himself assisting at an entertainment of such half-barbaric splendour, and held under such dramatic circumstances. Every man in the room knew that the commencement of a fierce campaign was only a question of weeks, perhaps days; and we snatched the enjoyment of the hour as gaily as did the guests at the Duchess of Richmond's famous ball in Brussels on the eve of Waterloo.

Indeed the parallel between Osman Pasha's ball and the historic ball at Brussels which Byron has celebrated was a very real one. In both cases the dancers were dancing on the edge of a battlefield. In both cases the existence of an empire hung on the issue of the coming struggle. In both cases many of the brave men gathered there amid the music and the flowers and under the flags and lamplight were soon to be lying out upon the blood-soaked plain, cold and deserted—the *débris* of a dreadful festival. We had no "*Brunswick's fated chieftain*" there that evening; but the courtly old Turkish colonel who sat up cross-legged on the divan, and watched me so intensely while I danced, makes in my eyes a far more vivid picture. I saw him afterwards, again in a sitting posture, outside a redoubt near Radishevo, when the tide of battle had ebbed back, only to flow again in fiercer volume. His head had fallen forward on his knees, and when I touched him I found that he was dead—cut almost in two by a Russian shell.

However, the shadow of the impending war only served to throw the brightness of the ball into stronger relief, and I gave myself up to the business of pleasure with all the ardour of two and twenty. There were only about a dozen of us, mostly members of the medical staff, who were dancing men, and we were consequently kept busy. I generally divided one waltz into three parts; and as the other men followed my lead, we were able to give all the ladies a turn occasionally, and there were no wall-flowers. A big ambulance tent had been pitched in the garden to serve as a supper-room, and we paid for the refreshments as we had them, the money going the hospital fund. I used to take my partners out after every dance, and the champagne corks were flying almost as thickly as the bullets later on.

I recollect that I spent just £9 on suppers and refreshments during the evening. A man is not inclined to be economical when he knows that before long he may have no mouth to put champagne in and no head left to get dizzy with it. Zara Dilber Effendi had got in a splendid supper from Crajova in Roumania, where he also obtained the favours for the *cotillion* which was danced in perfect style under the direction of the experienced Madame Kronberg and Madame Busch.

Among my partners that night were three very charming sisters, who had been born in Roumania, but whose father was a Greek. They spoke German very well, and consequently I danced more often with them than with the other ladies, with whom I found greater difficulty in conversing. The sisters were good enough to take quite an interest in me, and they invited me to call at their house during the week, following up their verbal invitation with a note next day. At the end of a sheet of dainty little handwriting on scented notepaper was a remarkable postscript (I find that ladies generally put the most important part of their communications into the postscript) setting forth that their grandfather had a rooted aversion to all Englishmen, myself in particular, and that he would certainly shoot me if he found me calling on his granddaughters. In campaigning times one is not discouraged by trifles, and soon after the ball I called upon my three charming partners, who entertained me with coffee and music at their beautiful home.

Suddenly a step was heard on the stairs, and the eldest of the sisters with a blanched face whispered that it was their grandfather, and bade me fly at once. I dropped from the window into the lane below, and as I did so the irascible old Greek opened fire on me with a blunderbuss. Fortunately for me his anger had affected his aim, and I escaped unscathed. A few years more or less make little difference in national proclivities. Old Lambro, the Greek pirate who attacked Don Juan, is said by Byron to have been "*the mildest-mannered man that ever scuttled ship or cut a throat*"; and the grandfather of my fair partners seemed to have inherited something of the same temperament with a certain difference.

In April of the year 1877 we began to realize fully that war was imminent, and the Turkish commanders set to work to prepare their troops for a stern and fierce fight. Every day almost the small, flat-bottomed, single-masted boats that plied up and down the Danube kept arriving with cargoes of flour and maize for victualling the town, and also with reinforcements of fresh troops, who were packed on board as close as eggs in a basket. Most of the reinforcements were quartered in the large camp, which was pitched about two miles and a half out of Widdin towards the Servian border; and when all had arrived, we found about thirty-five battalions of infantry there, with several batteries of artillery and squadrons of cavalry, the whole making up an imposing *corps d'armée*.

As the camp increased in proportions, it was found that more surgeons were required, and I received orders to give up my hospital work in the fortress and report myself for duty at the camp. I was appointed one of the ambulance surgeons, and rejoined my old regiment, the Kyrchehir, which had been sent out from the fortress. The camp was situated on a long, green slope of rising ground, several miles in length; and here the long lines of bell tents were pitched, among them the tent of my old comrade the paymaster, with whom I once more foregathered.

About half a mile from the camp was a large marsh or swamp, where great white arum lilies grew, with jonquils, narcissus, and the different kinds of iris, in magnificent profusion, as well as millions of the tiny white snowflakes. I had a trench dug outside my tent, and once a week our two servants, the paymaster's and my own, went down to the swamp, and brought back barrowfuls of flowers, which I planted in the trench. Here too the orderlies made me a great seat of turf, and every morning from six o'clock till half-past nine I sat there among the flowers to receive my patients, who used to come up from the different battalions to have their various ailments treated. Epsom salts formed a sovereign remedy for most of the trifling sicknesses, and my method of giving the physic was extremely primitive. As I sat on my throne of turf, I had a sackful of Epsom salts beside me, together with a bucket of water and a *pannikin*; so that when the patient had swallowed a handful of the salts I presented him with a *pannikin* of water, and he washed the nauseous mouthful down. The men never complained, and accepted these simple ministrations with exemplary *sang-froid*.

As a rule the Turks have excellent teeth; but in such a large assemblage of men there were of course many exceptions, and I had a good deal of tooth-drawing to do. Some of those Mussulman molars were dreadfully obstinate, and resisted every effort of the Giaour with fanatical determination. One man with a huge aching grinder in his upper jaw came to me three mornings in succession, for with the simple appliances at my disposal I was unable to extract it in one sitting. At last I made him sit down on the ground in front of me, and, grasping the forceps in my right hand, I braced my feet against the pit of his stomach, and put forth every effort. There was a crunching, grinding noise, a sound of breaking and rending, then a "*plop*" as when a recalcitrant cork comes out of a bottle of pale ale, and I was lying on my back in the trench among the arum lilies, with the forceps and the molar in my hand at last. As for the Turk, he spat the blood out of his mouth, piously remarked that *Allah* was very good, and went back to his company.

If any of my patients were seriously ill, or showed symptoms of malarial fever or dysentery, which was very prevalent, I had them placed in *arabas*, and sent back to the hospital in Widdin. Then, when my work of inspection was over, which was usually the case by about nine o'clock, the rest of the day was my own, and I spent it in improving my knowledge of Turkish and consuming large quantities of coffee and cigarettes with my brother officers. Every day the camp was in a state of great activity, with never ending drills and ceaseless inspections by the commandants, who spared no pains to see that everything was ready before the expected outbreak. The discipline throughout the camp was admirable, and the men were in excellent good humour.

Nearly every day I used to ride into Widdin to hear the news, and return to camp in the evening, generally reaching it before sunset. Only life in a Turkish camp can enable one to realize how deeply the Turks feel their religion, and how diligent they are in the practice of their devotions. No dour old Covenanter with a verse of a psalm on his lips ever flung himself with more dogged courage on the pikes of Graham of Claverhouse, than did those Turks charge down upon the Russian steel a few months later, with the cry of *"Allah"* upon their lips and the assurance of paradise in their heroic hearts. Perhaps the best qualification for a good soldier is to be a fanatic—as the next best is to be an *infidel*. After "Praise-God-Barebones," the most striking figure in a *mêlée* is Sergeant Bothwell, who died *"believing nothing, hoping nothing, fearing nothing."*

Every evening at the camp near Widdin the men were formed up in long, double lines just before sundown; and as the sun sank below the horizon the cry of *"La ilaha illallah Mohammed Rasul Allah"* started at one end of the lines, and was taken up by man after man, dying away in the distance *diminuendo*, and travelling back again *crescendo*, until it reached the starting-point in a mighty shout of religious fervour. The effect resembled nothing so much as a *feu de joie* of musketry, delivered with the precision and clearness attainable only by the daily practice of a lifetime.

When the men were dismissed from this mighty church parade, they would scamper off like so many schoolboys, and indulge in all kinds of games with the keen joy of living, and the unblunted faculties of sensation which are seldom found in the alcohol-drinkers of other nations. Wrestling was a favourite pastime with the men; and it was no uncommon sight to see five thousand spectators gathered in a huge ring, in the centre of which picked competitors, stripped to the waist, engaged each other in a catch-as-catch-can struggle. Hassan Labri Pasha, one of the principal officers in the camp, was an enthusiast in the sport of wrestling, and used to get up great tournaments in which the men wrestled each other for prizes of tobacco and other inexpensive little luxuries.

After three weeks of this life in camp, I was ordered back to Widdin again, and took up my quarters at the little Bulgarian hotel on the bank of the Danube where I had been before. Things were looking very serious at this time; and though war was not actually declared by Russia until April 24, 1877, still it was quite certain long before this date that Roumania would espouse the Russian cause; and when the Russian Army which had been quartered on the Pruth entered Roumanian territory, the Government of the Porte communicated with the Roumanian Government, intimating that they construed the act of Roumania in allowing Russian troops to cross her frontier as an act of hostility towards Turkey.

About a week before the declaration of war, two Roumanian officers came down the Danube from Kalafat, and landed at my hotel, where they were stopped and told that they could go no farther. One of them was a Captain Giorgione, whom I met and asked to dine with me before he went back to Kalafat. He accepted my invitation, and after a long and pleasant conversation about the general situation and the prospects of war he gave me a cordial invitation to go across the river to Kalafat and pay him a visit in his quarters. As hostilities were expected to break out at any moment, no one was allowed to cross the Danube from our side without a special permit from Osman Pasha; and as there was no probability that he would grant me the necessary permission, I determined to make the trip on my own account. Possibly this was an indiscretion on my part; but indiscretions are apt to be the most enjoyable things in life, and I was getting tired of the humdrum routine of the camp.

I had my English passport with me, which ensured my safe conduct until the actual declaration of hostilities; and armed with this precious document, I got one of my colleagues to act as *locum tenens* during my temporary absence from my practice, and hired a boat and a crew of boatmen to take me over the river, which at this point is nearly a mile wide, and flows with a current of extraordinary velocity. I dressed myself in a suit of mufti, but had no hat, and must have presented rather a piebald appearance with a Turkish *fez* surmounting a suit of English tweed. The Roumanian customs officers stared at me pretty hard, but they franked me through on my English passport, and I went into Kalafat, leaving my boatmen on the Roumanian side of the river to bring me back the same night.

I strolled into a *café* in Kalafat, which was then a town of about three thousand people; and the experience of living again in the European fashion, eating at a table, sitting on a chair, and seeing men in ordinary coats and trousers and hard black hats, struck me with all the charm of the unexpected. I felt the sensation of a Robinson Crusoe transplanted suddenly from his desert island and set down in the Hôtel Bristol.

Almost the first person that I met after I had finished breakfast was my friend Captain Giorgione, who expressed his delight at seeing me, and took me off at once to introduce me to the general commanding the division, after which I went to the captain's quarters in a house in the town. Most of the ordinary residents of Kalafat had already left the place, fearing that the bombardment of the town by the Widdin batteries was imminent, and the houses were filled with Roumanian officers and men. I lunched with Captain Giorgione and his brother officers, many of whom spoke German, and evinced a capacity for hearing news which was hardly disinterested. However, they were excessively polite, and in the afternoon we strolled on the promenade, and listened to the strains of an excellent military band.

As evening drew in my conscience began to trouble me, and I had the qualms of a schoolboy who has broken bounds, thinking of Osman Pasha and the remarks that he would be likely to make if he found out where I was. However, my newly found friends would not hear of my leaving them that day, and insisted upon my staying to dinner, at which I was given the seat of honour next to the general. What a capital dinner that was! Perhaps I enjoyed it all the more from the little circumstance that Osman Pasha might have me shot as soon as I got back. The Roumanian band played English airs in my honour, and the officers kept my glass always filled with Pommery. By the time we had reached the walnuts I found myself developing a surprising talent for mendacity, and the more questions that my polite hosts asked me the more astonishing grew my answering taradiddles.

Of course they tried to pump me as to the number and disposition of the Turkish troops, and of course, guileless youth that I was, I lied wholesale. Even when I had put down the troops in Widdin at a hundred thousand men and expanded the artillery to four hundred guns, I was almost as astonished at my own moderation as they were at the magnitude of the force which Turkey had already mobilized in Widdin. One of the Roumanian surgeons who was at that dinner was green with envy when he discovered that I ranked as a major in the Turkish army while he was graded as a lieutenant. We had a very merry night of it, and I hope that all the fibs I told will not be remembered against me. Then at daybreak I made my way to the river, found my boatmen, and was back by six o'clock at my hotel with no one a bit the wiser for my escapade.

I met some interesting men at Widdin just before the war, notably a splendid young fellow named Frank Power—who, by the way, was a nephew of the late Sir Peter Lalor, once speaker of the Victorian Legislative Assembly, and long ago a picturesque figure in the fight at the Eureka Stockade near Ballarat. Frank Power was a young Irishman, who had joined the Austrian military service, but afterwards was sent up to Widdin to act as war correspondent for the London *Daily Telegraph*. He lived with me; and I found him a most delightful companion, full of romance, and generously endowed with the love of adventure, and the enthusiasm, fire, and wit which are characteristic of the best Irishmen. He was a splendid rider and keen all-round sportsman, had read widely if not deeply, and with the mercurial temperament of the adventurer he combined more than a trace of the artist nature. He had the happiest knack of producing charming sketches in black-and-white or water-colours of bits of picturesque Bulgarian peasant life, groups of Turkish soldiery, or glimpses of the iris-spangled country that was soon to be coloured in a deeper dye.

Poor Power was almost heart-broken when they sent up Nicholas Leader from Constantinople to replace him as the correspondent of the *Daily Telegraph*. He returned to Vienna, and thence to Dublin, where he resumed his old journalistic life for a time. But to such a man as Power a life of comparative inactivity was impossible; and when the troubles broke out in the Soudan, he soon found his way over there, and eventually reached Khartoum,[1] where General Gordon appointed him British consul. Shortly before the fall of Khartoum, Gordon sent him down the Nile in a steamer with Colonel Stewart and an Arab escort to take despatches to the force advancing

---

1. *Gordon: the Career of Gordon of Khartoum* by Demetrius Charles Boulger also published by leonaur.

to the relief of Khartoum.

However, before the steamer had got far the smouldering fires of disaffection among the natives on board broke into flame, and they succeeded in running the steamer aground. Lured by the friendly demonstrations of the Arabs on the shore, Colonel Stewart and Frank Power went ashore with their escort while efforts were being made to lighten the steamer and float her off again. The full details of what followed will never be known with certainty; but news of a massacre reached the British column eventually, and the bearers of the despatches were among the missing. Those who are familiar with Dervish methods may picture for themselves the sudden rush of bloodthirsty fanatics, the desperate hand-to-hand combat, and the deaths of Colonel Stewart and of my gallant young comrade when they fell pierced by Arab lances on the scorched and dreadful desert that lies along the banks of the Nile from Wady Halfa to Khartoum.

Nicholas Leader, who was sent up from Constantinople to take Frank Power's place in Widdin, had already had an adventurous career, and had smelt powder in many lands. After seeing service with the British troops in Canada, he resigned on the declaration of war by France upon Germany in 1870, and took service with the French arms. He was attached to the ill fated army of Bourbaki, and was interned with other prisoners of war in Switzerland. Afterwards, when the Carlist insurrection broke out in Spain, he joined the standard of Don Carlos, and took part in the fierce guerilla warfare which the Carlists waged against the Spanish Government. The war correspondents of those fighting days in Spain were as daredevil a crew as ever lived; and Leader described to me with many a laugh the circumstances under which he first met Edmund O'Donovan, another Irishman, as gay and reckless as himself.

Leader was in command of a small fort in the north of Spain during the height of the insurrection, when one day he espied a strange figure clad in a long, dilapidated overcoat approaching the walls. The Spanish sentries yelled to the suspicious visitor to halt; and as he took no notice of them, they fired on him, and the bullets kicked up the dust all round the stranger. The only result, however, was that he increased his pace, and came on at the double until he reached the walls off the fort amid a rain of bullets. "Cease firing, ye blackguards!" he shouted in the simple dialect of Southern Cork. "I'm Edmund O'Donovan, and how the blazes can I get in unless you open the gate!" Leader was summoned to interpret the strange language of the foreigner, and he let him in. Thus it was that Edmund O'Donovan, who was attached to the government troops, walked alone into the enemy's fortress.

Nicholas Leader, after all his wanderings, found a grave in Turkish soil; for after a few weeks in Widdin, he joined the army of Suleiman Pasha at the Shipka Pass, and died there of fever.

About the time that Leader left Widdin the town was in a state of suppressed excitement, for everyone knew that the declaration of war was imminent, and the slightest incident was sufficient to cause a demonstration.

Once I went with two others by boat to a small island on the Danube, where there were numbers of wild duck. We got to work upon them in great style, and soon had a full bag; but when we were in the middle of the fun, half a squadron of Roumanian cavalry came galloping down to the opposite bank to see what the firing was about. It would not have taken much at that moment to provoke a conflict.

CHAPTER 4

From Widdin to Plevna

Although we knew that war was coming, still the actual declaration fell with the suddenness of a bombshell. On April 25 I had done my hospital work, and was walking down the street, when I noticed a great commotion, and saw groups of people talking excitedly together and orderlies galloping about in all directions. Presently Tallat Bey, a nephew of Osman Pasha and one of the headquarters staff, came cantering down the street. I stopped him to ask what all the excitement was about, and he told me that war had been declared by Russia on the previous day. A regular hum pervaded Widdin all that day, as the people repeated to one another the ominous news that Turkey would have to fight once more for her very life. We had been arranging all our ambulance work beforehand; and old Hassib Bey undertook, in compliance with my request, that I should be attached to the first troops that took the field.

But strangely enough, though war had been declared, and though we could see the Roumanian troops busily engaged in completing the fortification of Kalafat, several days went by without a shot being fired from either the Widdin or Kalafat batteries, and we were left looking at each other in grim expectation and suspense.

I remember well the first time that I ever heard a shot fired in war. I was sitting in my little Bulgarian hotel on the bank of the river with Colonel Stracey, who afterwards commanded the Scots Guards. He had been inspecting the Russian Army at Kischeneff, and between the time that he left them and his arrival at Widdin war was declared. When he came to the hotel where I was staying, I was delighted to see him, since he was the first Englishman, apart from the war correspondents, the notorious Dr. Black, and my friend Jack, the engineer of the Government mill, whom I had met in the town. We were having lunch together, when we heard a loud "*boom*" apparently close at hand, followed almost immediately by the distant roar of a heavy gun; and before we could realize what was happening, a shell struck the end of the hotel and crashed through two rooms, bringing bricks and plaster down in all directions with clouds of dust.

The bombardment from Kalafat had begun at last, provoked by a shot from a Turkish gunboat on the river; and within a few minutes the shells were shrieking over us, the women were screaming, and valorous old Turks were running out of their houses armed with rusty flintlocks or anything in the shape of a weapon that they could get hold of. Now and then a shell came crashing into the hotel; and as it stood in an isolated position on the bank of the river affording a capital target for the enemy's fire, it soon became too hot a corner to remain in. So it was shut up, and Stracey and I, both of whom were then under fire for the first time, moved farther back into the town, where I had secured a house for myself on the previous day in anticipation of some such trouble.

The firing went on for about three hours, and all the women in the town were of course terribly frightened, and were rushing about shrieking and weeping, not knowing what to do. It was curious to see the behaviour of the different nationalities in the hour of danger. Most of the Spanish women gathered together under the walls of the fortress, where they erected a roof of mats with the fortress wall as a support. Here they were perfectly safe from the Roumanian shells, which either struck the wall on the outside or else passed over it, dropping much farther in the natural course of their trajectory. The Turkish women huddled together in two large alcoves in the wall of the archway leading into the fortress, refuges which were almost like dungeons hewn out of the solid masonry, and which were absolutely safe from projectiles.

When the firing was over I went to the hospital, and found that four or five people had been wounded. A Spanish boy had lost his arm, and a Turkish woman had been killed by a shell bursting in her room. One unpleasant result of the bombardment was that Stracey and I had nothing to eat all night, as all the butchers and bakers in Widdin were down in their cellars, and no amount of money would induce them to come out. They put their heads above-ground next day, cautiously emerging like rabbits from their burrows, but always went back at night.

That evening when I was dozing off to sleep there was a terrific crash of artillery, the vibration of the firing breaking every window of the house; and as it was quickly replied to by the batteries of Kalafat, I jumped into my clothes, and rushed out to find the cause of this sudden eruption of hostilities. It was plain enough. A Roumanian vessel loaded with troops was running the gauntlet down the river in front of Widdin; and as she steamed past in the night on the far side of the long island opposite the town, the smoke of her funnel betrayed her, and the earth-shaking roar of the forty heavy siege-guns in the Widdin batteries told that the attempt was discovered.

Only the vessel's smoke-stack could be seen over the island by the sparks flying upwards in the dark, and through this phantasmal target the big shells hissed and shrieked in vain, bursting in mid-air and burying the fragments in Roumanian soil across the river. The batteries at Kalafat took up the tale at once, and for a few hours we had a lively time of it. It was the adverse fortune of war for the Roumanian vessel; for after she had dodged the storm of shells from our siege-guns and got safely out of range, she was blown up by a Turkish monitor lower down the river, and every soul on board perished.

On June 1 I was detailed for duty in the main hospital, which was just then receiving an unusual amount of attention from the Kalafat batteries. Unfortunately for the wounded, this hospital was situated a few hundred yards from one of our batteries; and while the Roumanians were finding the range for this battery, a good number of their shells, which had too much elevation, dropped on the hospital and on the surrounding houses. I was sitting in my room in the hospital one day when a shell burst with an awful crash in the middle of a ward full of sick and wounded men. It struck the lattice of a window, and at once exploded. When I rushed in, the ward was full of dust and smoke, out of which came terrible screams and cries. Four of the patients had been killed on the spot, and seven others had been wounded.

One man, who was delirious from malarial fever, had his side ripped open from hip to shoulder by a fragment of the shell. He was still alive, but wildly delirious. Another had his arm fearfully mangled, and I took it off at the shoulder there and then. The only nurses that I had were the men supplied by the different regiments for hospital duty. One of them, a stalwart private from my old regiment the Kyrchehir, was among the four who were killed by the shell. A great outcry was made outside Turkey about the Roumanians violating the Convention of Geneva and the principles of humanity by firing on the hospital; but my own opinion is that they could not avoid hitting it in the position which it occupied, and that it should never have been placed there at all.

One strange and grim incident happened during the bombardment, and, to the Turkish mind especially, seemed to illustrate the doctrine of fatalism with appalling vividness. In the height of the firing, when the shells from the heavy siege-guns at Kalafat were dropping incessantly within the fortress, one of them, as it exploded, tore a great hole in the ground large enough to contain a horse. A Turkish woman, who was cowering with three children under the shadow of the wall, determined to take refuge in the newly made hole, reckoning by the doctrine of chances that it was about the least likely spot to be again disturbed.

Hardly had she crept in and drawn the three children after her than another shell, leaving the cannon's mouth at Kalafat nearly two miles away, dropped into the very same hole and blew the four hapless creatures who were hiding there to atoms. On another occasion I saw a shell strike the angle of a house, tear two walls down, and reduce one half of a room to ruins. In the other half of the room were a Turkish woman and two children, all of whom escaped unhurt.

As soon as the war had fairly started and the troops had smelt blood, the Circassians began to display the wild courage and the love of pillage inbred in them in the mountain fastnesses, which they only left to become the troublesome members of the Turkish Empire that they generally turned out to be. Of their bravery and resourcefulness there could be no question; but their rapacity was inextinguishable, and no one who did not wear a uniform was safe from them. Soon after the commencement of the bombardment, a party of about fifty Circassians organized a private raid on their own account into Roumanian territory, and carried it out with extraordinary dash and brilliancy.

One dark night, when the flash of the guns at Kalafat and the answering stream of fire from the Widdin batteries illuminated the blackness with fitful gleams of light, the Circassians crossed the Danube in boats, towing their horses behind them by ropes. They had made ingenious lifebelts for the horses out of the inflated pigskins which were used as wine casks in the country, and thus equipped each hardy little animal swam easily behind the boats and crossed the river without mishap. When the Circassians reached the opposite bank, they removed these novel lifebelts, mounted their horses, shot a couple of Roumanian sentries, and galloped off in the darkness with the instinctive knowledge of the whereabouts of plunder that is born in the blood of hereditary cattle-stealers.

Before long they had rounded up a goodly mob of the small black cattle of Roumania, and had them headed for the Danube. The Circassian is an expert stockman, and for the party to bring four hundred cattle down to the river was an easy task while the Kalafat gunners, blissfully unconscious of the *coup* that was being executed under their noses, kept pounding away at the Widdin fortifications. To bring a mob of cattle across a river nearly a mile wide and with a current of great velocity would need some skill in daylight; but to bring them across in pitch darkness, and under the guns of the enemy, was a feat which few but Circassians could accomplish.

Those black cattle, however, that are found along the banks of the Danube are almost amphibious, and they take to the water like dogs. As soon as the front files had taken to the water the others followed them readily, and the Circassians followed in the boats, rounding up the stragglers with their whips, and towing their horses, re-equipped with the pigskin lifebelts, behind them. So in darkness and rain, across the hurrying flood of the Danube they brought four hundred head of Roumanian cattle, and left behind them two dead sentries lying with their faces turned towards the sky.

All that May the bombardment of Widdin was continued at irregular intervals; but there were occasionally several successive days on which there was no firing, and at these times life in Widdin was inconceivably dull. While these voluntary armistices were in progress, we could see the Roumanians hard at work constructing new batteries, which made the Turkish troops in Widdin chafe at their enforced inactivity.

Owing to the conditions under which the bombardment took place and the strong fortifications of Widdin, the Turkish loss in killed and wounded was remarkably small; for on June 27, after several weeks of intermittent firing, we only had about twelve killed and twenty wounded.

The Roumanian gunners seemed to have great difficulty in finding the range; for on June 26, when I was sitting on the verandah of the Austro-Hungarian Consulate, all the Roumanian batteries, six in number, opened fire apparently on the consulate, though it was said afterwards that their target was a Turkish monitor lying a little farther down the river. The first two shells flew over the consulate, the next exploded in the adjoining house, and the next fell into the river about twenty yards from where we were sitting. Despairing, it seemed, of hitting the consulate, my quondam entertainers, with whom I had dined not so long before, directed their efforts upon the fortress, but without doing any serious damage.

On the following morning they commenced operations at seven o'clock, and from that hour until three o'clock in the afternoon the screaming of the shells was incessant. This was decidedly the biggest day that we had had, and the Turkish batteries responded very vigorously. Osman Pasha took the keenest interest in the artillery practice, and remained in one of our largest batteries for the greater part of the day. While there he told one of the gunners to direct his fire upon a certain battery. The gunner fired three times, and on each occasion he dropped the shell right into the Roumanian battery. Osman Pasha was so delighted that he embraced the man, and made him a sergeant on the spot.

In spite of the stunning noise of the projectiles, many of which weighed sixty pounds apiece, one soon got used to the cannonading; and while the bombardment was going on, I often sat on the battlements with my legs dangling over the side, and watched the Roumanian gunners at their work.

Our friends the Circassians, whenever they found time hanging heavy on their hands, were in the habit of relieving the monotony by private forays across the river, during which they made things very unpleasant for the Roumanian outposts. Osman Pasha himself admitted that he could put no reliance upon the Circassians. In his treatise on the campaign, he sums up this branch of his troops in one fitting sentence: "*En résumé, leur concours fut plus invisible qu'utile.*" At the same time he points out that the savage excesses of the Circassians were equalled, if not surpassed, by the exploits both of the Cossacks and the Bulgarians, who never allowed an opportunity of massacre or pillage to escape them.

At the same time, while admitting the excesses of the Circassians, he is careful to point out that the regular Ottoman troops were kept in a thorough state of discipline by their officers. "We can affirm," he declares, "that the Turkish regulars never committed an act similar to the massacre of the defenders of Lovtcha, nor to the inhuman treatment of which the Turkish prisoners were the victims after the fall of Plevna."

It may not be out of place here to give a brief sketch of the plan of campaign which Osman Pasha submitted to the commander-in-chief, Abdul Kerim Pasha, about the end of June, and which, had it been adopted, would probably have changed the whole issue of the war. From the official records, since collated under the *muchir's* personal supervision, it appears that Osman Pasha proposed to the commander-in-chief to leave about twelve battalions of infantry for the defence of Widdin, and to unite the remainder of the forces at his disposal, namely, nineteen battalions, so as to make a *corps d'armée*, at the head of which he (Osman Pasha) should leave Widdin. He would pick up on the march a few battalions from the garrison of Rahova, make for Plevna, and there join the division of Hassan Hairi Pasha, who would quit Nicopolis without waiting for the enemy's attack. Then passing Lovtcha, the whole column would march upon Tirnova, where Osman Pasha would effect a junction with the eastern army from Shumla under Mehemet Ali Pasha, and then with the two combined armies march in the direction of Sistova. If this junction were prevented by the movements of the Russian Army, Osman Pasha could occupy the position of Lovtcha, which was better situated than Plevna for the defence of the Balkan Passes.

However, Osman Pasha could not obtain leave to carry out his plan, and he even encountered opposition in making the necessary preparations. His idea was of course to assume the offensive, and hurl the Russians back upon Wallachia before their reinforcements arrived, instead of being compelled, as afterwards happened, to act on the defensive at Plevna.

Afterwards, on July 10, the Sultan gave Osman Pasha a free hand, but it was then too late; and so it came about that delay at the critical moment, combined with the incapacity of Redif Pasha, the Turkish minister of war, who was responsible for the defective organization of the Ottoman army, its reduced strength, and its lack of proper transport and commissariat services, operating together, neutralized the brilliant generalship of Osman Pasha and the devoted courage of the men who fought under him.

On the evening of July 12 we heard the news that we were to march next morning, and every heart beat high at the prospect of an early escape from the demoralizing inactivity of life in the bombarded town. Among the troops left in Widdin for garrison duty was my old regiment the Kyrchehir; and on the evening of July 12, just eight days before the first battle of Plevna, I rode out to the camp to bid farewell to my old comrades, from whom I was now to part, for in accordance with my own request to Hassib Bey I had been appointed to go on duty with the troops about to take the field. My relations with both the officers and the men of the Kyrchehir Regiment had been of the most cordial nature ever since I joined them in Constantinople. They all expressed their regret at the separation, which, I need hardly say, I felt as keenly as they did. My leave-taking with my little comrade Mehemet Ali the paymaster, whose tent-mate I had been, and who had taught me most of the Turkish that I knew, was specially affecting; and I can say with truth that, as I cantered back to Widdin that night to take the field against the enemy, I carried with me the good wishes of all my old comrades.

On July 13 at five o'clock we marched out of Widdin, bound, as we afterwards understood, for Nicopolis. Osman Pasha's army consisted of nineteen battalions of infantry, fifty-eight guns, and one regiment of cavalry;[1] while Izzet Pasha was left behind with the remainder of the troops to garrison Widdin. I was attached to the Shumla Regiment, which had the reputation of being one of the finest fighting regiments in the Ottoman Army; and two other surgeons, Weinberger and Kustler, both Austrians, accompanied the advance guard with me. We said goodbye to the others before we started, and we all drank each other's healths, and wished each other good luck in the unknown struggle that was before us.

The men of Osman Pasha's army were all in splendid fettle, and were looking forward with longing to the time of coming to close quarters with the enemy. Since the close of the Servian war they had all been well fed and well clothed, the horses were in tiptop condition, and the men set out upon the march with a light heart, carrying each his seventy rounds of ammunition and his accoutrements reduced to the lightest marching order as if the weight was nothing. We had a baggage train consisting of waggons full of ammunition; but there was no commissariat service, and we had to rely for sustenance solely on the great army biscuits, each as big as a soup-plate, of which every man carried a supply. Water was obtained from the water-carts, which followed the column in case streams or wells should fail us *en route*.

It was the height of summer, and the weather was terribly hot when we started on the morning of the 13th, the line of march following the course of the Danube, though at some distance back, this precaution being adopted for two reasons—first, to conceal our objective from the enemy and, secondly, to minimize the danger from

---

1. Lieutenant Herbert's reckoning gave the field state of Osman's marching out strength at 19 battalions, 6 squadrons, 9 batteries; in all 12,000 men, with 54 guns. *Vide The Defence of Plevna*, by Lieutenant V. Herbert.

their guns.

The Roumanians of course were quickly aware of our departure, and they followed us with their field-guns on the other side of the river. When they began to shell us, however, at Vidpol, we diverged from the main road, and, striking farther back, continued our march without sustaining a single casualty. At five o'clock in the afternoon the column camped near the village of Artzar, and I rode into the village on a foraging expedition to see if I could not supplement the biscuits, which were very hard fare, and had to be broken with a hatchet and soaked in water before they could be eaten.

I managed to buy some *kabobs*, or small pieces of meat fixed on skewers; and Weinberger, Kustler, and I made a fire, and cooked a modest supper, which we ate with the best of appetites. We determined to camp about a mile away from the main body, and tied our horses up to the branches of a huge walnut tree, while we admired the novel sight of the bivouac. The column had halted in a wooded valley among the hills and along the bank of a river; so that the lights of a thousand camp-fires danced on the quiet water, and the hum and laughter of thirteen thousand men came to our ears on the soft night breeze that was whispering through the walnut trees. Gradually one by one the lights died down; the men, tired with the long and dusty march, wrapped themselves in their great-coats; and the camp was sunk in slumber.

At about nine o'clock it began to get very cold, and Weinberger, Kustler, and I decided to shift our quarters, and move in among the main body to warm ourselves by the smouldering camp-fires. Picking our way gingerly among the sleeping forms that lay thickly on the bare ground, we came to a water-cart, to which we tied our horses, and then lay down to sleep. In the middle of the night there was a tremendous uproar, and I woke with a start, fancying that the Russians were upon us; but the scare was groundless. Our horses had pulled over the water-cart, broken their bridles, and were galloping mad with fright among the sleeping men; while the cries of the sentries and the curses of the rudely awakened sleepers speedily put the whole camp into confusion. In the middle of it all Osman Pasha put in an appearance to see what the noise was about, and the disturbance ceased as quickly as it began. With a few blessings from the sentries, we dozed off again to snatch what sleep we could, knowing that we had a hard day before us on the morrow.

On the following day the marching was terribly severe, for the heat was intense, and the distance we had already travelled had told on the men. About half a dozen fell down from sunstroke, and we had to leave them by the side of the road on the chance that the arabas bringing up the rear would pick them up. We came to several small rivers which were not bridged and had to be forded, while the roughness of the country caused much trouble to the artillery.

In many places the path was so precipitous that the horses had to be taken out, and the guns pulled up to the summit by the men with drag-ropes. At four o'clock in the afternoon the column reached Krivodol; and here Osman Pasha received an urgent telegraphic message from Said Pasha, the Sultan's private secretary, instructing him to push on with the utmost possible despatch, and declaring that the Turkish Empire was then between life and death.

In order that the fatal consequences of the long delay in Widdin, at a time when every moment was precious and when every Turkish soldier was needed on the frontier, may be clearly understood, it is necessary to take a bird's-eye view of the disposition of the Russian forces and their plan of campaign during those momentous days in July.

As the Franco-German war opened with a race to the Rhine, so the Russo-Turkish war opened with a race to the Balkans, and the Russians got there first. By July 5, while we were still in Widdin, three Russian army corps had crossed the Danube at Sistova, with a division of cavalry and several Cossack regiments. General Gourko, with a strong advanced guard, including infantry, cavalry, artillery, and mounted pioneers, had crossed the Balkans by the bridle-path of Hain-Bogan, an exploit requiring extraordinary efforts, and debouched near Hainkioj on July 14. Here Gourko's dragoons easily routed a regiment of three hundred Anatolian Nizams; but a single Turkish regiment properly informed and properly led could have barred the pass for days.

On July 19 the Shipka Pass was taken, a considerable Turkish force was dispersed, and a panic was struck at Constantinople. Meanwhile General Krüdener, with the Ninth Russian Army Corps, left Sistova on July 12, on the 15th invested Nicopolis, and on the 16th received the surrender of that fortress, upon which Osman Pasha was then marching. Ahmed Pasha, Hassan Pasha, with seven thousand men, were made prisoners, and one hundred and thirteen guns, with a large quantity of miscellaneous stores, fell into the hands of the Russians. Had Osman Pasha's propositions for an earlier departure from Widdin been carried out, Nicopolis would probably have been saved and the course of the campaign entirely changed. It was the news of the imminent attack on Nicopolis, which was communicated to Osman Pasha while we were lying in camp at Krivodol, which caused him to break up the camp after a few hours' rest and push on with that terrible forced march to Plevna.

We reached Krivodol at about five o'clock in the afternoon of July 14, and bivouacked near the village. It was a most picturesque little place, dotted down as it were in the middle of a sheltered valley which was watered by a little river. Here and there in the valley I saw curious mounds of earth about twelve feet high, and on inquiry I found that these were the tombs of Greek inhabitants who had settled here under the Byzantine Empire. After a successful forage for eatables in the village, I decided to bivouac on the top of one of these tombs which had a small hollow in the summit very enticing to a tired man; but before I wrapped myself in my great-coat for a sleep, the spirit of antiquarian research got hold of me, and I resolved to investigate the contents of my uncanny sleeping-place.

By the offer of a few *piastres* apiece, I got a dozen men from my regiment with picks and shovels, and under my direction they dug down into the tumulus until they came to an old stone coffin containing some bones, two pretty Greek vases, and a few Byzantine coins. I left the bones in their place, and filled up the tomb again, taking with me the coins and the vases. The coins I afterwards gave away, and the vases, which I wrapped up in a sheepskin and tied to my saddle, were broken by a little accident which occurred next night on the march.

Before midnight the march was resumed, and for the remainder of the night and all next day the journey was continued, until we reached the village of Veltchiderma late in the afternoon. Weinberger and myself rode on in advance of the column to the village; and I was so thoroughly done up by the intense heat of the day and the exhaustion of the march, that I made straight for the Turkish *khan* or hotel, and after getting my horse something to eat I fell fast asleep in the only decent-sized room in the place. When I woke up, I found Osman Pasha and his staff in the room talking. I apologized for my presence, and he was most good-natured about it. "A soldier sleeps when he can, my boy," he said; "for he never knows when he may get another opportunity."

After my sleep I went down to the river and had a splendid swim, while the main body of the column, which extended several miles in length, arrived at the camping-ground. We were just preparing to make ourselves comfortable for the night, when I noticed that there was an unusual amount of excitement about my regiment; and I found to my disgust that an advanced guard of about seventeen hundred men, including my regiment, had orders to march right through the night, and push on to Plevna with the utmost possible speed. Osman Pasha had received news by telegraph that Nicopolis, which was his objective, had been taken by the Russians; and he made up his mind to march straight to Plevna, which was distant sixty-nine miles from Veltchiderma.

Oh, the monotonous horror of that march! We were dead tired when we started; and all through the dark night the men stumbled blindly on, forbidden to sing or even to speak, lest they might betray their presence to the scouts of the enemy. Silent, sleepless, footsore, sick for want of food, and faint for want of water, they marched on the long road to Plevna. Our commander was Emin Bey, and we had about fifty cavalry scouts with us, but no guns. I rode behind Weinberger, and at about two o'clock in the morning his horse pitched head foremost into a deep hole in the track, and I went after him. The two of us with our horses floundered out of the hole somehow or other, and we fortunately escaped with a few bruises; but my archæological treasures were lost, my Greek vases tied up in the sheepskin were smashed to atoms, and all my sacrilegious enterprise had gone for nothing.

Next night the men were so tired that we had to camp for a couple of hours in the open plain, as they could positively go no farther without a rest. My horse had had hardly anything to eat all day; so I rode away a hundred yards from the main body to a place where there was some good grass, and decided to let him have a feed. I tied the reins round my wrist, and went to sleep on the open plain. When I woke up all was silent, for the troops had gone, and so had my horse, while I knew that the country all round was swarming with Cossacks. It was not a nice predicament to be in; but luckily my horse, a beautiful little Arab stallion and very quiet, had not strayed far, and I easily caught and mounted him. Then I went in pursuit of the troops, and by a combination of luck and judgment I found them before I had ridden many miles.

We lost half a dozen men next day from sunstroke; and I could do nothing to save the poor fellows, who simply dropped in their tracks, and had to be left to die at the side of the road. We had hardly any water, and the men suffered terribly, the feet of numbers of them being quite raw with continual marching. I bound up their feet as well as I could with linen and old rags, but the men who wore sandals were much better off than those who wore boots; and the severity of the march may be guessed from the fact that, while the advanced guard consisted of one thousand seven hundred men when it started, there remained only one thousand three hundred when it reached Plevna. The others had dropped out on the way, and those that remained alive were picked up by the waggons following the main body behind us.

That afternoon we crossed the River Isker, the men wading through the water, which reached to their shoulders. Weinberger and I found that the troops were to halt for a couple of hours near a Bulgarian village, and we rode in to see if we could not get something to eat. Since leaving Widdin we had eaten nothing but a handful of kabobs, some maize plucked in the fields, and our hard biscuits.

The first thing that attracted my attention as I rode into that village was a flock of geese, and I remember saying to Weinberger, "Look here; I don't know what you are going to do, but I am going to have a goose for dinner." We saw a Bulgarian, who was evidently the proprietor of the geese; and Weinberger, who spoke Bulgarian fluently, opened *pourparlers* on the subject, and offered a *medjidie* apiece for two of the birds. The Bulgarian was obdurate, and refused to sell at any price. We talked to him politely, we urged the claims of hospitality, and we descanted upon the high price which we were prepared to give, but all to no purpose. The idea of losing a splendid dinner which was already practically in my grasp enraged me, and I made Weinberger cover the Bulgarian with his revolver while I secured the materials for a meal. With the revolver barrel levelled at his head, the Bulgarian was obliged to watch me sulkily as I chased the flock of geese with my drawn sword. The blade was as keen as a razor, and with a couple of swishing strokes I smote off the heads of two of the birds. We plucked them, cleaned them, and roasted them; Weinberger ate one, and I ate the other.

When we had finished this hearty meal, we found that the troops had gone on; so we rode after them, and travelled right through the night, finding ourselves next morning about four miles from Plevna. This was the sixth day after leaving Widdin, and we had done one hundred and twenty miles altogether, having covered the last seventy miles in three nights and two days of almost continuous marching—a feat which will bear comparison with the greatest forced marches on record. The men had subsisted on two biscuits per day with a very small allowance of water, and each man had carried seventy rounds of ammunition as well as his accoutrements. Few of them, moreover, had received a single penny of pay for the past twelve months, and yet they stuck to their work with indomitable pluck and good humour.

When we reached the bridge across the Vid, about three miles from our destination, on the morning of July 18, the column could go no farther, and we halted for the last time in sight of the minarets of Plevna.

Alouf Pasha with three battalions had been in the town for some time, and Osman Pasha had sent us on in advance to assist him in holding Plevna until the main body could arrive.

When I rode into Plevna at eleven o'clock in the morning of July 18, I went straight to a *khan* and had a Turkish bath, after which I sallied out to survey the town.

CHAPTER 5

The First Battle of Plevna

The town of Plevna is built in the valley of the Tutchenitza, a small affluent of the Vid, about three miles from the meeting of the two, and just south of the confluence of the former with the Grivitza, which gave its name to the celebrated Grivitza redoubt. Before the war Plevna contained about seventeen thousand inhabitants, eight mosques, and two Christian churches. All round the angle formed by the confluence of the Grivitza and Tutchenitza are rolling hills, rising to their highest on the north near the villages of Opanetz, Bukova, and Grivitza. To the east one could see a number of small isolated hills, forming natural *mamelons*; and on the south a huge natural rampart defends the town. On the left bank of the Tutchenitza rise a succession of knolls, which were called by the Russians the "Green Hills"; and here some of the heaviest of the fighting afterwards took place.

When we of the advance guard arrived at Plevna on the morning of July 18, the uncut maize stood high on the hill-slopes round the town, and in places even a cavalry trooper might be hidden. The Green Hills were covered with vineyards, and there was plenty of timber, consisting mostly of oaks and beeches, which speedily vanished as the campaign progressed, until the hills were desolate in their absolute bareness. When Osman Pasha arrived, the fortifications consisted of a single blockhouse, between the Vid and the Tutchenitza on the Sofia road, of the kind which one saw all along the Servian and Albanian frontiers. The position, however, offered splendid opportunities for defence, enclosed as it was on three sides by hills, which afforded admirable sites for defensive works, hiding the interior and allowing reservesto be concentrated out of sight ready to be directed on any threatened point.

The deep ravines which break up the country and for the most part converge on Plevna rendered the lateral communication of the attacking force very difficult, so that the tactical contact, which is so important to the success of a combined attack on two points, was scarcely possible. It was easy to see that the ground was difficult for the movements of cavalry and guns; and the maize, vineyards, and scrub combined to prevent the rapid movement even of infantry.

In a short but highly suggestive sketch entitled *Le Petit Village*, Zola describes a modest little hamlet, nestling in a valley, remote from the busy world outside, and screened by a curtain of closely planted poplars from the eyes of curious strangers. It is watered by a small gurgling stream, along the banks of which are built the simple cottages of the country folk. Today, (as at time of first publication), the very existence of the hamlet is unknown, even to the dwellers in the neighbouring towns. Tomorrow the curtain of poplars has been rent by shot and shell, the little river runs red with blood, and the name of "Woerth" is blazoned in letters of fire upon the page of history. So has it been with Plevna. The little town had never been heard of before the campaign of 1877-1878, and it is not even mentioned in Von Moltke's sketch of the defensive advantages of Bulgaria. Now its name is known to every schoolboy, and the mere mention of it makes the pulse beat faster wherever pure patriotism and unflinching devotion to duty in the face of fearful suffering are recognized and honoured.

I walked through the narrow streets of Plevna on the day before the first battle, and saw a town already deserted by most of the wealthy inhabitants. Here and there I noticed a Turkish civilian dressed in the long, loose caftan, and the wide trousers tucked into high boots, which formed the universal dress of the Turks; while the Bulgarians wore the sheepskin caps and suits of coarse yellow frieze which I had seen before in Widdin and Sofia. The streets were paved with cobblestones, and the main street formed the principal bazaar of the place; while sundry evil-smelling lanes, running off to the right and left, were inhabited by scowling Bulgarians, who looked as though they would have cut my throat with the greatest pleasure. The Tutchenitza ran right across the main street; and here I saw the women washing clothes and chattering together, apparently unconscious of the dreadful trials before them.

At the lower end of the long, straggling main street, however, there was a collection of dirty little huts occupied by the Gypsies; and when they saw the troops coming, they seemed to recognize that the horrors of war were near, for they set up a prolonged wailing, while they wrung their hands with gestures of the deepest grief.

Leaving them to their lamentations, I proceeded to investigate the resources of the town, and was overjoyed to discover a European doctor, upon whom I promptly called and introduced myself. He was a very original character this Dr. Robert, and how he came to Plevna in the first instance I never found out. Born at Neuchâtel in Switzerland, he disappeared from the paths of European civilization when he had finished his medical course, and eventually settled down in Plevna, where he had been for ten years before I met him. He was not a bad-looking man, apparently about thirty-three years of age, with a fair beard and moustache. He had a good practice among the Bulgarians, and had evidently become a fashionable physician who commanded his own price.

Dr. Robert lived in the best house of the town, and drove the finest team of four black cobs that I ever sat behind. He had a regular menagerie in his gardens, which were fenced with wire, and contained a collection of storks and herons, a tame animal which I took to be a jackal, and four deer, which we afterwards ate. He had some good ideas as a landscape gardener too, and had tapped the Tutchenitza for water to irrigate his domain by means of channels.

After calling on Dr. Robert, I went off to pay my respects to the *kaimakan*, or Turkish governor of the town, who had his quarters in the *konak*, or town hall, a fine structure, built from the stone taken from an old Roman ruin which once occupied the site. We afterwards used this building as a hospital. The *kaimakan* was very courteous, and placed a clerk at my disposal, who found me quarters in a small, isolated Bulgarian house at the extreme north of the town.

After making these necessary arrangements I joined Weinberger, and we both went to dinner with Dr. Robert, who had not seen any European except his housekeeper for ten years, and was naturally eager to meet visitors who could tell him of the haunts of his youth. The housekeeper was a Viennese woman, decidedly unprepossessing in appearance, but a most excellent cook; and Weinberger and I, who had quite recovered our appetites after eating the two geese at Veltchiderma, enjoyed that dinner thoroughly. The doctor's house was furnished with every luxury. There were knives and forks and chairs, not to mention a piano; and as it was the first European meal that I had eaten for many months, with the exception of my dinner with the Roumanians at Kalafat, it is needless to say that I made a first-rate repast.

We drank a great many bottles of Bulgarian wine, and the more Dr. Robert drank the more loquacious he became, recounting his early bacchanalian and amatory exploits in German with a particularity of detail that was most edifying. Then he sat down at the piano and thumped the keys furiously, while he roared out convivial ditties in French, German, and Bulgarian until the whole house shook as if under the concussion of a bombardment. Even the Viennese housekeeper, who made her appearance upon the festive scene with a threatening aspect, failed to keep him quiet; and Dr. Robert was still chanting the praises of *"Wein, Weib, und Gesang"* when I made my way to my new quarters and sank into a deep and dreamless slumber, which even the manifold insects of Bulgaria were powerless to disturb.

Next morning I rode out to my regiment, which was camped on the hills, and asked the colonel to supply me with a servant. He ordered up six men for my inspection, and I chose a particularly smart-looking young Circassian named Mehemet, who afterwards became my faithful adherent, and performed his duties as groom and cook most satisfactorily. Then I rode away to the bridge over the Vid, and watched the arrival of Osman Pasha with the main body. They were all pretty well fagged out with fatigue and want of food and sleep; but there was no time to be lost, for the Russians were already advancing from Nicopolis upon Plevna, so Osman Pasha and his staff rode out at once and selected tactical points for the disposition of the troops. A strong force was sent out to the Janik Bair facing due north, another detachment was sent to the village of Grivitza in the hills facing east, and there was also an outpost in front of the village of Opanetz.

After seeing the troops arrive, I went to lunch with Dr. Robert, who had arranged to go with me and see the fighting if there should be any. At one o'clock I heard the boom of the Russian cannon which marked the opening of the protracted hostilities round Plevna, and the challenge received an immediate response from our batteries. Immediately all the Bulgarians in Plevna retired to their cellars, or any other place of security that they could find; and Dr. Robert and I rode off along the Nicopolis road to the Janik Bair, where the Turkish batteries were in position. By keeping just below the crest of the hill, Robert and I were safe from the shells, which either fell short on the far side of the hill, or else flew over our heads in the direction of the town. The hills were lined with our troops, who were all under cover, and, tying my horse to a tree, I walked up towards the summit. On my left I could see the villages of Bukova and Opanetz, while on the rising ground in front of me a mile away I caught an occasional glimpse of the gleam of Russian bayonets.

Looking out from the crest of the hill on which the Turkish batteries came into action, I saw the ridge of a smaller hill in front of me, and beyond it a second slope of rising ground, upon which the Russian artillerymen had planted their guns. These formed part of the force which General Schilder-Schuldner had under his command, and with which he advanced next day with the greatest confidence to a crushing defeat. The hill upon which the Russian guns were planted was thickly timbered, and at first I could see nothing but puffs of smoke followed by leaping flashes of flame. Then came the scream of the shell, which in the great majority of cases either buried itself in the hill-face below our batteries, or else flew overhead and dropped half a mile behind us in the valley towards Plevna. We had eighteen guns right on the summit of the hill extended in line, with hastily thrown up entrenchments in front, and the firing was almost continuous.

I made my way to the extreme left, where I took up a position in rear of the battery, and watched the firing. The artillery horses had been left under cover in the rear, and the men settled down steadily for an afternoon's practice at long range. It was the first time that I had been under fire in the open field, and I watched the proceedings with the closest interest, having my box of instruments and my packet of *tiftig*, or lint, ready for treating the wounded. Both sides were firing common shell, apparently rather as an evidence of willingness than with any hope of doing serious damage at so long a range. I counted about forty Russian guns in action, and after a while I could see the shells in the air quite plainly, and could pretty well judge where they would fall. When they struck the hill-face below us, a cloud of dust would fly up as they exploded in the earth; and when they flew over us, I could hear them buzzing like hornets as they sailed away into the valley behind.

While I was making my way up to the left of our line, I saw three Turkish artillerymen lying dead. One had been shot in the abdomen, and presented a terrible spectacle with his intestines all hanging out. The two others had had their legs carried away by shells. When I reached the farthest battery, I found one of the gunners with his hand ripped open by a splinter of iron, and I rendered surgical aid to my first wounded man under fire, washing the injury with water from my water-bottle, sewing up the hand, and dressing it with *tiftig* from my wallet. Then I sent the man to the rear, and told him to report himself at the hospital.

Here it was too that I saw my first man killed in the open field. It happened this way. I was lying on my stomach exactly on the summit of the hill, and about twenty-five yards from the end gun of the battery, watching the Russian practice, when I saw six simultaneous puffs of smoke and six flashes of fire dart from the oak wood on the distant slope. One of the gunners at the end gun in the battery next to me was in the act of "laying" it, and was squinting along the sights to get the elevation of the Russian battery, when the six shells started on their journey. Those flashes of fire were the last things he ever saw on earth, for one of the shells struck him full in the face and took his head clean off. There was a spirting from the blood-vessels in the neck, and then the headless corpse spun round in a circle, the legs moving convulsively like those of a chicken when its throat is cut.

I was so close to the man that I could see every movement, and the sight affected my nerve centres in the way that the normal system is affected by any sudden and horrible sight; that is to say, I turned cold all over, and was very sick on the spot. A few months later the frequent repetition of similar spectacles had so dulled the sensitiveness of my nerve centres, that I could look upon the most shocking casualties without experiencing the slightest physical inconvenience. We dragged the gunner's headless corpse to the rear, where it was buried the same evening.

Both sides ceased firing at about six o'clock, at which time we had only nine men killed and three wounded. I heard afterwards that the Russian loss was also small. The demonstration hardly rose to the dignity of an engagement, and doubtless the Russians regarded it more as an appetiser for the solid fare to follow than anything else. At Russian dinner parties there is always a preliminary course called the *zacuska*, consisting generally of caviar or sardines devilled with cayenne, with which the guests are expected to sharpen their appetites. This artillery duel was the *zacuska* to prepare the combatants for the *pièce de résistance* on the morrow.

Everyone knew when the fields-guns ceased talking on the evening of the 19th that we were in for a big fight next day, and that the Russians were preparing to make an infantry attack. Hassib Bey, the principal medical officer, and Reif Bey, his second in command, were busy making preparations for the reception of the wounded; and the owners of several of the largest houses were unceremoniously evicted by the military authorities with the curt notification that their residences were required for hospital purposes. Weinberger and I dined with Robert that night at his house, and had a tremendous *"shivoo,"* the expatriated Swiss surpassing all his previous bacchanalian exploits, and adding sundry incoherent battle-songs to his *répertoire* of selections, until the Viennese housekeeper finally asserted her authority and closed the festivities. I went off to bed at my own quarters about midnight, and found that my Circassian had arranged all my effects in order and made me fairly comfortable.

All the medical staff had received instructions to assemble at the main hospital at seven o'clock in the morning; so I tumbled into bed at once, and slept until I was awakened at about six o'clock by the roar of the field artillery in action once more. The guns had already been firing for a couple of hours, and the engagement was in full progress, when I hurried to the large Bulgarian schoolhouse, which had been converted into the principal hospital.

At this stage it will be convenient to sketch briefly the main features of the attack which General Schilder-Schuldner delivered on Plevna on July 20, and of the manner in which he was defeated by Osman Pasha.

The total Russian force operating against him was supposed by Osman Pasha, from information which we obtained, to amount to thirteen thousand men. The total available strength in Plevna was about fifteen thousand men, most of whom, however, were in poor trim for fighting, having just arrived after a long and arduous march, and having been deprived of sleep for many nights in succession. On the night before the battle Osman Pasha gave strict orders to the outposts to exercise the greatest vigilance, so as to prevent a night surprise, and instructed the commanding officers to group their men as much as possible, and not allow them to straggle. An attack was imminent; but it was difficult to foresee in what direction it would be made. Roughly speaking, the Turkish line of defence extended from the village of Grivitza on the east of the town, along the slopes of the Janik Bair, and away through Bukova to Opanetz on the north-west, the right wing being at Grivitza and the left at Opanetz.

Soon after four o'clock the battle began by the Russian artillery opening fire upon the Grivitza positions, and the Turkish batteries at once replied. Then a brisk fusillade was heard on the hills in the direction of Opanetz, and the general advance of the Russians began. Five battalions of Russian infantry advanced to the assault, and threw themselves upon the Turkish left wing, forcing it backwards.

Osman Pasha quickly despatched supports, and the Turks charged home with the bayonet, whilst the Russian troops stood firm against the attack. The heaviest of the fighting took place on the slope of the Janik Bair extending towards Plevna, and here the loud "hurrahs" of the Russians were answered by cries of "*Allah,*" "*Allah,*" from the Turkish lines. After three hours' fighting the Russians, who had sustained enormous losses, were repulsed and driven off in full retreat, while the reserves sent up to support them retired without having taken part in the engagement. The initial success of the Russians in forcing back the Turkish line of defence no doubt conduced towards their defeat; for, encouraged by the result of the first attack, they straggled on in disorder, and fell in with a hot fire from the hedges and walls all round them.

While our troops were holding the enemy in check on the left, a Russian infantry attack was developed on our right wing, where two lines of trenches were carried; and finally the third and last trench was also carried at the point of the bayonet, nearly all the Russian officers having been killed. Turkish supports were hurried up, and the Russians, who had suffered terrible loss, were driven from the positions which they had taken, and were put to complete rout.

When I reached the building where I was instructed to report myself, I found that it consisted of two large rooms, the outer of which contained fifty beds, while the inner was furnished with three or four benches intended to serve as operating tables. The rooms were high and well ventilated with many windows, and fortunately there was an abundant water supply, while the building stood in about two or three acres of ground. This had originally been the playground of the Bulgarian children who attended the school. Now it was filled with wounded men, and the laughter of the children was replaced by groans of agony. Already the courtyard was full; and as I looked up the Nicopolis road I could see a long string of Bulgarian *arabas*, each drawn by two little white oxen, bringing the wounded down from the battlefield.

Only the men who were gravely wounded were brought in these *arabas*, and hundreds had to drag themselves down on foot. As the rough, springless *arabas* jolted over the cobble-stones of the Plevna street, the sufferings of the wounded men must have been excruciating. There was no field hospital to render first aid, and it is not easy to imagine the misery of an unfortunate wretch, say, with a compound fracture of the thigh, transported in a cart and without any surgical attendance from the field to the base hospital. The two ends of the bone jarring together with every movement of the cart could not but cause the most exquisite agony.

As far as the eye could reach stretched the long line of *arabas*, each with its load of suffering men. Every cart was driven by its Bulgarian owner, and escorted by a Turkish soldier to see that the Bulgarian did not despatch the unhappy victims before their time. The foremost carts had already arrived, and the entrance was blocked by the jostling drivers all anxious to get rid of their loads, while every minute fresh wounded kept staggering in on foot. Even the stoical Turks could not help moaning when they were lifted out of the carts by unskilful hands and dragged into the hospital, which was quickly assuming the appearance of a slaughter-house. Dead and dying were lying one on top of another in many of the *arabas*, matted together with clotted blood.

Other ambulances had been established in different parts of the town; but this was the principal one, and there were six other surgeons besides myself attached to it. I pulled off my coat, and went to work at once. The first man whom I tackled had walked down from the field. He had been shot through the jaw, and was much blanched from loss of blood. I plugged the hole with lint, and passed on to the next unfortunate, who had been shot through the liver by a fragment of shell. Part of the liver was sticking out through the wound, and the man, who was much collapsed, although quite conscious and in great pain, formed a shocking spectacle. He had a great tear in his liver. I stitched it up and washed the wound; but the case was a hopeless one. If I could have given him chloroform, thoroughly opened him up, and washed everything out, I might have been able to save him; but there was no time for that. He lingered on in great agony, and died on the following day.

In dealing with gunshot wounds, where the variety is practically unlimited and no two cases are the same, the surgeon has to be resourceful and inventive. I was here brought face to face with conditions which were quite new to me, and with extraordinary complications, which required the most delicate and careful operations, but which had to be dealt with out of hand and in a few minutes. Looking back now I am filled with wonder that so many of our wounded recovered, considering the unfavourable conditions under which they were treated. The third man whom I tackled had been struck in the abdomen by a piece of shell, and about one foot of his intestine was projecting through the wound. In that condition he had been carried from the hill where he was shot, and, needless to say, he was in a horrible condition. I washed the intestine, enlarged the wound, again shifted the intestine back into its place, and stitched the wound up. In a week or two the man recovered, and went back to his place in the ranks.

All day on that terrible 20th of July I worked in the Bulgarian schoolhouse among the wounded men, and all day the *arabas* kept arriving with fresh loads, until there was absolutely no place left in which to lay the sufferers. In all my surgical experience I have never known men to exhibit such fortitude under intense agony as these Turkish soldiers, nor have I ever met patients who recovered from such terrible injuries in the remarkable way that these men did. They were magnificent material for a surgeon to work on—men of splendid physique, unimpaired by intemperance or any excesses. Occasionally one found isolated cases of intemperance among the higher officers in the Turkish Army; but I never saw a private soldier under the influence of liquor during the whole time that I was in the country.

There were many of these men whose lives I could have saved if I could have persuaded them to take stimulants; but it was impossible to get them to touch alcohol, even as medicine. The principles of their religion forbid the use of alcohol, and the humble Turk clings so tenaciously to his religion that he would rather meet death itself than violate its precepts. On account of another remarkable religious prejudice many of the men who came under my hands absolutely refused to submit to amputations, believing that the loss of a limb would prevent them from entering paradise. Owing to this curious prejudice many of my patients lost their lives.

The booming of the artillery was soon varied by the sharp crackle of the rifles, which indicated that the infantry fusillade was commencing in earnest, and men began to come in who were wounded by the heavy conical bullets from the Berdan rifles, with which a large proportion of the Russian forces were armed. This rifle carried a bullet with a very high velocity; and several cases came under my notice which illustrated its destructive power. The Berdan rifle-bullet, however, often drilled a clean hole right through a man, thus simplifying the surgical treatment; while the older Krenke rifle, with which the bulk of the Russians were armed, inflicted a much larger wound, and not infrequently left the bullet embedded in the body.

Among the others whom I attended that morning was a splendid young Turk who had been shot through the head. The Berdan conical bullet pierced the left side of the skull about an inch and a half below the crown, and passed out in a straight line through the other side, leaving two holes, one at each side of the fez which the man was wearing. It bored a hole clean through the upper portion of the brain; but the sufferer, though he was weak from loss of blood, was perfectly rational. I put a syringe into the orifice, and cleaned the lacerated portion of the brain with a solution of carbolic, afterwards dressing the skull with an antiseptic pad and bandages. The man was put into the hospital, where he remained for about six weeks, and at the end of that time he was discharged cured. He went back to his regiment, and I never saw him again.

In one of the *arabas* which discharged its load at the hospital door was a wounded sergeant. The poor fellow had had both his eyes taken out by a bullet, and was in great agony. We took him in and treated him, keeping him in the hospital till he recovered. Some weeks afterwards we discharged him cured, but sightless, and he went down to Sofia.

Many men were shot right through the chest, of whom nearly all died. In cases where we could not readily locate the bullet we did not waste time looking for it, and several men who recovered from their wounds went back to the ranks with an ounce of Russian lead hidden somewhere in their bodies. Occasionally a bullet would take a most erratic course. One man whom I attended had been shot in the back of the neck, and the bullet travelled along his shoulder and down his arm just under the skin. I took it out at the wrist.

A peculiar instance came under my notice of the extraordinary vitality which a human being sometimes displays. A couple of men brought in a young Circassian and laid him on the floor, all the beds in the hospital being already occupied. He was deathly pale, and when I went to him I found that he had a terrible wound in the chest. At first I thought that he had been struck by a whole shell; but I found on examining him that a rifle-bullet had struck his cartridge case which was strapped across his chest, and exploded one or more of the cartridges. The explosion had blown away a great portion of the chest, and exposed the heart, which I could see beating. I plugged the cavity as well as I could, and he lived for four or five days in the hospital, perfectly conscious all the while, and eager for news of the fighting. I think it was on the fifth day after his admission that I was examining the wound, when I found the brass butt of a cartridge embedded in the muscles of the heart. I pulled it out, and dressed the wound again; but the shock was too severe, and the man died soon afterwards.

We had no skilled attendants attached to the hospital, and no one to do the dressing but a few soldiers who had been told off for the purpose. Blood was everywhere; and as I went my rounds as quickly as possible among the moaning sufferers, I had an attendant carrying my box of instruments, a basin of water, and a supply of bandages after me. On all sides I heard the piteous moan, "*Verbana su, effendi,*" "*Verbana su, hakim bashi,*" meaning, "Give me a drink of water, doctor"; and fortunately we were able at least to assuage the intolerable thirst which afflicts men when the moisture of the body has been depleted by great loss of blood. All the cases which required operations were put aside, and left for the following day, as it was necessary, in the hurry of endeavouring to overtake the work, to deal with the larger number of less serious cases first. Whenever I saw that a case was hopeless, and that the man was sure to die, I simply made him as comfortable as I could on the floor, gave him a drink of water, and left him there.

I remained in the hospital until three o'clock in the afternoon, and during the whole of that time the carts were jolting over the stones bringing us in fresh cases. I never stopped for a moment whipping out bullets, sewing up wounds, cleaning wounds, and putting up fractured limbs in splints. Sometimes when the carts came in I did not know which of the men were alive and which were dead, the living and the dead were lying so closely one on the top of the other.

At three o'clock Hassib Bey, the principal medical officer, sent a message for me, ordering me to go to another place which had been turned into a temporary hospital. It was an isolated building, about a quarter of a mile away from the schoolhouse, and was on the other side of the Tutchenitza. The building had been a private house, and here I found about a hundred wounded men, many of them officers, who had been lying there helplessly since early in the morning, with no attendance except the small services which two *jarra bashis* were able to afford.

A Turkish colonel shot through both jaws was my first patient. The bullet had cut through the base of the tongue, and the poor fellow was unable to speak. His mouth was wide open, and blood was issuing from it. I picked away the broken pieces of bone, put a bandage round the jaw to support it, and, having made the colonel as comfortable as I could, I went on to his brother officers. All the rest of that day I worked by myself, with only the two *jarra bashis* to assist me, among

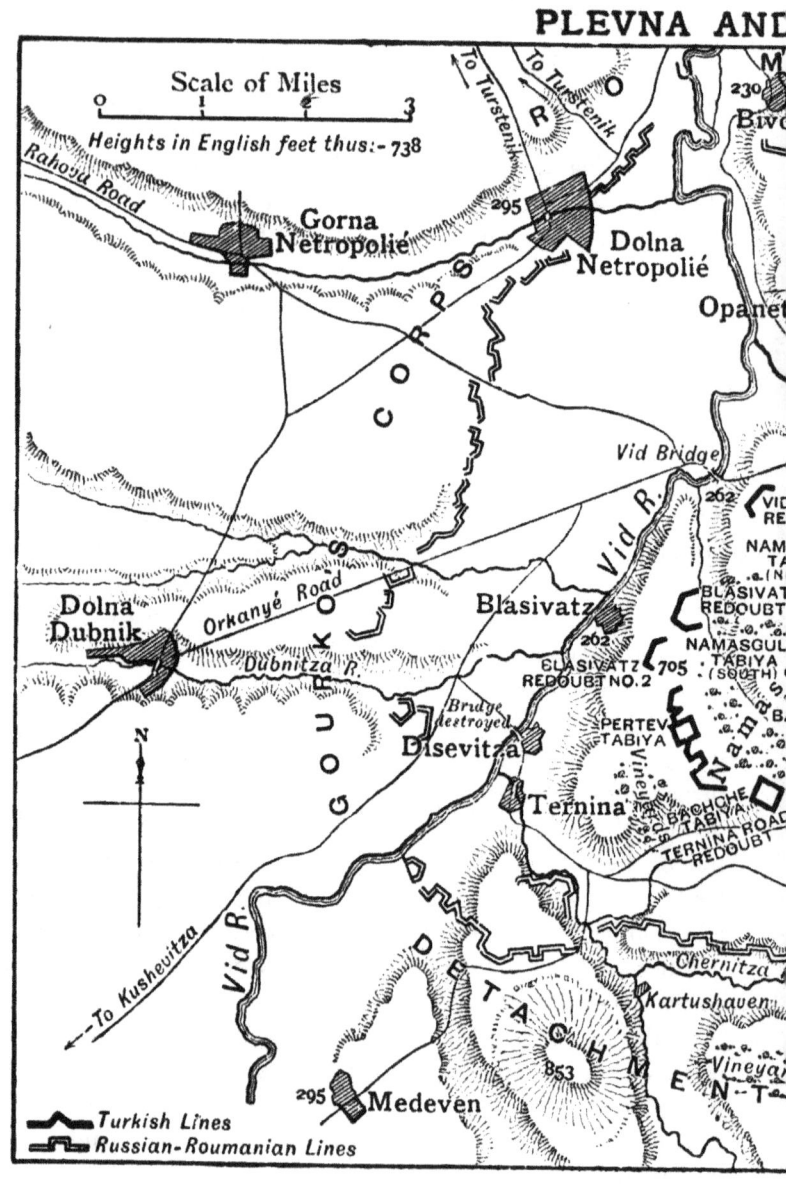

ENVIRONS.

the wounded men, and when it grew dark I went on with the minor operations by the light of four candles stuck on bayonets. At eleven o'clock that night I dragged myself off to bed.

It was a beautiful summer night, with moon and stars shining, as I walked back to my quarters utterly fagged out with that tremendous day's work. A couple of miles away to the north I could see the long ridge of the Janik Bair shining in the moonlight. More than a thousand Turks and more than one thousand two hundred Russians lay stretched on the other side of the hill, and along the line of the fighting from Bukova on the left to Grivitza on the right.[2] All was silent now, but the hills were not deserted yet, for the burial parties were hard at work, and the Circassians, ever on the lookout for plunder, were gathering in the dreadful harvest of the battlefield.

I slept soundly till six o'clock in the morning, and then went back to the house where the wounded officers had been brought. There were about a hundred wounded men there altogether; and as we had no beds to put them in, we had to lay them on the floor pillowed on their own great-coats. There were plenty of provisions in the town, and I had supplies of broth, beef-tea, and milk brought up for the patients from the central depot. Still, in spite of everything that we could do, it was an experience never to be forgotten. As one moved amongst them one heard piteous moans on every side, coming from forms which in some cases could scarcely be recognized as human, so terribly had the shrapnel done its work. Those who believed that they were dying were saying their prayers out loud, calling upon Allah to receive them into paradise; and here and there an officer in the delirium of fever was fighting the battle over again, sitting up in his blood-clotted, shot-riddled uniform, and calling upon his men to follow him, until he fell back breathless and exhausted. A good many of them had died in the night while I was away, and I told off a couple of men to bury them at once.

While I was going round the house, I found that we had two young Russian soldiers there among our own people, and I gave them

---

1. No statistics of Turkish casualties, other than the above, were ever published. The Russian figures far exceed those in the text. The Russian losses, according to official enumeration, were 22 officers killed and 52 wounded, and 2,771 men killed and wounded; nearly two-thirds of the officers and over one-third of the men were therefore *hors de combat*. Of the three colonels commanding regiments two were killed; a general commanding a brigade was wounded; of the six field officers present with the 19th regiment two were killed and two wounded. Schilder-Schuldner's force consisted of 6,500 men and 46 guns.

as much attention as I could. One was a fair-haired young fellow, quite a lad. His case was hopeless from the first, for he had been shot through the lungs, and he died that day without being able to leave any message. The other had his leg from the knee downwards shattered by a shell, and he lived for about a fortnight.

Osman Pasha had made arrangements to send all the wounded away to Sofia, and nearly all of those whom I attended were placed in waggons and sent down *viâ* Orkhanieh. Many of them, however, as might be expected, died on the way, and the road could have easily been traced by the dead bodies.

I requisitioned some beds for my hospital; and when I had got all the wounded men dressed and fed, I thought that my day's work was finished. Just as I was going out for a short rest, however, an orderly came and told me that a number of wounded men were lying in a Turkish mosque without any help at all, and asked me to go to them. I found a most beautiful little mosque nestling down in a grove of trees on a slope of ground to the west side of the Tutchenitza, and, mounting the half-dozen steps which formed the approach to the main entrance, I looked inside.

It was indeed a hideous sight. The square floor of the mosque was covered with dead and wounded men, who had been placed there on the day before, and apparently forgotten. There were about eighty of them altogether, and the first thing that we had to do was to separate the living from the dead, which was not an easy task, as the dead were lying across the living and the living across the dead. We took out twenty-seven dead men first, and found that in some cases a man with faint signs of life in him had been lying all night, half suffocated by his own blood and by the inert mass of a dead comrade lying across him. The walls, which were whitewashed, were plentifully bespattered with blood, and soon I was a shocking spectacle myself.

I put on a soldier to go round with a bucket and *pannikin* to assuage the fiery thirst of the poor wretches, and then I set to work extracting bullets and sewing up wounds and washing them as fast as I could, with a soldier to help in the dressing. I undertook no big operations simply because I had not time. It was a race for life with many of the men; and while there were cases there which would have required at least an hour to deal with properly, the most that I could spare was ten minutes.

By July 22 all the wounded that could travel had been sent to Sofia, and we had about two hundred of the graver cases left, most of them being cases requiring serious operations. We selected a convenient building on the banks of the Tutchenitza, right under the shadow of a mosque, and there we set up operating tables under the trees in the open air. It was strange every day to see a flock of white doves circling round the minaret of the mosque, and every evening at sunset to watch the old Mussulman priest as he climbed the tower and solemnly invited the faithful to prayer.

CHAPTER 6

The Interval Between the First and Second Battles

We sent away about eight hundred of the wounded to Sofia within a few days after the first battle; and of those who remained behind many died, and the remainder resolved themselves into cases for simple operations. Amputation of the arm or leg was necessary in many instances, and whenever the sufferer would permit it this was carried out. With the large medical staff attached to the army, the work ought to have been very easy; but as a matter of fact many of the surgeons could not or would not undertake any important operation, and in the few instances when they did muster up courage to lop off an arm or a limb the spectacle was not an edifying one. Almost all the operations were performed either by Osman Effendi, a Circassian, who was a really brilliant surgeon and a capable anatomist who had learnt his profession in Paris, or by myself.

Both of us were very young and inexperienced; but in spite of these drawbacks it is not too much to say that we saved many lives which would otherwise have been lost. The foreign doctors seemed to lose their heads in an emergency; and it was not an uncommon thing for Osman Effendi or myself to find some poor unfortunate wretch, who had been smashed up by a shell or drilled through by a Berdan bullet, absolutely rotting away in a hospital ward simply because the surgeon in charge would not operate. Whenever we made a discovery of this kind, we used to bring the patient out to the operating table under the willow tree, and do the best we could for him under the circumstances; but it cannot be denied that, owing to our lack of experience, we often made serious mistakes. I will candidly confess that if I had possessed my present knowledge at that time, and if I had

had command of all the best appliances, I could have saved many lives which unfortunately flickered out in that shady little grove on the banks of the Tutchenitza.

In addition to the grave cases which involved the removal of an arm or leg, we had a large number of minor injuries to attend to, especially wounds in the hand, which were remarkably frequent. When the troops were in the act of firing, their fingers and hands were naturally exposed; and though later on, when the firing was mainly done from behind entrenchments, finger wounds became far more frequent, still we had a good many of them even after the first battle.

A splendid lesson in stoical fortitude was afforded by those fellows, who tendered their maimed hands for operation without the slightest flinching. The stump of a willow tree which had been cut down stood near the bank of the stream, and here I was accustomed to take my seat, after providing myself with a basin of water from the stream and a sharp knife. I put a little carbolic in the water, and with these simple preparations I was ready for my patients, who sat cross-legged in a row close by me. There was no administration of chloroform by a skilled anæsthetist, no careful dressing of the injury by a white-aproned nurse, none of the usual accessories of the ordinary hospital; for my operating theatre had a carpet of greensward starred with wild flowers, and its ceiling was the deep blue sky of midsummer.

Instead of the rows of students who usually grace these scientific ceremonies, scores of the snow-white doves that are considered sacred throughout Turkey paused now and then in their cooings, as they fluttered round the minarets of the ancient mosque above the willow grove and looked down upon the strange scene below them. The wounded soldiers took their turns each in his proper order; and as I sat on the willow stump a man with a thumb or finger, as the case might be, mangled into a shocking pulp of festering flesh, would hold up his injured hand to me as he sat on the grass at my feet, and would look on without flinching while I cut away the rotting flesh, trimmed up the place, and washed and dressed the bleeding stump that still remained. I did over a dozen of these cases in one morning; and later in the campaign, when the fighting in the redoubts began, I have amputated as many as twenty-seven fingers in succession.

One result of the frequency of these finger wounds was that they formed a convenient pretext for escaping service in the ranks; and though the Turkish soldiers were too brave to think of malingering, there was one Arab regiment in which the offence became very common. This was the regiment which had already shown the white feather during the battle, and which was only induced to hold its ground by the threat of Osman Pasha that unless the men stood firm he would himself open fire on them from headquarters, and catch them between the Russian fusillade and the fire of their own side. Compelled by this unpleasant prospect, the regiment rallied, and afterwards gave a good account of itself; but, as might be supposed, the men were not in love with fighting, and many of them hit on the device of deliberately blowing off the trigger-finger so as to be unfit for further service. We had a good many of them to treat, and at last Osman Pasha got to hear of it, and of course was very savage at the malingering. He at once issued an order that the next man found guilty of maiming himself in this way would be instantly shot, and the threat, as it turned out, was no idle one.

One morning, just as I finished my round in the hospital, I was summoned by an orderly to attend Tewfik Bey, and when I reached his tent I found three men from the Arab regiment standing there under a strong guard. Their arms had been taken from them, and each man had a hole through the index-finger of the right hand. Tewfik Bey desired me to decide whether the appearance of the injuries indicated that they had been self-inflicted; and when I learnt from him that if I answered in the affirmative the men would be instantly shot, I declined to take the responsibility, and requested that a small medical board might be appointed to deal with the matter. Tewfik assented, and invited me into his tent to wait while an orderly fetched two other surgeons.

Presently Weinberger and Kustler arrived, and we three, after inspecting the prisoners, retired to a little distance to consult. There could be no doubt whatever about the fact, for the mutilated finger in each case was blackened with gunpowder, showing that the man had placed his finger on the top of his rifle-barrel and pulled the trigger, probably with a piece of string. The three men watched us as we sat at a little table under a tree and drew up a short report confirming that the injuries were self-inflicted. I presented the report to Tewfik, who was smoking a cigarette nonchalantly in front of his tent; and as soon as he had read it, he ordered out three firing parties of twelve men each, six of each squad having their rifles loaded with ball, and six with blank cartridge.

A sergeant stepped up and bandaged the eyes of the culprits, who were placed on their knees in a row a few yards distant from each other. A few moments were granted to them to say their prayers, then a naked sword-blade flashed in the sunlight, a quick word of command rang out, a volley startled the camp, and the victims fell dead riddled with bullets. It was a sharp remedy, but a sure one, and after that we had no more malingerers.

Osman Pasha was a strict disciplinarian, and the splendid order which he maintained in Plevna all through the campaign was really remarkable. At first the Bulgarian shop-keepers wanted to close their shops; but the commander-in-chief compelled them to keep them open, promising that any attempt at looting by the soldiery would be promptly and severely punished. A military police force was organized for the protection of the townspeople, and the soldiery were given to understand that any excesses would be visited by the only penalty known to the martial code in war-time—the penalty of death. Owing to this decisive action, the Bulgarian population regained confidence, and carried on their respective businesses without let or hindrance.

For several days, indeed, after the first battle the spoils of war stripped from the dead Russians on the field of action by the roving and predatory Circassians were on sale in every bazaar. One could buy good Russian great-coats for a few *piastres*, while boots, caps, and arms all had a ready sale. A large number of crosses in bronze, silver, or gold were taken from the dead Russians, and exposed for sale in the bazaars. It was strange to go shopping in the narrow, malodorous Plevna by-streets, and watch the chaffering that was going on over the poor small personal effects of the brave fellows who lay out yonder on the slopes of the Janik Bair. Many of the Russians had gone into action with the photographs of their wives or sweethearts in little leather cases, which they carried in an inside pocket next to the heart; and the Circassians, prowling round the field on the first night after the battle, robbed the corpses of these simple treasures, and bandied them from hand to hand with brutal jests round the bazaars next day.

The simple faith which is such a dominant feature in the Russian national character was strikingly exemplified in some of the articles found upon the dead bodies. I saw a Circassian offering for sale a little painting of the Virgin Mary and the infant Jesus, which he had taken, according to his own statement, from the body of a dead Russian, a mere fair-haired lad, who had been killed by a bayonet thrust in the hand-to-hand fighting. The painting was done on a wooden plaque about one foot long by six inches wide, and was evidently of great age, probably at least two hundred years old, from its appearance. It was found beneath the tunic of the dead boy, and was perhaps a family treasure given to him by his mother before he went away to the war. There is at least no doubt that it was worn as a charm against danger. But the simple faith of the Russian mother could not save her son in the grim reality of battle, and the steel of the *infidel* Turk pierced the sacred figure of the Virgin before it reached the soldier's heart.

Many of the Russians wore steel plates covered with chamois leather over the region of the heart. These plates would stop a rifle-bullet in those days, although the ball from a more modern Lee-Metford, Lebel, or Mauser rifle would have pierced them like tinder.

No scruples were shown in appropriating the valuables of the enemy; and the Jews in Plevna made a handsome profit by buying Russian *roubles* for a few *piastres* apiece from the Circassians and Bashi-Bazouks who had gone through the pockets of the dead, and by taking the foreign coin away to the ordinary markets of exchange.

I bought a Russian signet ring in the bazaar one morning from a Circassian. It lies before me on the table now, and brings back vivid memories. It is a heavy gold ring, with a large red stone like a cornelian, carved with the figure of Æsculapius, easily recognisable from the traditional accessories of the snakes and the cock. It was surely a curious coincidence that the figure of this legendary founder of medical science should have fallen into the hands of one of his own disciples!

Of course Osman Pasha strongly discountenanced this looting of the dead; but it was impossible to control the predatory instincts of the Circassians, and in spite of the prospect of instant death if detected they continued to prowl round the battlefield in search of treasures. One night five of them were taken red-handed, and hanged at daybreak *pour encourager les autres*; but Osman Pasha's attention was so much taken up with the necessary work of fortification, that the looting went on afterwards just the same.

To show, however, that the *muchir*, far from oppressing the Bulgarian inhabitants in the manner imputed to him by contemporary press writers, was always throughout the siege absolutely fair towards them, one significant incident may be mentioned for which I can vouch, as I was myself a witness of it. One morning, while I was passing by the yard of a Bulgarian butcher, I found an altercation going on between the Bulgarian and a free-lance from one of the Circassian irregular bodies. Although I could not understand what was said, I was able to gather that the Circassian wanted some meat, which the Bulgarian would not give him. After a minute or two of heated argument, the Circassian drew his revolver and shot the Bulgarian in my presence, the bullet entering the man's foot. I reported the matter to Osman Pasha personally, and he ordered the instant arrest of the Circassian; but the man was never seen again. Recognising that death would be the penalty of his act if he were discovered, he escaped from Plevna that night, and we saw no more of him. The butcher died from his wound.

There was plenty of work for the men of all ranks to do between the 20th of July and the 30th. We never knew when another attack might be launched; and though the Russians had disappeared from sight, our scouts used occasionally to bring in word that they had seen detachments as near as five miles off. Our men were working away as busily as bees fortifying outposts, digging entrenchments, and building redoubts on the cordon of hills that formed the natural rampart of the town. They also had to complete the work of burying the dead, and as the Russians had left us all their dead to inter as well as our own this was no light task. When I had finished my morning's work in the hospital, I used to call on Dr. Robert and borrow one of his smart little black cobs for a ride out to the hills to see how our fellows were getting on with their labours.

I often watched the burial squads at work, as I sat there on the black cob puffing a cigarette in the glorious summer weather, and saw them dragging the scattered bodies together into a little heap, and then digging a trench to hold them. Sometimes they would put twenty or thirty into one trench when they came on a patch where the troops had fallen thickly, and sometimes a dead soldier lying far away from his comrades would be buried in a lonely grave by himself. The Russian and Turkish dead were always kept distinct, for the Moslem will not sleep by the Giaour, even in the grave.

As I rode over the crest of the hills four or five days after the battle, and down to the hollow where the Russian lines received the hottest of the Turkish fire, I saw that in most cases the Russian dead had not been buried deep enough; now and then, indeed, scarcely more than the three handfuls of dust prescribed by the old poet had been thrown over the corpse, which protested with a faint, sickly odour at these maimed funeral rites.

In one little hollow I saw some locks of curly fair hair sticking up from the ground, and, scraping the earth away with my sword-blade, found a dead Russian there. In many places a foot, a finger, or a hand protruding from the ground revealed the presence of the dead; and as I advanced farther down into the valley from the Turkish line of defence, I came across a great number of bodies which had escaped the notice of the burial parties altogether. There they lay, with the hot July sun beating down upon them, and the cool moisture of the earth teeming with horrible living things beneath them. The faces of many of the Russians, as is often the case when death is due to gunshot wounds, were placid and composed; while the skin, tanned to the consistency of parchment by the rays of the sun, showed as yet no sign of putrefaction. With others death had come with such instantaneous force that the expression of the face still reflected the tumultuous passions that chased each other through the brain of the living man in the supreme hour of battle. One could see, to quote the vivid words of the soldier's poet,

Anger and pain and terror
Stamped on the smoke-scorched skin.

But while the part of the body exposed to the action of the sunlight was preserved in a mummified condition, the lower part, which rested on the earth, had already undergone the first stage of decomposition. Anyone who has ever turned over a great stone embedded in a bank of mossy earth, and seen the swarms of noxious living creatures battening on the underneath side, will recognize without further description the sight that met my eyes as I prised over a dead body here and there with my scabbard to ascertain its condition.

After the battle fresh troops kept pouring into Plevna from Sofia, and it soon became evident that Osman Pasha did not intend to content himself by remaining in the town purely on the defensive.

Lovtcha, as we knew, had fallen into the hands of the Russians before we reached Plevna, having been occupied by General Sobatoff on July 16; and Osman Pasha, having had time to look about him, determined to recapture that town. Its importance from the strategical point of view was obvious, inasmuch as it commanded the main road to Sofia, from which our reinforcements were to come. The possession of the town was also indispensable to Osman Pasha in order to cover the operations of the Plevna Army, and to complete his front line of defence, which should serve him as a base of operations whenever the moment might prove propitious for assuming the offensive.

The town of Lovtcha lies in the valley of the River Osma, about twenty miles from Plevna, and twelve miles from the Trojan Pass.

Roughly speaking, the river divides the town into two parts, one of which was inhabited by the Mussulman population, and the other by the Bulgarians. Before the war the great majority of the inhabitants were Mussulmans, who numbered about twelve thousand; and Lovtcha was then one of the richest towns in Bulgaria, boasting no fewer than twenty mosques, three orthodox churches, ten primary Moslem schools, and many schools for Christians. It was placed at the junction of several main roads, and its position rendered it therefore important both to the invaders and the invaded. Sobatoff had occupied it with a column composed of the second squadron of Cossacks of the Guard, two squadrons of Don Cossacks, and two field-pieces with a detachment of infantry.

As soon as the fight of July 20 was won, Osman Pasha made all his preparations for recapturing Lovtcha by a surprise. He first reconnoitred the position with a detachment of cavalry, and then, taking six infantry battalions, a battery of field artillery, and a troop of Circassian light horse from the reinforcements which had arrived from Sofia, he formed a column, the command of which he entrusted to Brigadier Rifaat Pasha, who had Tewfik Bey as his next in command. The column marched from Plevna at six o'clock in the evening of July 25, and arrived at daybreak before Lovtcha. An attack was immediately delivered on the town, which was defended by three or four squadrons of Cossacks and a large number of Bulgarians who had been armed by the Russians. Only the merest semblance of resistance, however, was offered by the enemy, and Rifaat Pasha's column occupied the town almost without striking a blow.

Thus within the space of a week the Russian arms had sustained two serious reverses, and the Russian commanders were evidently preparing an attempt to rehabilitate their prestige. Avoiding any serious engagement, and only showing themselves at great distances, they confined themselves to long-range artillery practice while they concentrated their forces. Meanwhile the Turkish Army was strengthened by additional reinforcements of regular troops and of auxiliary cavalry. The only other event of importance between the first and second battles of Plevna was the recapture of the village of Trestenik, situated about ten miles from Plevna, on the left bank of the Vid. This village had fallen into the hands of the Russians; but Hassan Labri Pasha and Mehemet Nazif Bey, with a few battalions of infantry, a couple of field-guns, and a troop of Circassian horse, retook the village on July 25, and drove out the Russians, who retreated towards their main body.

While these stirring events, which can be described in a few words, but the success of which was of vital importance to Osman Pasha's plan of operations, were taking place outside Plevna, I remained on duty at my hospital in the town, hearing only at times the faint echoes of artillery in the distance to remind me that fighting was still going on.

Although hastily organized and furnished with few of the articles which are deemed necessary to the equipment of civil hospitals, our hospitals were fairly efficient at the commencement of the campaign before our resources became overtaxed. Hassib Bey, the principal medical officer, was a capital organizer and administrator; and although he never interfered in the actual surgical work, he was always ready to listen to suggestions and to furnish us with any necessaries that we asked for.

During the early part of my stay in Plevna, I had my quarters in a small Bulgarian house which was nearly a mile away from the general hospital, so far, indeed, that I afterwards moved into a more convenient spot, and my little house was given over to the French journalist Olivier Pain. My first landlord—who was landlord in name only, for of course I never paid him any rent—was a Bulgarian, and his daughter was one of the few pretty women that I ever saw in Bulgaria. Conversation, however, was restricted by linguistic limitations, for I knew scarcely any Bulgarian, and the only word of English that she could say was "London." Wherever I saw that girl, she would show her white teeth with a charming smile, flash her big black eyes, and with beautiful irrelevance ejaculate "London!" Whether she knew what London meant I cannot say, but her limited vocabulary expressed more in its way than the gushing phrases of many more brilliant conversationalists.

When she said "London" with a bright air of welcome and a frank smile as I came home at night tired out with the day's work, I knew that she meant, "Good evening, doctor; I hope you haven't had a very bad day today; and see, here is your *pilaf* and coffee ready." When she uttered the word with a backward turn of the head as she passed out of the door and a pretty coquettish glance, it was very evident that she was really saying, "Goodnight now, doctor; pleasant dreams to you, and I hope a Russian shell won't find you in the morning." My domestic arrangements, however, which were very primitive and did not include much preparation of eatables, were mainly attended to by my

Circassian servant, who proved himself to be a very handy fellow.

Hassib Bey instituted the excellent plan of getting all the medical staff to meet at nine o'clock every morning at the administrative block, where the main hospital was placed; and after breakfasting on coffee, *pilaf*, and eggs when I could get them, I used to ride up to the rendezvous. Hassib Bey and Reif Bey, his next in command, used to meet us all there, and the whole lot of us used to have a smoke together for half an hour or so, and discuss any interesting cases that we had to deal with. If we had any complaint to make about the food supplied to the hospitals, or if we wanted anything extra in the way of appliances, our representations were listened to on the spot. It was a capital idea, and worked very well indeed.

After the first rush of work was over, I had my own hospital to attend to. This was a two-storey Bulgarian house, the ground floor of which was unoccupied, while upstairs there were three large rooms, in which I had about twenty-five patients. Beds and blankets were provided, and I was able to make the sufferers fairly comfortable. Two Turkish soldiers were allotted to me to act as hospital orderlies, and they proved apt pupils at their work. I trained them to act as dressers and nurses, and found that they carried out their novel duties excellently. We had a good many deaths at first, and news was always conveyed to the Moslem priests, who came and laid out the dead, wrapping the bodies in white linen sheets, and taking them away for burial in the Turkish burial-ground. Good, nourishing food was provided for the convalescents, who had plenty of beef-tea, soup, *pilaf*, eggs, and bread; and possessing as they did an extraordinary recuperative faculty and constitutions unimpaired by intemperance, a very fair percentage recovered.

CHAPTER 7

The Second Battle of Plevna (July 30)

Although I could speak Turkish sufficiently to make myself understood for ordinary purposes, I found myself in difficulties when my patients began to talk to me about their private affairs, or to go into long accounts of their adventures on the battlefield. Sometimes, however, I was able to gather a few startling illustrations of the ferocity with which the engagement had been fought.

One of my patients was the colonel of a Kurdish regiment, a magnificent specimen of a man, who had been shot in the thigh by a rifle-bullet. The ball had entered the left thigh on the outside, passed clean through it, and also through the right thigh, making four distinct wounds, which had occasioned a great deal of hæmorrhage with inflammatory conditions and high temperature. I refrain from giving this patient's name as he may be still alive, and he probably would not desire to remember the incident which he related to me.

He told me that he received his wound in the height of the action, and became for a while unconscious. When he came to himself, he commenced to crawl on his hands and knees towards the Turkish lines, and on his way he came to a Russian officer lying wounded on the ground. I give the story now in his own words. "I saw him lying there before me," whispered my patient to me as I dressed his wounds, "and the impulse to kill him came into my mind. I suppose he read my purpose in my face, for he pointed to his wound, and then he held up his hands to me as if to ask for quarter. As I crawled over on my hands and knees, I knelt over him and pointed to my own wounds in reply. Then I drew my revolver and shot him through the head.

My servant, who had come to look for me, was close behind me.

He was a Kurd, and he took his long Kurdish knife and cut off the Russian's head before he was dead. The air made a gurgling, bubbling sound as the knife went through the windpipe. The Russian officer had a long fair beard. He was a fine man, and I shall never forget his face. You are horrified. Well, it was war. I was not a man then, I was a wild beast. I killed him as he lay there because he was in my power. If I had been in the same position, he would have killed me. It was destiny."

Each of the members of the medical staff had a similar hospital to attend to, and all were managed on much the same lines. As a rule I finished my work in the forenoon, and had the rest of the day more or less to myself, except when it was my turn to attend at the main hospital, where once a week I had to be in attendance all night on emergency duty.

I was on friendly terms with the colonels of most of the regiments, and especially with Tewfik Bey, who used to keep me supplied with the latest news until he went to Lovtcha, and then I was thrown back on my own resources; but I found plenty of entertainment in watching the progress of the fortifications, trenches, and redoubts, which the troops were constructing with ceaseless activity under the direction of Tewfik Bey, who laid out the works before he went to Lovtcha.

Although not very particular as to what I ate, I got very tired of the incessant *pilaf* and scrambled eggs which my Circassian cooked for me, and both Weinberger and I always looked forward with lively pleasure to an invitation to dine with Dr. Robert, who was certainly very liberal in his hospitality. On these occasions we had European food admirably cooked by the Viennese housekeeper, and Robert always produced his best Bulgarian wine. I think I can see him now, dressed in his dirty yellow suit of Bulgarian *frieze*, with his long, sinuous fingers flying over the keys of his piano as he yelled out song after song in half the languages of Europe until far into the early hours of the morning. Peace to his ashes! He used to give us capital dinners; but I never could find out what happened to him eventually.

One little incident connected with him is perhaps worth recording here, though it occurred at a later period in the campaign. When the shells were falling fast in Plevna, Robert dug a large hole in his garden, and was accustomed to bury himself in it like a mole whenever the firing became particularly hot. One day, when I was watching outside his garden, I saw the housekeeper bring in his midday meal, steaming hot and very appetizing. Just as Robert sat down to it a shell exploded on the top of the house, and Robert was off to his hole in the ground like a fox with a pack of hounds at its heels. As he lay there quaking, it seemed a pity that the dinner should be allowed to get cold, so I vaulted the fence and ate it myself. The cutlets were simply delicious.

Of course Robert had nothing to do with the wounded men. He was simply a Bulgarian doctor, and was, moreover, strongly suspected of Russophile proclivities. Long afterwards I heard a rumour that he was shot as a spy before Plevna fell.

In those days of comparative quiet which preceded the second battle we only gleaned stray pieces of news from the outside world. The telegraph wire was closed to all private despatches, and the information which filtered into the town was consequently of the vaguest. The soldiers who came up from Sofia certainly brought us news as to the progress of the campaign in other parts of the Turkish Empire; and we learnt that while the Army of the Lom was doing fairly well, Suleiman Pasha's forces had sustained a serious disaster at the Shipka Pass. The untrustworthy nature of the news, however, may be understood from the fact that for some days a persistent rumour was current that Great Britain had declared war against Russia, and that twenty thousand British troops were even then at Sofia.

In order to get a clear idea of the significance of the second battle of Plevna it is necessary to comprehend the position from the point of view of the Russian commanders, who realized that if they did not blot out their crushing defeat of June 20 by a great victory they would be compelled to abandon the initiative and fall back upon a tedious defensive policy with all its attendant disadvantages. It was clear that the most natural course to attempt was to crush Osman Pasha's army, for Plevna was much more accessible than either Rasgrad or Eski-Zagra; it was easier to concentrate a force there, and there was no immediate danger in any other quarter.

To attack the Turkish Army of the east would probably necessitate protracted siege operations; while if Osman Pasha were defeated, it would be easy to reinforce General Gourko, and afterwards advance against Suleiman Pasha's army. Thus it was that the Russian general staff, who were sixty miles away at Tirnova, resolved to attack Plevna, and entrusted the task to Prince Schahoffskoi and General Krüdener. Let us see with what result.

On the 27th and 28th of July our scouts reported the proximity of large bodies of Russians coming from Nicopolis and Poradim, and we all recognized that an attack was imminent. The 29th was quiet; but on the morning of the 30th, as I was at breakfast, I heard the boom of the heavy guns once more, and recognized that the Russian artillery preparation for the attack had commenced, and that the Turkish batteries were replying. The early morning had been damp and foggy; but when the fog lifted the sun came out strongly, and it became blazing hot. I had received no special instructions from Hassib Bey, my superior officer, and I resolved to see as much of the fighting as possible. So, when I had finished my work at the hospital, I saddled my horse, and galloped off as a free-lance with my pocket-case of surgical instruments and two large bags, one containing *tiftig*, or lint, and the other bandages.

For weapons I carried a sword and a revolver, but no carbine. No field ambulance had been organized, and it occurred to me that I might be of some service to the wounded. So I headed in a south-easterly direction, where the firing seemed particularly heavy; and about a mile from the town I rode up the slope of a small *colline*, below the crest of which a regiment of Turkish infantry were lying under cover. The day was very hot, and the men had had nothing to drink since they took up their position five or six hours before. When I got there it was about ten o'clock, and the first thing I saw was a long procession of Turkish women of the poorer class, who were carrying earthen pitchers of water from a small stream at the foot of the hill to the thirsty troops lying in position. Some were ascending with full pitchers, and others were descending again with the empty vessels to replenish them at the stream.

At this time the roar of the guns was terrific, and the Russian shells were screaming over our heads, some of them exploding in the air and others striking the ground behind us. The women, who were all dressed in white, with their *yashmaks* over their faces, and only their eyes showing, went steadily on with their self-appointed task, carrying their pitchers of water up to the men and back to the stream without a falter. When I was about two hundred yards from the crest where the troops were lying, a shell burst within a few yards of me, and a fragment of it struck one of the women in the arm. She screamed out as the artery spirted up over the white dress, and I made her my first patient in the battle.

As soon as the other women saw that she was wounded, they made a great fuss, chattering away like magpies. They placed her under a tree, and at first refused to let me attend to her, for a *Giaour* must not touch a Turkish woman under any circumstances; but when they could not stop the bleeding themselves, they became alarmed, and offered no objections when I approached with my bags of lint and bandages. I slit up the sleeve of her dress with a pair of scissors and stanched the bleeding; but the injury was only a flesh wound, and not serious. Osman Pasha got to hear of the women being there somehow, and presently an *aide-de-camp* came galloping up and cleared the whole lot of them off. They went back into the town, and I saw no more of them.

When I reached the crest of the hill and looked round, I saw an immense panorama of country thickly sprinkled with hills, and from every individual summit a battery of field-guns seemed to be roaring. No Russian infantry were visible, and it was impossible to say which were the Russian guns and which the Turkish. The noise was terrific, and everywhere I saw clouds of dust, with here and there a Russian battery with six horses going at full gallop, as the guns came into action at a new position. Over towards Grivitza and over by Radishevo and on the crest of every hill we had men placed, and our batteries were answering the Russian fire. I attended a few wounded men who had been struck by fragments of shells, and then I rode off due east towards the village of Grivitza, which was the objective of both the attacking columns.

On the way I met Osman Pasha and his staff, and saluted them. Osman looked careworn and very anxious. He was riding a little bay cob, which he always used when any specially dangerous operations were in progress, preferring not to run the risk of getting either of his two other valuable chargers killed. That little bay cob was a capital barometer by which to gauge the warmth of the fighting; and whenever he made his appearance on the battlefield, it was safe to assume that affairs were pretty critical. Just as I passed Osman Pasha, I heard the whistle of rifle-bullets for the first time in the engagement.

Looking over towards Radishevo, I could make out a strong Russian force in the village. They were sending their guns on in front, and the infantry were advancing, also following the guns, which were going at a furious gallop. I could see Osman Pasha and his staff riding over towards the Bulgareni road, which lay at the foot of the Janik Bair, with the Grivitza brook running alongside it. As I followed them I met several wounded men dragging themselves slowly and painfully from the front to the hospital at Plevna, and I was able to reduce their sufferings a little, though of course I could not attempt any operations even of the simplest kind.

Gradually I became aware of the general disposition of the opposing forces, and found that the Turks, roughly speaking, occupied the arc of a circle south and south-east of Plevna, while the Russian troops were advancing in converging lines upon them with the village of Grivitza evidently as the main object of their attack. From the top of the hill where I stood I could make out the advancing lines of the Russians, while our troops by this time were below me, standing in hastily constructed trenches which they had dug for protection against the increasingly heavy fire. Some idea of the infernal tumult which was going on may be gathered from the fact that over one hundred and fifty heavy guns were firing incessantly, while the infantry fusillade extended in an unbroken line from one end of the arc of defence to the other.

From where I stood I could see the attack on the village of Grivitza quite plainly. The Russians attacked in column of front half a mile wide, while our men waited grimly breast high in the trenches in front of the village. The whole place was so thickly covered with smoke, and the area of the battlefield was so extended, that sometimes I scarcely knew who were Turks and who were Russians. I rode back a little way from the crest of the hill to get cover, and presently my friend Czetwertinski galloped up with eighty troopers, who formed the bodyguard of Osman Pasha. We had a talk together, and presently, as we could not see much from where we were, we agreed to go up and inspect our first line of defence.

Just below the crown of the hill we found four thousand Turkish troops entrenched and blazing away at the Russians who were developing the attack on the position. Czetwertinski and I rode together to the extreme end of our line of infantry, and I could hear the bullets whistling like hornets all round us. Czetwertinski, as he sat there on his horse, leisurely rolled a cigarette for himself, and then looked round for a light. Seeing that the soldier in the trenches nearest to us was puffing calmly at a cigarette himself in the intervals of business, Czetwertinski sang out to him, "*Verbana a-tish*," meaning, "Give me a light." The man clambered out of the trench, saluted, and handed his lighted cigarette to Prince Czetwertinski. As he stood there in the act of saluting a rifle-bullet went through his head, and the man threw up his arms and fell dead. Czetwertinski remarked to me that it was not good enough to stop there any longer; so we retired to the other side of the hill again, and rejoined the cavalry, who were waiting there under cover.

Just at this juncture the Russians, who were advancing in two lines of company columns, a formation totally unfitted for modern warfare, began to falter under the terrific fire from our trenches. The faltering grew more decided, and in a few moments the advance was changed to a retreat. This was our opportunity. The bugles sounded for the Turkish cavalry to advance; and almost before I could realize what was happening, I saw old Mustapha Bey, the colonel of the regiment, and the eighty troopers, with Czetwertinski among them, going off at full gallop straight towards the retreating Russian infantry, who had already begun to run. For a moment I hesitated what to do. Then old Mustapha Bey waved his sword, and sang out to me to come along with them; so I forgot that I was a simple medical officer. I drove the spurs into my horse, and in half a minute I was riding alongside Czetwertinski in a wild charge against the flying Russians.

We climbed the hill at a gallop, rode through our own men at the top, and charged down the slope towards Schahoffskoi's fugitives. There was a large field of ripe maize on our right as we went down the hill, and I could see the Russians running through it as hard as their legs could carry them, believing of course that a strong body of cavalry was swooping down to cut off their retreat. Next to the field of standing maize was a field of barley, which had been reaped and piled in stooks. I could see the Russians dodging in and out among the stooks as we rode towards them, our troopers yelling and cheering as they emptied their carbines and revolvers into the mass of the fugitives. The Russian officers were trying to rally their men, and parties of them began to make a stand under some trees and to reply to our fire.

In a moment more, when the most venturesome of the troopers had got within forty or fifty yards of the fugitives, the Russians suddenly faced round, and, recognizing that they were attacked by a mere handful of men, took up a formation and poured their fire into us in earnest. Hassan Labri Pasha, who was watching the whole thing, foresaw that our retreat was likely to be cut off, and he sounded the retreat. We wheeled our horses just in time, drove the spurs in, and galloped back for our lives.

Probably no man except one who has been in a similar position can even faintly guess at the rapid change of feeling which comes over one at such a crisis. A few moments before, while we were galloping forward against the fugitives, I felt as brave as a lion; but when once I had turned my back to them and heard their bullets whistling round me, a mortal dread came over me, and if I had had a hundred millions in the bank I would have given it all to be a furlong farther from the muzzles of those Russian rifles. It was every man for himself of course, and we did not attempt to preserve any sort of formation. The instinct of a hunted animal flying for cover made me turn towards the maize-field, and I galloped into the friendly shelter of the tall stems, bending my head low over my horse's neck and urging him forward with voice and spur.

The maize was tall enough to conceal a horse and man completely, so that the Russians could not take aim at any individual mark; but they poured incessant volleys into the field, and many a bullet fired at random found its billet. As these hundreds of bullets cut the maize stalks in all directions round me, I must confess that my previous recklessness had given place to a ghastly, overmastering terror. Wherever I turned, danger was by my side, and I could only press blindly forward and hope for the best. A trooper close by me suddenly threw up his arms, and seemed to spring several feet up from the saddle before he fell with a thud among the blood-soaked maize stalks. It occurred to me then that he must have been shot through the heart.

By this time the entire Russian force which had been attacking our position on the hill was in full pursuit; and as I came out on the other side of the maize-field with the other survivors of that mistaken charge, I saw with dismay that our retreat had affected our own infantrymen with a panic. They had held their ground stubbornly while the Russians were developing the original attack; but when they saw us galloping back pell-mell with the returning Russians behind us, the moral influence of our retreat was too much for them, and they started to run from the position. It was a critical moment; but the threatened retreat was stopped as quickly as it began; for Osman Pasha, who had been watching the affair with his staff from the top of the hill, took prompt steps to rally the men.

The slope of the hill, from the crest down to where the men were entrenched, was extraordinarily steep; but when we rode up it, and the men in the trenches began to follow us, Osman Pasha and his staff came down it at full gallop, with shouts and direful threats, emptying their revolvers at the advancing body of their own men. This drastic remedy had the desired effect, and the men rallied, took their places again in the trenches, and opened fire upon the Russians.

By this time it was beginning to get dusk; and as the firing showed no signs of diminution, I made my way back to Plevna as fast as I could go, in the full conviction that it was all up with us, and that the Russians would be in the town soon after me. What actually happened was this. The Russians took our first line of trenches, when Osman Pasha, seeing that the northern attack had died out, ordered down two fresh regiments along the Nicopolis road to reinforce the position. The men were quite fresh, and they "doubled" the whole way, covering the intervening two miles in about twelve minutes, and arriving just in time to bar the farther advance of the Russians, who fell back after some desperate hand-to-hand fighting.

When I reached the town, the bullets were falling pretty thickly in the streets, showing that the Russians had penetrated unpleasantly close. I saw a Bulgarian coming out of a house with a bucket to fill it with water from a small fountain in the middle of the street; but before he reached the fountain he fell dead drilled by a rifle-ball.

Coming to the hospital, I was soon up to my neck in work. Gradually the firing died away, and all night long the wounded kept coming in, some walking and others in *arabas*. We had thirty-seven medical men on the staff at this time, and there was plenty for all to do. No one knew exactly what had happened; and I remember telling several of the wounded men, who inquired how the day had gone, that we had been beaten. Later on, however, I found that we had won a great victory, and that the Russians had been decisively beaten all along the line; Krüdener's and Schahoffskoi's columns having suffered terrible loss, while Skobeleff who had been fighting on the Green Hills, had retired his force in good order, and with lighter loss. The Russian total loss was given as one hundred and sixty-nine officers, and seven thousand one hundred and thirty-six men, or about one-fourth of the total force. Even this figure, however, is believed to be largely underestimated. The Turkish loss was about eight hundred killed and nine hundred wounded.

In spite of this splendid victory, the great chance of the campaign was missed owing to the want of cavalry. If we had had a strong body of cavalry, scarcely a Russian would have reached the Danube alive; and even as it was the panic among the Russians at Sistova was so great that a rush was made upon the bridge, and many waggons were actually pushed over into the river by the crowding fugitives.

As for my little troop of cavalry with whom I made that desperate charge and still more desperate retreat, it had been absolutely decimated, though Mustapha Bey the colonel, Czetwertinski the captain, and the Turkish lieutenant, all escaped as fortunately as myself.

In the town of Plevna we had plenty of accommodation for the wounded, and all the arrangements for attending to them were in far better order than on the occasion of the first battle. When the main hospital was full, we sent the men off to the smaller hospitals, and many of the less serious cases lay out in the open air all night. It was a repetition in many respects of our experience after the first battle; for we had forty-eight hours of almost continuous work, and then the great bulk of the men were put into carts and sent away to Sofia. On the first night after the artillery firing had ceased, all was quiet, and the only sounds to be heard in the town were the cries and moans of the wounded and the loud creaking of the great wooden-wheeled waggons as they rolled over the cobble-stones outside.

As I have said, we were much better prepared for the reception of the wounded than after the first battle; for we had plenty of instruments, chloroform, antiseptic solutions, and bandages, and, moreover, we had trained a number of the soldiers to act as an ambulance corps. These assistants were able to help us very materially, and had become quite expert dressers. In the majority of cases the wounds were very severe, as the men had fought principally in the trenches, and when hit they were generally shot either through the head or right through the chest.

On August 1 I got away from the hospital at about five o'clock in the afternoon, and rode out to have a look at the battlefield. Near the spot where the Grivitza redoubt was afterwards built the Russian dead lay thickest, and within a space of about two acres on this rising slope I counted fifteen hundred bodies. The spectacle was a horrifying one. Turkish burial parties had already been out burying our dead; but the Russians were left where they fell. Nearly all of them were absolutely naked, for the Bashi-Bazouks had been there already, and had stripped them of arms and clothing completely. I could not help noticing the difference in physique between the Russian soldiers and the Turks. The Russians were far less robust, and many of them seemed to be mere lads, hardly equal to the task of carrying the heavy Berdan or Krenke rifle. Broken gun carriages lay on every side, and the ground was scarred and torn in all directions.

A number of wounded horses, lying on the ground unable to rise, were neighing pitifully, and farther off two or three more with broken legs and entrails hanging out were dragging themselves slowly and painfully to a pool of water that had collected in a hollow at the foot of a hill. I shot four of the unfortunate creatures with my revolver, and put them out of their misery.

Some of the wounded men were in very strange attitudes. One man was kneeling as if in prayer; another was on his hands and knees; another was lying in his own brains. All three had been stripped by the Bashi-Bazouks. The Russian line of retreat could be easily distinguished, for it was marked out by a track of dead bodies laid as plainly as the track of a paper-chase. Here and there I could see where groups of them had tried to make a little stand, and had been shot down thirty or forty or fifty at a time. I saw one dead man in a most extraordinary position. He was stuck in the fork of a tree about fifteen feet from the ground, having evidently climbed it for safety, and then been shot by a stray bullet.

Returning from my visit to the dead, I devoted myself again to the wounded in the hospitals, and performed a number of amputations together with Osman Effendi, who worked splendidly with me. In the intervals of work next day I rode out again to the battlefield, which was beginning to smell terribly, so that we had to send out more burial parties to bury them in large trenches containing eighty or a hundred bodies each. So terrible had been the slaughter that some Russian regiments had literally ceased to exist.

Within a very few days after the battle we had sent away the greater number of the wounded, and only the cases for operation remained. All of these were removed to the main hospital, and Osman Effendi and myself resumed our work upon this new supply of patients. All our operations were done out of doors in the same place under the willow tree near the bank of the Tutchenitza. A great number of cases ended fatally which in a civil hospital would probably have resulted differently; but we did not attempt any intricate operations, and we were also hampered by the fact that the patients frequently preferred to die rather than undergo the amputation of a limb.

If a man had a bullet in his knee, for instance, such a thing as excising the knee or laying it open was never thought of, and we simply took the leg off. This is a legitimate course for a surgeon to adopt in time of war, because the skilled attention necessary to the after treatment of a delicate operation was not available, and it was often better surgery to take a man's leg off and preserve his life than to perform an intricate operation in order to save the leg with the probability of the patient succumbing for want of careful nursing afterwards. As in the case of the wounded in the first battle, there were a large number of men whose fingers we had to amputate.

Trade revived quite briskly as soon as things began to settle down again in the town, and the bazaars were all in full swing. Many Spanish Jews, scenting large profits from afar, put in an appearance, and bought Russian coin and arms from the Circassians who had secured the plunder. A Russian *rouble* was to be had for two pence, and an officer's sword could be had for a *franc*. I myself bought two beautifully mounted Russian revolvers, which I still possess.

Osman Pasha was overwhelmed with congratulations upon his brilliant victory from all quarters of Europe, and I was a witness of an impressive scene when he was the recipient of the highest military honour that the *sultan* can bestow. It was a few days after the battle, and I was standing close to the headquarters camp, behind which all the reserves were stationed, when I heard the bugles sounding the "fall in." Everything had been perfectly quiet, and there was no sign of the proximity of the Russians, so that I was at a loss to understand the meaning of the order; but it was carried out with astonishing celerity. Within five minutes several thousand men were on parade under arms, and I was looking round to see what was the matter, when I saw a Turkish officer in gorgeous uniform galloping up to the headquarters camp accompanied by a troop of cavalry. It proved to be an *aide-de-camp* of the *sultan*, who had come up from Constantinople with an escort bearing despatches for Osman Pasha.

Soon all the camp was in motion, and as the bugles repeated the call troops came pouring down to the parade-ground from the different redoubts and the earthworks on the Janik Bair and at Grivitza, and formed up into square. All the field officers were present, including Adil Pasha, the second in command. The *sultan's aide-de-camp* and some of the officers went into the tent of Osman Pasha, who presently appeared with the first order of the Osmanli, the highest Turkish military decoration, pinned upon his breast, with the cordon. The *aide-de-camp* read out a special despatch from the *sultan*, congratulating Osman Pasha upon his recent brilliant victory. He then presented him with a splendid sword, the hilt of which was set in diamonds, and he presented Adil Pasha with a brace of magnificently mounted pistols as a token of the *sultan's* appreciation of his soldierly qualities.

All the officers came forward with the standard-bearers, and Osman Pasha then delivered a stirring address to the troops. He said that his Imperial Majesty the *Sultan* had done him the honour of decorating him with the order which he then wore, and had presented him with that magnificent sword in token of his pleasure at the decisive defeat which had been inflicted upon the Russians. Though the *sultan* had decorated him personally, yet the credit of the victory did not belong so much to him as to his brave officers and troops, who, he felt certain, were still eager and ready to try conclusions again with the enemy. He added that the battle which they had just fought was not to end the campaign. They were fighting for hearths and homes, for wives and children; and though the fighting still in store for them would probably be even more severe than that which they had already gone through, still he placed the fullest confidence in their bravery and their patriotism. The troops all cheered their leader lustily, and the ceremony came to an end with a great, united shout of *"La ilaha illallah Mohammed Rasul Allah."*

During those days after the second battle the work of fortification proceeded with ceaseless activity under the direction of Tewfik Pasha, who was rapidly rearing a chain of redoubts connected by trenches and subterranean passages to bar the passage of the Russian troops into Turkish territory. These earthworks were marvels of intricate construction, and at this period the greater number of our troops lived underground like moles, tunnelling communications between the different redoubts, the largest of which was the famous one at Grivitza, which contained four thousand men.

When we had finished our work with the wounded and sent them all away, I had practically nothing to do, and used to spend my time riding about the hills either on Dr. Robert's trotting pony or my own charger. I got tired of my quarters in the Bulgarian house, and decided to flit to some place more convenient to the hospital. I found the place I was looking for in another Bulgarian house, situated in the extreme north-west of the town on the bank of the Tutchenitza, and within a couple of minutes' walk of the hospital. It was a remarkable house, for it had no front door and no staircase inside, although it was a two-storey edifice. There was a large yard at the back, and in one corner of it was the shed, which did duty for a stable.

I saw that there was a fine garden attached to the house, and that it was separated from the Tutchenitza by a fence. The ground floor was inhabited by a forbidding-looking Bulgarian and his family, and I took possession of the upper rooms, which were reached by a flight of stone steps from the outside. There I installed myself in the best bedroom as comfortably as possible under the circumstances, and Ahmet, my Circassian servant, occupied an adjoining apartment. He had no trouble about arranging the furniture in my room, because there wasn't any, with the exception of a wide divan running round the wall.

Cordial hospitality was not at that time the strong point of the average Bulgarian, and my host downstairs was an unusually surly person. I was a tenant at will—that is to say, at my own will, not at my landlord's—but the heads of the household took no more notice of me than if I had been dead—probably indeed not so much. There was one little chap, though, a yellow-haired, blue-eyed Bulgarian boy of about thirteen, who used occasionally to visit me; and he endeavoured without success to explain to me his views upon the position. I encouraged his confidences with an eye to subsequent advantages, and reaped the reward in milk, which the little chap used to bring me from his father's dairy cow. With the addition of the milk to my daily fare, I was enabled to boil my rice in a new way and to improve my *menu* considerably.

In the beautiful garden which surrounded the house were some of the most magnificent specimens of china asters, zinnias, and balsams that I have ever seen. I sent some of the seed home to Australia, and can still, even after long years, pluck flowers which are the lineal descendants of those that bloomed for the first time in the blood-stained soil of Plevna. But sometimes that garden produced another and a ghastlier crop. About ten days after the battle we had a terrific downfall of rain. It poured for about twenty-four hours in torrents, and the Tutchenitza was soon running a banker. Presently the flood-waters encroached, and poured across the low-lying flats, through the fence, and over our beautiful garden. When the rain stopped and the water receded, I walked in the garden one morning, and found *débris* of all sorts, which had been brought down by the stream, still sticking in my favourite gooseberry bushes.

Among the flotsam and jetsam gathered there was a grisly relic from the battlefield a mile or two away. It was a human head, with most of the flesh worn off the skull by the action of the water, and the teeth set fast in a horrid grin. It was impossible to say whether it was the head of a Turk or a Russian, and I buried it under the gooseberry bush where I found it.

A day or two after this great rainstorm I rode out again over the hills and visited the battlefield. Far down on the lower ground, where the main Russian attack upon Grivitza was delivered, I came upon a gully, down which the recent rains had poured a miniature mountain torrent. The water had scooped away the earth that was thinly laid over the Russian dead, and had robbed the shallow graves of the corpses, carrying the bones away to the lowest lying ground, and depositing them there to whiten in the sun. Hundreds of skulls which had been separated from the bodies were lying there. I thought of the Kurdish colonel, and of the fate which his Circassian servant meted out to the wounded Russian officer, and I guessed the shocking reason. These were the heads of wounded men whom the Circassians had decapitated.

CHAPTER 8

The Fiascos of Pelischat and Lovtcha

My own Circassian servant, Ahmet, was an excellent attendant, and I seldom had any trouble with him. Once, however, an incident occurred through which I nearly lost him. It all arose through a pig. Next door to my quarters, and between them and the house occupied by Dr. Robert, was the residence of a Bulgarian, who was rather more affable than most of his compatriots, and who allowed me to use a right-of-way through his place to get to Dr. Robert's, so as to avoid the necessity of going a long way round. I often saw this Bulgarian as I went through his garden, and one day he told me that he was going to kill a pig, and that if I sent Ahmet in to him he would give him some fresh pork for me. When I conveyed my wishes to Ahmet, I was met by an unexpected obstacle. Ahmet was a good Mussulman, and hated pork as the devil hates holy water. He refused to touch the accursed thing, and it was in vain that by turns I bullied and entreated, threatened and cajoled him to fetch the material for an appetizing plateful of pork chops.

He positively refused, and at last I told him that if he would not obey my orders I would have to send him back to his regiment. This was an unpleasant alternative, for with me he had light duties, comfortable quarters, plenty to eat and drink, and no fighting, whereas if he were sent back to his regiment he would have to spend long hours digging in the trenches, with the certainty of being sent under fire on the first reappearance of the Russians. In spite of all this he steadily refused to fetch the pork, and I admired his steadfastness so much that at last I went and fetched it myself. I took it over to Dr. Robert's, and we had a splendid dinner.

It was about this time that I first met that remarkable adventurer Olivier Pain, whose history forms one of the strangest pages in the book of political martyrs. Tewfik Bey told me one morning that a Frenchman had arrived in Plevna; and as I was extremely anxious for some news of the outside world, I determined to call on the visitor. He was established in the Bulgarian house which I had not long quitted, and was receiving the scant attention which the black-eyed daughter of the house found time to bestow upon him, and the conversational treat which her one remark "London" occasionally afforded.

When I visited the stranger in my old well known quarters, I found a tall, sallow man, apparently about twenty-five years of age, with a small, pointed beard, and an air of intelligence and almost of distinction. He was arranging his few possessions in the room when I entered and introduced myself to him. As my eyes wandered round the room, I was thunderstruck to see this Frenchman pinning upon the wall a photograph of Sydney Harbour, and I asked him at once if he knew Sydney. He replied that he did; and when I told him that I was a native of Melbourne, he said that he had also been in Melbourne, and knew it well. He seemed somewhat troubled at my recognition of the photograph, and at last, speaking in very tolerable English, he said to me, "Sir, I have a very high idea of the honour of an English gentleman, and I take you to be one. If you will promise not to betray me, I will tell you who I am."

"Like yourself," I replied, "I am alone here, and it does not matter a straw to me who you are. You are evidently an intelligent and educated man, and that is quite enough for me." Then he told me that he was Olivier Pain, and that during the stormy days of 1871 in Paris he had embraced the cause of the Commune, and been deported for life to New Caledonia, in company with the fiery and *intransigéant* Henri Rochefort. He had escaped in 1874 with Rochefort to the Australian coast, and had reached Sydney in safety, afterwards making his way to Melbourne, and thence to America, where for some time he lay *perdu*. Venturing back to Europe, however, after many adventures he reached Geneva, and on the outbreak of the Russo-Turkish war was engaged as a war correspondent by one of the principal Geneva newspapers.

Now war correspondents were regarded with the utmost distrust in Turkey, while Osman Pasha positively hated them, and strict instructions were given that no stranger should be allowed into Plevna without a special *firman* from the *sultan*. It was characteristic of the audacity of Olivier Pain that he should have made his way from Constantinople unprovided with the necessary *firman*, and should have "bluffed" himself into Plevna, in the belief that among the hundreds of departing wounded men and arriving reinforcements his presence would not at first be noticed. As a matter of fact, however, he was noted at once, and eventually had to leave the town temporarily; but for a fortnight he continued to inhabit my old quarters, and I saw a good deal of him.

Little skirmishes between our pickets and the Russian vedettes used to occur from day to day, and Pain began to exercise his *metier* as war correspondent at once, writing the most picturesque descriptive articles to his Geneva newspaper. I was shown afterwards a copy of that journal, in which a long account appeared written by him, and purporting to be a description of some heroic exploits performed by myself. Upon the slender foundation of my participation in one of the trifling cavalry skirmishes which were constantly taking place, he had built up a remarkable narrative, in which he portrayed me, I am afraid with more vividness than veracity, cutting down Russian troopers by the score. However, fortunately for himself, Pain was an enthusiastic admirer of everything Turkish, and he found in Osman Pasha a model of all the military virtues. It was fortunate for him that he adopted this view in his letters, for unknown to him they were all opened and read by Tewfik Bey before being despatched from Plevna.

Of course Tewfik Bey apprised his superior officer of the contents of the letters, and the result was that Osman Pasha's antipathy to war correspondents was mollified in this particular case. War correspondents are not usually thin-skinned; and when at last it became necessary absolutely to turn Pain out of Plevna because he had no authority to be there, Osman Pasha himself gave him a letter to the executive in Constantinople recommending that the necessary permission should be given to him to return to Plevna. He was unable to return at once as the road was blocked; but Chefket Pasha, coming up in October with fresh troops, reopened it, and with him came back Olivier Pain. He survived all the horrors of the fall of Plevna, and lived to seek for new adventures in the service of the *mahdi* in the Soudan.

The quixotism of Pain's politics was well revealed in his conduct in going to the Soudan as a colleague of Rochefort's, with the idea that he could assist the *mahdi* against England, and so injure the traditional antagonist of France. In that book of fascinating interest *Fire and Sword in the Sudan*,[1] Slatin Bey tells the story of Olivier Pain's appearance in the *mahdi's* camp while his troops were marching on Khartoum, and

---

1. *Fire and Sword in the Sudan*, by Rudolph C. Slatin Pasha is also published by Leonaur.

of his acceptance with suspicion both by the *mahdi* and the *khalifa*. A few days after Pain joined in the march he became ill with fever, and was placed on an *angareb*, or couch, slung upon a donkey. Growing weaker and weaker, he slipped at last from the donkey, fractured his skull, and died miserably when the column was within three days' march of Khartoum.

As I knew him at Plevna, Pain was capital company. He told us what Europe was thinking of us set there to repel the repeated assaults of the Russians; and he gave us many stories of wild life as a political convict in New Caledonia and a refugee ever since in half the countries of the world.

My friend Czetwertinski had come to stay in my quarters as his health was very delicate and he could not live under canvas; so he and Pain and myself generally dined together, and gathered for a smoke and a chat in the evenings. One night a slight contretemps occurred which came near depriving me of one of my friends, if not both. Czetwertinski conceived the brilliant idea of converting some of the milk which the Bulgarian boy used to bring me into butter, and with this object he extemporized a small churn and turned himself into an impromptu butter factory. The volatile Frenchman could not resist giving his communistic feelings expression, and he made some remark about "the butter-making prince" which grievously incensed the haughty Pole.

An instant challenge to a duel followed, and I had the greatest difficulty in preventing my two friends from exchanging shots according to the recognized code. Finally I pacified them, and had the satisfaction of seeing them fall upon each other's necks in a cordial embrace. When Pain finally left us in response to a peremptory order from headquarters, he bequeathed his stock of firewood to me as an acknowledgment of the hospitality which he had received; and I secured possession of this coveted luxury in spite of the loud objections of Pain's Bulgarian landlord, who regarded the wood, which was now becoming a scarce commodity in Plevna, as his lawful perquisite.

A curious superstition on the part of the Turks came under my notice one night soon after Pain's departure. I was tossing about feverishly in bed, suffering agonies from the assaults of the domestic insects which in Bulgaria attain to stupendous proportions, when I heard a tremendous volley of guns, and for the moment I believed that a night attack was taking place. However, after a few minutes of independent firing, the noise died away, and I went to sleep again.

Next morning it appeared that there had been an eclipse of the moon on the previous night, and the townspeople were acting in accordance with an ancient superstition when they fired off every available gun, believing that in doing so they would scare away the monstrous animal which was endeavouring to devour the silver queen of night. They were curiously alive to an empty superstition, yet curiously insensible to hard facts, for they appeared to tolerate the ever-present annoyance of the insects with equanimity. When I resorted to the device of putting the legs of my bed in vessels full of water, so that the fleas and other hopping and crawling visitors could not climb up to attack me, the pertinacious creatures thought out a way to circumvent me. They simply crawled up the wall and along the ceiling until they were in a position to drop down upon me, which they did. It was the most marked display of reasoning power in the lower creatures that ever forced itself upon my notice. The only way that I could baffle the voracious crowd was by moving my bed out into the open air, and this I did.

In the forenoon of August 31, while I was pottering about my hospital, I heard guns at a distance of about five miles, and jumping on my horse I galloped off to the headquarters camp, only to find it deserted. Information was obtainable, however, showing that Osman Pasha had suddenly moved off eastward in the direction of Poradim before daybreak with nineteen battalions of infantry, three batteries of artillery, and all the cavalry at his disposal. He had gone out really for the purpose of getting information and ascertaining the position of the Russians. It was a huge reconnaissance ending in a battle.

As I had received no orders to remain in camp, I rode off in the direction of the firing, and after going a couple of miles I saw three or four mounted officers. Fearing that I might be sent back, I went a little aside, and passed them, as I thought, unnoticed; but they speedily ordered me to halt, and when I went up to them I found that one was Hassib Bey, the principal medical officer.

"Where are you off to in such a hurry?" he said to me; "you are the very man we want."

I told him that I was anxious to see the fun, and he advised me, with a laugh, to curb my ardour, and ordered me to remain with him.

We rode on together for another couple of miles, when we came to an ambulance at work. It was the only ambulance that I ever saw in the field with the Turkish troops, and was a very simple affair, managed by four surgeons, who had brought tables, instruments, water, basins, and bandages with them. A number of wounded men were waiting to be treated, and a long stream of others were coming in from the direction of the fighting. Hassib Bey ordered me to assist the other surgeons working at the ambulance, and I took up my duties among the wounded forthwith. We were stationed on the lee side of a hill in comparative safety and out of the line of fire; but the battle was so close to us that we could hear the roar of the heavy guns, the sharp rattle of the breech-loaders, and the loud hurrahs of the troops engaged.

Presently a rumour reached us that our men had captured two Russian guns on the crest of the long ridge between Pelischat and Sgalevitcha and a few minutes later those field-pieces, which were made of bronze and were the first Russian guns that we had yet seen closely, were taken past us at a gallop by Turkish drivers heading for Plevna. When the wounded men who were lying all round us waiting for their turns saw the captured guns, they were excited to the wildest enthusiasm. Many of them rose to their feet in spite of their wounds, and many more propped themselves up painfully on their rifles as they cheered the capture that had been made.

I remained with the ambulance for several hours, and the record of work there shows how much can be accomplished in the way of surgery under active-service conditions. I had a small chamois-leather bag in my pocket which I used generally for carrying coffee; but I devoted it on this occasion to holding the bullets which I extracted from my patients. I was the only operator; and when the afternoon's work was done, I counted nineteen bullets in it—not a bad record of operations all performed within three hours.

If a wounded man came in with the bullet in anything like a handy place I whipped it out at once, and in no case did we give chloroform. Most of the men were walking back or crawling along as well as they could, and a few were being brought in on stretchers by their comrades.

Among the wounded arrivals was an infantry captain who was a nephew of Hassib Bey. He was shot through the calf of the leg, and he was able to give us some details of the fighting. He told us that the Turks had taken a Russian redoubt, or rather a small entrenchment fortified with sandbags, and that there were a good many wounded men there, but no doctor.

I saluted Hassib Bey, and asked him if I could go forward.

"All right," he replied, "you can go; but, for goodness' sake, take care of yourself."

I promised to do so, and galloped off towards the sound of the fighting. On my way I passed a long string of wounded men making their way back to the ambulance, and was able to stanch their bleeding in many cases, and place them in a better condition for continuing their journey. Presently I came across several dead men, and the shells began to fly about. As I advanced farther the numbers of the dead increased, and the bodies of several Russians among the Turks marked the spot where the fighting had been hand-to-hand. Soon I saw the Russian camp about a mile away. It consisted of a number of little wooden huts on a slight slope in front of the village of Pelischat, and there were a good many tents as well. I could see the Turkish troops engaged; but as I came up to them, they were beginning for the second time to fall back under a hot fire from the Russians.

The country was very open, and lightly timbered, with here and there a few beeches and walnut trees, under which little groups of wounded men were resting on their way to the rear. It was plain that the Russians had recently occupied the ground which our troops at this moment were holding, for lying on the plain were many wounded Russians who had been left behind when their regiments fell back, and those hapless creatures received short shrift from the irregular troops fighting under the Turkish flag.

One instance of the savagery with which the conflict was conducted I witnessed personally; and though it shows the Turkish irregulars in very lurid colours, I can vouch for the performance of similar and even worse atrocities on the part of the Cossacks a few days later.

As I was looking at the firing and wondering how much longer our men would be able to hold the advantage which they had gained, I saw a Circassian, with a most diabolical expression on his face, stooping down to pluck some of the long grass that grew there abundantly and wiping his *camer*, or short sharp sword, upon it. I rode up to see what he was doing, and found that he had just cut the head off an unfortunate wounded Russian. The headless trunk, still quivering with muscular contractions, lay on the ground at his feet, and he was holding up his horrid trophy by the hair.

I rode on to the small earthwork which our men had captured. The regiment which had taken it still held possession, and the Russian troops were advancing in strong force to recapture it. I gathered that desperate fighting had gone on here, and that the redoubt had already been captured and recaptured two or three times. The men who were then holding it were the remnant of the attacking party, and when I was about a hundred yards from the fortified spot I passed an immense number of Turkish dead. They were the first company in the column of assault which perished to a man.

The Russians in the redoubt must have reserved their fire, for nearly every man of the first company had five or six bullets through him. The redoubt itself was full of dead and dying men, and the Russians, having rallied, were already coming back beyond their foremost line, being within about five hundred yards of the redoubt. It was plain that if our men did not retire they would be annihilated, and they began to fall back in good order, taking as many of the wounded with them as possible.

One of the first men I saw was Czetwertinski, who was captain in a cavalry troop. He told me that a few minutes before I arrived his horse had been killed under him by a shell which ripped the animal's side open. So perished the magnificent black charger which no man in the squadron could ride but Czetwertinski; the horse to whom he really owed his commission. Czetwertinski had been left unmounted for a minute or two; but he speedily took the horse ridden by his servant Faizi, who had to find his way back as best he could.

The shells began to come pretty thickly among us, and the Russian gunners were making very fair practice. I saw a Turkish regiment lying down close by some trees, when a couple of shells exploded almost simultaneously among them, killing seven men and wounding many more, whom I attended on the spot.

Osman Pasha with Tewfik Bey and his staff were there in the thick of it. The commander-in-chief had had three horses shot under him that day. Presently our men began to retire in earnest, under a perfect storm of shot and shell from the returning Russians. All our wounded men had been got away except two who were left behind in the redoubt. I saw them there, and, realizing what their fate would be when the Russians should have retaken the redoubt, I decided to make an effort to save them. I got into the redoubt, and found that one of the men had been shot through the neck by a rifle-bullet. He was bleeding terribly, and was already blanched to the colour of death.

The other man had been struck in the left thigh by a fragment of shell which had shattered the bone. I got them both out, and managed to get the man who was shot in the neck upon my horse. I placed him in the saddle, and I put the man with the shattered leg up behind him. I held the second man in position with my right hand, and led the horse by the bridle with the left. The man with the broken leg was suffering terrible agony, but he held up his comrade in front of him and prevented him from falling off. In this way we started to rejoin our troops, who were now nearly half a mile away, retreating slowly and firing as they went. The Russians were within about four hundred yards of the redoubt when I left it with the two wounded men and the horse.

The Russians were pouring in a hot fire on our retreating troops, and our men were answering at intervals, so that I was caught between two fires. I could hear the Russian shells screaming over my head as I made my way back. Our pace was necessarily slow, for I had to walk the horse all the way, and to take the utmost care lest the men should fall off. When we had got about half a mile from the redoubt, the man in front fell off the horse dead, and I left him there. I put the other man into the saddle; and after a period that seemed like a lifetime, I reached our foremost lines and went on through them, and out of the line of fire, without having received a scratch.

We saw several regiments of Russian cavalry detach themselves from the main body and come galloping down as if to cut off our retreat; so our officers ordered the field-guns into action, and we opened a destructive shell fire on them which stopped their pursuit. The main body of the Russians also drew back, and did not pursue us farther; so that without further misadventure we reached the site of the field ambulance, and I placed my man in one of the waggons after bandaging up his leg. When I took him off the saddle, I noticed a little pyramid of clotted blood, about three or four inches high, on the horse's wither. It had been caused by the slow *drip-drip* from the neck of the first man before he fell off dead.

I stopped at the field-ambulance depot attending to the wounded men until about six o'clock in the evening, when we all cleared off and went back to Plevna. This was the battle of Pelischat, otherwise named Sgalevitcha. We had about one thousand three hundred men killed and wounded, and we had gained absolutely nothing. I never could understand the exact object of this sortie from Plevna, since even if we had succeeded in capturing the Pelischat-Sgalevitcha position we could never have held it.

Early on the morning of September 4 an orderly came to my quarters before I was up, and said to me, "At eleven o'clock you will see some troops advancing by the Lovtcha road, and you will follow them."

I asked him where they were going, and he said that he did not know. I inquired how long we were likely to be away, and he said that he had no idea, adding that I had better take my instruments with me because I should probably want them.

After I had done my work at the hospital, I went up to the headquarters camp, and found that Osman Pasha and a number of officers, Hassan Labri Pasha, Emin Bey, Tahir Pasha, Tewfik Bey, Osman Bey, and Yalaat Bey, with sixteen battalions and three batteries, were marching out along the Lovtcha road, and I joined them at once. About a mile from Plevna on this road were some large vineyards laden with clusters of ripe grapes, which had attracted the attention of our troops some days before this. In fact, the Turkish soldiers, in their desire to get the ripe fruit, had been in the habit of stealing out by night past our vedettes into the vineyards, and several of them had been shot by the Russian outposts; strict orders had accordingly been given to the troops to refrain from indulging their appetite for grapes under the circumstances, and the Turkish sentries had been instructed to shoot any men who attempted to pass them during the night for the purpose of getting into the vineyards.

When, however, we were marching out towards Lovtcha in the daytime, it was impossible to keep the troops out of the vineyards; and many of the men who had not been too plentifully supplied with rations for some time past gorged themselves with fruit to such an extent that they became ill with dysentery, and I had to attend to them. On the outskirts of Plevna also I noticed many Turkish professional beggars who pestered the troops for money; and as it was considered lucky to give something in charity before going into action, the soldiers were very liberal, and the beggars reaped a rich harvest of *piastres*.

Almost as soon as we were well clear of Plevna and out into the open country, we fell in with some Russian cavalry vedettes, and began a period of intermittent fighting which continued all that day. When the vedettes saw that we were in strong force, they fell back upon a field where the corn had been cut and stood piled up at intervals in stooks. It was quite interesting to watch them dodging for cover from one stook to another, while our men tried to pick them off with their rifles. A good many of the Cossacks fell in the wheatfield, and the remainder were driven back without difficulty. Hardly had we got rid of those, however, when three or four Russian infantry regiments put in an appearance with a couple of batteries of artillery, and opened fire on us.

We were drawn up in very open order, and Osman Pasha sent a couple of batteries up to the crest of some rising ground, and we started to shell the enemy, still continuing to push forward with the main body. There was a small creek to cross, and we had a hard task to get the guns over the bridge under a heavy fire from the Russians. It was very exciting work; and as Tewfik Bey was directing the passage of the bridge, his horse was killed under him by a shell. At last, however, we got safely over, just as it was growing dusk, and sending out skirmishers in front we continued to advance. The firing went on for some hours, sudden sheets of flame appearing on both sides in the twilight as the opposing troops discharged volley after volley; but our casualties were very few, and at last there was a cessation of hostilities.

We camped in a wheat-field which had just been reaped, and Weinberger and I sat all night in one of the stooks, holding our horses. We had no rations with us; but I had had a good feed of grapes in the morning, and with some cobs of maize that I had put in my pocket before starting we managed to satisfy our hunger. As we squatted in the stook together, Weinberger and I discussed the situation seriously, and came to the conclusion that it was by no means reassuring. In point of fact we made up our minds that our last hour was all but come, for we made sure that before morning the Russians would bring up their troops and we should have to be struck by a flank attack.

Our communication with Plevna would no doubt be cut off during the night, and we apprehended that when the morning came our force would probably be annihilated. When day broke, however, we looked out of our stook, and found to our intense relief that there was not a Russian in sight anywhere. It was the most beautiful morning that I remember to have ever seen; and after the bare hills round Plevna and the narrow streets of the town, the well timbered, undulating country was a delightful sight.

The march was resumed soon after daybreak, and it must have been midday before we halted in the doghole Bulgarian village of Kakrinka, a little distance eastward of Lovtcha. A number of pigs belonging to the fugitive villagers were roaming about among the empty cottages, and the Circassians, who, like all good Mussulmen, regard the pig as a filthy and abominable creature, showed their religious zeal by shooting several of them. On the outskirts of the village we met a Bulgarian woman with two children, and from her we learnt the fatal news that Lovtcha had fallen two days before. Our march from Plevna had been with the object of relieving Rifaat Pasha, who commanded the garrison at Lovtcha; but we had arrived too late, for he had been attacked by an overwhelming Russian force, and the Turkish troops in Lovtcha had been cut to pieces.

What had happened was this. Skobeleff had advanced upon Lovtcha on September 1, with about twenty-one thousand men and eighty-four guns, exclusive of the Cossacks and their batteries. Aware that he was vastly outnumbered, Rifaat Pasha had sent an urgent request to Osman Pasha in Plevna for immediate assistance; but the commander-in-chief apparently considered that the Lovtcha position could hold out for a few days, and delayed to send reinforcements at once.

During the night of September 1, Skobeleff had thrown up entrenchments and established batteries on a hill two miles from Lovtcha, and opened fire early on the morning of the 2nd upon the position. Later in the day the main Russian body had come up, and thrown up entrenchments to prepare for the general attack, which took place on September 3. After three hours of desperate fighting, the position was carried, and the Turks withdrew their left wing across the river Osma. The attack on the second Turkish position was then commenced, and the citadel of Lovtcha was at last carried by Skobeleff and his Russians, after a general rush from all sides late in the evening.

Most of the Turkish fugitives had already fled towards Mikren, twelve miles south-west of Lovtcha, hotly pursued by Cossacks and artillery. Cut down by the Cossacks or killed by Russian shells, the Turkish force was practically wiped out. Ignorant of the details, however, and knowing only the bare fact that Lovtcha was in the hands of the Russians, we pressed on towards the position; and when we were about five miles from Lovtcha, we saw a couple of regiments of cavalry and a regiment of infantry drawn up on the bank of the Osma. They advanced over the plain to meet us; and as we were well posted on a fairly high eminence, we opened fire on them with artillery. I saw one of the shells drop right in the middle of a squadron of cavalry, and five or six men with their horses were all down on the ground together.

Under the stress of the artillery fire the cavalry scattered and retired, some remaining to pick up their wounded. We continued to fire upon these, and killed about twenty-five or thirty more of them. Below the eminence upon which our troops were drawn up was a wood of dwarf oaks, walnuts, and beeches running down into the plain which form the valley of the Osma; and Osman Pasha, believing that a Russian force was concealed in the wood, sent down a couple of battalions to clear it.

I sat on my horse on the top of the hill, and watched this interesting operation. There were little open spaces here and there in the wood, and I could see the red *fezzes* of the soldiers bobbing about among the trees as they worked the cover exactly like a pack of foxhounds. There was a great deal of shouting and indiscriminate firing, and we all expected to see the Russians bolting out of the wood on the other side. It was intensely exciting; but at last we saw the *fezzes* emerging on the far side of the wood, and we realized that they had drawn it blank. There was not a Russian in the place; but I had three wounded Turks to attend to who had been shot by their own comrades when the promiscuous firing was going on in the wood.

As we looked over upon Lovtcha from the hill where we were halted, the town appeared as if it was on the stage of a vast theatre, while we were in the dress circle. Below us was a long green plain with the silver thread of the river Osma meandering through it, and farther away was the town of Lovtcha nestling in the ranges. On the banks of the river were two Bulgarian villages, and we could see Russian troops in both of them.

Osman Pasha held a council of war on the top of the hill, and all the principal officers attended, the question debated being whether an attempt should be made to recapture Lovtcha or not. The general opinion was that it was inadvisable to make the attempt, and Hassan Labri Pasha alone was in favour of an attack. At last, after discussing all the arguments for and against, it was decided not to attack such a strong position occupied by an immensely superior force; and Osman Pasha, much against his will, was obliged to order a return to Plevna.

Meanwhile our cavalry and Circassians were sent down the hill to make a reconnaissance, and I went with them. After going some little distance, we came across a ghastly evidence of the ferocity of the fighting, for we counted nearly four hundred Turks all lying dead together. They had apparently tried to break away when Lovtcha fell, and had been cut down by the Cossacks when making a last stand under the walnut trees. Every corpse was fearfully disfigured. The faces had been slashed with sabres even after death, and the corpses had been subjected to the horrible indignities which are usually supposed to be practised only by the hill tribes of Afghanistan. Whether those atrocities were committed by the Russians or by the Bulgarians I could not definitely determine; but the sight enraged the Circassians to an appalling extent, and their threats boded ill for any Russians who might fall into their hands alive.

It was impossible for the column to return to Plevna by the same way that it had come, because we knew that the Russians had seized some important positions on the road, fortified them with earthworks, and brought up their artillery. Consequently Osman Pasha decided to make a *détour*; and as Lovtcha was about due south of Plevna, we headed at first in a westerly direction and gradually worked round to the north.

It was an intensely hot day, and we all suffered severely from thirst, having been without water for several hours. I managed to find a pool of dirty water, however, and I drank as much as I could, not knowing when the next opportunity for a drink might arrive. As for food, all that we had consisted of the cobs of maize that we gathered in the fields as we passed.

Later in the afternoon, however, we had another meal with a different *menu*. As I passed through a Bulgarian village with an advance party of Circassians, we came to a farmhouse on the top of a ridge well timbered with walnut trees. The Circassians made a hurried investigation of the premises, and then set fire to some outbuildings which were thatched with straw. They had found a hive of bees in the shed, and calmly burnt the place down to smoke them out, so that we secured an excellent meal of walnuts and honey.

Osman Pasha was very strict in putting down pillaging, and an instance occurred on the same afternoon of the severity with which he punished any infraction of orders in that respect. As the column passed through one of the small Bulgarian villages which were sprinkled at frequent intervals along the line of route, a small field of tobacco enclosed by a brushwood fence was espied, and a Turkish sergeant who was pining for a cigarette could not resist the temptation, but climbed through the fence and filled his pockets with the dry leaf. Osman Pasha happened to see the incident; and, putting his horse at the fence, he jumped over into the tobacco-field, seized the sergeant and tore the stripes from his shoulder, degrading him to the ranks for his insubordination.

After we had marched about five miles beyond the farmhouse where we had got the honey, we camped for the night, and a very unpleasant night it was. The bivouac was pitched in the middle of a wide expanse of swampy ground, which was so moist that the water oozed through as one sat on the grass. I procured a plank, and lay on it all night, snatching a few minutes of fitful slumber at intervals.

At about eleven o'clock I was roused by a terrific rattle of infantry fire, and we all leaped to our feet firmly convinced that the long expected Russian attack had come at last. All was confusion as the men hastily threw themselves into formation and rammed the cartridges into their rifles; but the firing stopped as unexpectedly as it had begun, and we were left staring into the darkness in anxious suspense. Soon we discovered that it was a false alarm. A white horse which had been wounded in the fighting round Lovtcha had dragged himself painfully all the way from that vicinage after our column, recognizing the bugle calls of the army to which he belonged. But the poor brute paid the penalty of devotion, for our sentries mistook him in the darkness for a Russian vedette, and an alarm was sounded which brought about a volley of musketry fire that put him out of his pain at once.

Next morning the column started very early, and marched through beautifully timbered, undulating country. We saw a couple of Russian vedettes galloping away from one of the Bulgarian villages, and guessed that the enemy were in the neighbourhood. But they kept out of our way, and did not provoke an engagement.

At about two o'clock in the afternoon, as I was riding with the Circassians in front of a battery of field artillery, I heard a terrific explosion, and, looking round, saw a column of smoke behind me fully a hundred feet in height. There were a number of small black fragments falling through the smoke, and I found that an explosion had taken place in one of the gun carriages. The ammunition had gone off in some mysterious way, and the black fragments falling through the air were all that was left of the two unfortunate gunners who had been sitting on the ammunition box. Both the wheel horses were killed on the spot, and one of the drivers was badly injured. No one ever knew how that mysterious explosion occurred. That night we camped in the open again, and at eleven o'clock next morning we arrived at Plevna. I went to my quarters, had a wash, and then resumed my work at the hospital. But there was not much to do, and at two o'clock I was free to take a walk through the town.

To my intense surprise I saw a man who looked like an Englishman; and as I had not seen an Englishman for several months, I shouted to him, half in Turkish and half in English, to ask him who he was. He proved to be a man called Drew Gay, the correspondent of the London *Daily Telegraph*, and he wore an extraordinary nondescript get-up, including a little forage cap, patent leather riding-boots, and an enormous cavalry sword. He was on his way to pay a visit to the *kaimakan*, and was accompanied by a German artist named Lauri.

This little Lauri was a charming fellow, and full of the spirit of adventure. He was a great friend of Hamdi Bey, who was the son of Edim Pasha, the grand *vizier*, and in this way he was able to exercise sufficient influence to secure a *firman* authorizing him to visit Plevna. Lauri had lived in Cairo for some time, and had earned some notoriety by painting a portrait of the *khedive*.

Next day occurred the third and greatest Battle of Plevna—a battle in which the enormous value of the breech-loader when backed by entrenchments was fully demonstrated, as were also the magnificent pluck and endurance of the Turkish troops.

CHAPTER 9

The Third Battle of Plevna

Those two factors in the Turkish defence, *viz*. rapid rifle fire and complete field fortification, were justly regarded by the Russian general, Todleben, the principal defender of Sevastopol, to have been the chief causes of the overwhelming defeat of the Russians in the third Battle of Plevna.

During the six weeks which had elapsed since we entered Plevna from Widdin, I had plenty of opportunities of watching the natural genius of the Turks for fortification unfold itself. The pick and the spade were never idle night or day since our tired troops first camped on the Janik Bair; and now on the eve of the great battle the splendid result of their labours was apparent.

Plevna was defended by a line of earthworks of tremendous strength, drawing a ring of fire almost completely round the town. The chain of redoubts extended in the form of a horseshoe, the toe of which, pointing due east, was formed by the Grivitza redoubt, while one heel was at Opanetz in the north, and the other at Krishin in the south.

Plevna itself lay, as it were, in the "frog" of the foot, the nearest earthworks on either side being the Bukova redoubts on the north, and a double redoubt facing the "Green Hills" and dominating a long stretch of sloping vineyard on the south. It was round the Grivitza redoubt in the toe of the horseshoe, and this double redoubt close into Plevna in the heel, that the fiercest fighting of the whole protracted series of engagements was centred.

In six weeks the Turkish troops, under the direction of Tewfik Bey, had constructed the most elaborate and perfect system of field fortification that the world had ever seen—a system which utterly routed the old military idea that a bold and well reinforced attack must always succeed against a defended position. It may be as well to briefly describe the main features in the construction of these works as they appeared to an untechnical observer.

The usual type of redoubt was a large quadrangular fort, the walls of which were about seven feet high on the outside, and about twenty feet in thickness, the earth of which the walls were formed being a stiff loam, admirably suited for the work. Field-pieces were mounted inside the fort and fired through embrasures protected by *bonnettes*. The troops fired over the top of the parapet from a *banquette* reached by steps from the floor which was excavated below the level of the ground outside. The Grivitza redoubt, which was one of the largest, was a perfect square, each side of which was about fifty yards in length. Inside, the redoubt was divided into four compartments by a huge traverse of earth about eight feet thick, which was designed to protect the defenders from reverse fire.

Communication between the four compartments was afforded by narrow passages left open between the cross-walls and the exterior wall. The ammunition magazine was stored in a great subterranean chamber excavated underneath the massive cross-walls; and so efficacious was this mode of storing the cartridges, that during the four days' bombardment only two explosions occurred, although it is computed that the Russians fired at least three hundred thousand shells into the redoubts.

In the Ibrahim Bey redoubt a segment of a shell found its way into the magazine, which blew up during the height of the attack, killing forty of the defenders, Colonel Ibrahim Bey himself falling at the head of his men soon afterwards. In the Yunuz Bey redoubt in the extreme south-west there was also a disastrous explosion. Yunuz Bey, who commanded all the Krishin redoubts, survived the assault of Skobeleff and was decorated for personal bravery, together with Tewfik Bey, after the battle.

Access to each redoubt was gained from the rear, and in some cases one side was also left open, as Skobeleff's troops found to their cost in the work of which they held temporary possession. Sleeping accommodation for the artillerymen was provided inside the redoubts, while the infantrymen were lodged outside in the trenches. There was something weirdly dramatic in the sight of those Turkish gunners, black and weary and smoke-begrimed with battle, sleeping, as I have often seen them, in their narrow resting-places scooped out of the stiff loam in the inner side of the great wall of the redoubt.

The Russian shells came crashing into the exterior face of the earth wall; but the gunners slept on calmly in their subterranean clay beds, and after a brief slumber mounted to relieve their comrades again, often indeed only to exchange their narrow beds in the thickness of the earth wall for couches in the cold, wet earth outside and the sleep that knew no waking. Immediately in front of the redoubt in every case was a ditch about fifteen feet wide and ten feet deep as a first line of defence. Farther in advance was a line of trenches, in many cases connecting with an adjacent redoubt; and a second line farther on down the slope of the hill provided another line of fire.

The trenches had breastworks about three feet high, pierced with loopholes for rifles at intervals of one foot six inches. Covered passages effectually connected the trenches, and a network of similar passages afforded ample living accommodation for the troops. The scale upon which all these works were carried out may be imagined when it is mentioned that one of the redoubts contained in interior area more than ten thousand seven hundred square yards, and was provided with subterranean chambers affording lodgement for troops and staff as well as ample storage room and stabling for horses.

Of course the redoubts were not all uniform in exact pattern, some of them being designed for artillery and infantry, while others were defended by infantry only. In many of the works a second line of rifle fire was obtained from a covered way leading outside, so that when all the resources of a redoubt and trenches were at work an unremitting fire of three and in some cases four successive tiers was obtained. The supply of ammunition was practically unlimited; and it is not difficult to recognize that, under such conditions, an assaulting force could not but be terribly scourged both by infantry and artillery.

During the night of September 6 the Russians brought up their artillery under cover of the darkness, and threw up cover for the guns with their entrenching tools. When the morning of September 7 broke in cold and drizzling rain, the Russians had surrounded us, the Roumanian divisions being placed in the north and north-east, while the Russian divisions lay in the south-east and south. All the west side was occupied by cavalry, who commanded the valley of the Vid and the Orkhanieh road, so as to cut off the Turkish fugitives who were expected to fly in that direction.

The Russians had about eighty thousand infantry, twelve thousand cavalry, and four hundred and forty guns; while the Turkish forces numbered about thirty thousand infantry with seventy-two guns and an inappreciable number of cavalry.[1]

Every precaution had been taken by the Russians to avoid a repetition of the previous disasters which had attended their attempts to force Plevna by assault, and they relied for success upon their vast preponderance in numbers and upon a prolonged artillery preparation which was intended to demoralize the defence.

At six o'clock in the morning of September 7 I heard the roar of the commencing bombardment from Opanetz in the north, and it quickly worked round, until the two Grivitza redoubts due east of Plevna were involved. Across the Bulgarian road, Ibrahim Bey's redoubt and three or four others connected with it sustained a fierce bombardment, and the line of guns extending southwards across the Tutchenitza ravine and the Lovtcha road added their voices to the general roar as far as the village of Brestovitz, where a heavy fire from siege-guns was concentrated on the Krishin redoubt. A short experience of the bombardment, however, showed our troops that they had little to fear from the Russian artillery, and casualties were few and far between in the redoubts.

What was called the "mammoth battery," consisting of a tremendous group of fifty heavy Russian siege-guns, was placed in position due east of Plevna, and bombarded Ibrahim Bey's redoubt all day, the guns of the redoubt replying with spirit. The garrison of the redoubt were so well covered that they lost only forty men in killed and wounded after the whole day's firing, and the damage which was done to the earthworks during the day was repaired at night.

Soon after the commencement of the action I rode over towards Ibrahim Bey's redoubt, taking Lauri, the newly arrived German artist, with me. As we rode along together a Russian shell struck the ground about a hundred yards in front of us, and, ricocheting, flew over our heads and lodged in the ground behind us. Lauri was tremendously excited. He rushed off and picked up the shell, which he held in his arms as if it was a baby, exclaiming at the same time in his broken English, "I am forty-three years of age, and this is the first time that

---

1. According to Russian official statistics, the force brought against Plevna numbered over 90,000 men, composed of 70,000 infantry, 10,000 cavalry, with 24 siege-guns, 364 field-guns, and 54 horse-guns. The losses were in all 18,216 men: killed, 75 officers and 7,558 men; wounded, 290 officers and 10,658 men. The Turkish strength given in the text is only approximate. The losses have never been stated; Osman Pasha admitted after the surrender that he lost more men on the Lovtcha road and its vicinity than did Skobeleff, who owned to the loss of 160 officers and over 8,000 men.

I haf seen a gun fired. Ah, what would my wife say if she could now see me!"

With some difficulty I induced him to moderate his transports and drop the shell, which I was afraid every moment would explode and dissipate poor Lauri into space. By keeping on the lee side of the hill and dodging up at intervals we could catch glimpses of the "mammoth battery" scarcely a mile away, and could see the spirts of flame enveloped in white smoke as the guns were fired in a tremendous volley. Sometimes the shells struck the redoubt, and clouds of earth flew up; while at other times the projectiles went screaming over the crest of the hill, and fell in the low ground near the town.

I occupied myself in my hospital for the next few days, riding out at intervals to watch the progress of the bombardment, which was being prosecuted with terrific force. On the 10th the village of Radishevo, where the Russian batteries were in position, caught fire, and the conflagration lit up the wet grey sky in the east. Little damage was done to our redoubts, and the artillery preparation was so far a failure.

On the 11th the general assault took place. I was working away in the hospital all the morning, as the wounded were beginning to come into Plevna in considerable numbers, when I saw a Turkish sergeant who had been slightly wounded by a splinter from a shell. He announced that he was going back to the fight, and I said that I would go with him. I rode out, while the sergeant followed on foot, and passing our farthest redoubt I found myself among some trees, with the shells flying about in all directions. When I looked round for the sergeant, I found that he had disappeared, and that I was there by myself about two hundred yards in the rear of our foremost fighting line in the trenches. The troops were almost hidden from me by smoke, and a few wounded men were crawling back towards the redoubt for shelter.

I formed a little field ambulance behind the trees, and proceeded to give first aid to the wounded; but the firing began to get so hot that I was obliged to abandon the position and ride back. As I crossed the Lovtcha road in the direction of the Krishin redoubts, I came across three or four isolated rifle pits in which a few old Turkish civilians, armed with antiquated rifles, were busily firing upon the Russian lines. They had evidently not been observed by the Russians, and the old fellows, showing nothing but a pair of gleaming eyes and the long brown barrels of the rifles above the level of the ground, were knocking over their men at long range.

How on earth they got there I could not conjecture; but they soon saw me, and resented my appearance strongly. They called out to me in most forcible language to take myself and my horse away, as they were afraid that I should draw the Russian fire upon them. I left them still diligently potting the unconscious enemy, and at about four o'clock in the afternoon I heard a terrific musketry fire back towards Grivitza. After crossing the headquarters camp I could see dense masses of troops advancing from the village of Grivitza, and a black cloud of men already in the valley, about five hundred yards in front of the Grivitza redoubt.

Meanwhile the Russian artillerymen were shelling the redoubt, which was evidently in imminent danger. The stables at the rear of the redoubt, which were roofed with boards and hurdles, caught fire from an exploding shell, and blazed up as I was watching. I could hear the Russians cheering when they saw the fire.

Seeing the Russians in the valley, I galloped on the lee side of the hill, where I was under cover, to the Grivitza redoubt. I went into the redoubt which was being shelled, and, climbing upon the banquette where the men were firing, I could see large bodies of Roumanians attacking us on the north, while a detachment of Russians were advancing from the east. I found Sadik Pasha, who was in command of the redoubt, and told him that I had seen a strong body of troops in the valley below us and invisible from the redoubt. A shell exploded in the redoubt while I was there, and I was glad to clear out as quickly as I could.

Jumping on my horse again, I galloped off to the south, where Skobeleff was attacking the Krishin redoubts and the neighbouring works. As I rode across the Lovtcha road the firing was something terrific. Skobeleff's troops had taken the second crest of the Green Hills on the previous day, and this morning they had taken the third crest and driven our men back from the trenches into the two redoubts described afterwards by Skobeleff as the Number 1 and Number 2 Plevna redoubts. In spite of a furious counter-attack by the Turks, the Russian regiments remained in possession of the height, having thus carried each successive ridge of the Green Hills and driven our men back into the redoubts.

It was now about half-past two in the afternoon, and as I approached the rear of the two redoubts which were the objective of the main assault the intensity of the fire redoubled. The Turks were running out of the back of the redoubts in hundreds, and I tried in vain to rally them and get them to return. I saw a Turkish lieutenant, who was one of the fugitives, endeavouring to climb over a paling fence at the back of one of the redoubts and get away to Plevna. I upbraided him, and thumped him in vain with the flat of my sword. As he was getting over the fence he was struck by a rifle-ball, and fell with his back broken.

As I was shouting, entreating, threatening, and striking the fugitives to try and get them to rally, I saw two old Turkish civilians in long beards and caftans. They came up and caught me by both hands, saying, "*Sen choki adam,*" which means, "You are a noble fellow," or words to that effect. I remember this incident because it was one of the highest compliments I have ever received. Troops were flying pell-mell for Plevna, and shells were exploding at the rate of twenty or thirty per minute on the side of the hill. The roar of the artillery, the rattle of the musketry, the explosion of the shells, the loud hurrahs of the Russians, and the cries of the wounded made up a perfect hell. I met Czetwertinski near the redoubts, and he and I made renewed efforts to rally the men; but we were powerless to stop the mad tide of fugitives. Czetwertinski drove the point of his sword into a man's leg without being able to stop him; and at last, as it was getting hotter and hotter, he said to me that it was hopeless stopping there, and we had better be off.

As I returned to Plevna the men were flying like wild animals. It was a regular panic. They were like sheep before a bush-fire. When I got into the town there was a panic among the townspeople. A universal cry of, "The Russians are coming! the Russians are coming!" went up on all sides; and wounded men, old, bed-ridden, half-naked women, and screaming children were all crowding towards the head-quarters camp. I learnt then that Skobeleff had taken the two redoubts within half a mile of the town, and that the Grivitza redoubt was also in the hands of the Russians.

Skobeleff, it seems, had given the order to attack at three o'clock; and the Vladimir and Souzdal Regiments, supported by *chasseurs,* rose and rushed forward with bands playing and drums beating. They had to descend the wooded slopes covered with vines from the third ridge, to enter the valley, cross the stream at the bottom, and climb a stiff slope, completely bare for about seven hundred yards, on the summit of which the redoubt was placed. The attacking force received a terrible fire from the artillery and infantry in the redoubt attacked, as well as an enfilading fire from the Krishin redoubt; but when reinforced by the Revel Regiment, they pushed on doggedly under the hail of bullets, which had already killed nearly half of their number, flung themselves into the trenches, and finally climbed the parapet and took the redoubt. The second redoubt, which was connected with the first, also fell immediately afterwards after a desperate struggle.

Raked by the guns of the Krishin redoubts and by the fire of the Turkish infantry, who sallied out from the camp at the rear of these redoubts, Skobeleff's troops had a fearful night in the defences which they had captured.

Successive assaults were delivered upon them all through the night by the Turks; but time after time our men were driven back by the murderous fire of the Krenke and Berdan rifles. On the exposed side of the Number 1 redoubt the Russians had built up a parapet of the dead bodies of friend and foe alike; and sheltered behind this dreadful barrier, they poured a hail of bullets into the Turkish ranks. When morning broke I could still hear the rattle of the rifles; and working away in my shirt sleeves in the hospital, I could hear the rifle-bullets pattering on the red tiles of the houses in the town. At daybreak I went back to my quarters for a sleep. The Russian batteries had advanced to closer range, and two shells exploded in my garden. A bullet came through the door of the room where I was lying, and buried itself in the wall just before I fell asleep.

When I awoke and went out the firing was still going on, and there were about one thousand five hundred wounded men lying out in the open square. We started to dress them at once. All the wounded men who had been in the hospital were removed for greater safety to the south end of the town, so as to be as far away as possible from the scene of action. We cleared out a number of small Bulgarian hovels belonging to people of the poorest class, and installed the wounded in them.

I had not been at the hospital long before my Circassian servant came down and informed me that the firing at my house was getting very hot, and he wanted to know what he should do. He said that he thought the town was on the point of being taken. I told him to go back, pack up my things, and put them on my horse. I said, "If you see the Russians coming over the crest of the hill, come down here at once with my horse, but not otherwise." My horse had not come out of it scatheless, for a bullet had gone through the muscles of his neck; but he was still full of pluck and able to carry me well.

Meanwhile let us see what had been happening at the redoubts. Attack after attack was delivered through the night without success; and at last, at half-past ten a.m., a vigorous assault, backed up with a telling shell fire, shook the defence, and the Russians began to pour out of Number 1 redoubt, their example being followed by those in the adjoining work. Some of the foremost Turks had already penetrated into the redoubts; but they were sacrificed in vain, for Skobeleff, with his extraordinary personal magnetism and great courage, rallied his men again, and staved off the inevitable moment a little longer. I got away from the hospital at three o'clock in the afternoon, and rode out towards the redoubts where the Russians were sustaining a last furious assault by our troops under Tewfik Bey.

As I neared the redoubts this assault was at its height, and this time the Turkish troops would not be denied. The columns deployed under fire and formed lines of skirmishers, who received continuous support from fresh accessions of men behind, carrying the assault forward in successive waves. Soon the Turks were over the parapet once more, cutting down the Russian defenders, and driving the remainder out on the other side and down the slope again towards their own trenches on the Green Hills.

Thus the third Battle of Plevna ended, after five days' fighting, in the complete defeat of the Russians, who lost nearly twenty thousand men in the long bloody struggle, and gained nothing but the Grivitza redoubt, which was absolutely no use to them, and which fell mainly through the instrumentality of the Roumanian, not the Russian, troops.

It is amusing to observe how the Russian official documents describe the result. "The points chosen for attack," we read, "were the following: the redoubt of Grivitza, the works in the centre opposite the heights of Radishevo, and the third crest of the Montagnes Vertes. After superhuman efforts and enormous losses, our troops carried the first and last of these points. The Grivitza redoubt and two of the redoubts south of Plevna were in our possession; as to the central works, our troops, notwithstanding that they showed a bravery beyond all praise, could not carry them. Consequently we had obtained some partial successes; but fresh troops were necessary to profit by our gains, and these were not forthcoming. It was decided, therefore, to keep the Grivitza redoubt, and to abandon the Montagnes Vertes."

When I think of that last tremendous charge of the Turkish infantry, when the cry of *"La ilaha illallah Mohammed Rasul Allah!"* rent the air and rang from one redoubt to the other, as it went like the flame in a train of gunpowder round the whole circuit of the defences, I cannot help smiling at the polite official statement, "It was decided to abandon the Montagnes Vertes."

I was inside the Number 1 redoubt two minutes after the men of the front firing line, and I shall never forget the scene of carnage that I saw there. The redoubt was literally choked up with dead and dying men, and the ground was ankle deep in blood, brains, and mutilated fragments of humanity. The Turks became almost delirious with the excitement of the victory. Everywhere men were shouting, praying, and giving thanks to *Allah*. About three hundred of them got dragropes, and took the captured Russian guns off in triumph to the headquarters camp; and inside the redoubt the soldiers fell on each other's necks, danced, and sang in a perfect frenzy of delight. The excitement of the five minutes following the recapture of the redoubts was worth a lifetime of common-place existence; but all the while in the Grivitza redoubt, three miles away, the enemy stood watching with cannons ready—a silent warning of the conflicts yet in store for us.

After the battle, the Russians withdrew from their positions and retired on Radishevo.

The Turkish Army was mad with joy. We attached but little importance to the capture of the Grivitza redoubt by the Russians, because the Turkish garrison simply fell back upon the sister redoubt, which was only one hundred and eighty yards distant from the other in a north-westerly direction, and really commanded it. The unimportance of the loss of this redoubt was proved by the fact that, though the enemy occupied it during the whole of the remainder of the siege, they did little or no damage from it.

On the night after the battle, the Russian troops in the Grivitza redoubt Number 1, or the Kanli Tabiya, made a desperate sortie with the object of capturing the Number 2 redoubt, or, as we called it, the Bash Tabiya.

It is strange how the sleeping brain adjusts itself to circumstances—sleeps with one eye open, as it were. I could always sleep soundly under the fire of the heavy guns, even in a redoubt, because my brain recognized that they were practically harmless when we were under cover; but as soon as the rattle of the rifles began, I invariably awoke at once with an instinctive knowledge that the fight was approaching a crisis. So it was on the night after the battle. The Russian cannon continued to boom sullenly at intervals, and, worn out with fatigue as I was, they only lulled me to a deeper slumber in my quarters in the town.

Presently, however, a rifle volley rang out, quickly answered by another and another. In a second I was out of my sheepskin rug and on my verandah, from which I could see the night attack three miles away. The night was dark and drizzling; but looking in a north-easterly direction towards the line of the Janik Bair redoubts, I could see the flash of the volleys and the spirting flame of the artillery as the Russians leaped from their redoubt upon the Bash Tabiya, only one hundred and eighty yards distant from them. The Bash Tabiya was strongly garrisoned. Its heavy guns swept every yard of the ground between it and the newly captured forts; and its defenders poured an incessant hail of bullets from a triple line of rifle-barrels upon the attacking troops. To succeed under such circumstances was well nigh impossible, and after a few minutes of this awful fire the Russian remnant broke and fled back to the protection of the redoubt.

It was only on the morrow that we realised what a complete victory we had won in the battle of the previous day, because we could then see plainly that the Russians had suffered terrible losses and had achieved absolutely nothing. We began to feel more secure of our position; and the wounded, who had all been sent away to the lower end of the town, were brought back again and placed in temporary hospitals near our central depot. In the previous battles we had been accustomed to send the wounded away to Sofia at once, and the wisdom of Osman Pasha's decision in this matter was now made apparent. Insufficient as was our hospital accommodation, it was doubly fortunate that we were not encumbered with the wounded from the previous battles as well, because we now had about four thousand patients to deal with, and there was no chance of sending them away because we realized at last that we were in a state of siege. The Russians were all round Plevna, and they barred the Orkhanieh road.

We of the medical staff had four days of real hard work after the battle. There were an immense number of operations to perform; and as Osman Effendi and myself had to perform the greater number of them, our energies were taxed to the utmost. There were about forty doctors all told in Plevna, to deal with four thousand cases or thereabouts. Owing to the continuous nature of the work, I never went back to my quarters during the week after the battle, but used to sleep at the hospital. My Circassian servant cooked my food, such as it was, at my house, and brought it down to me while I was at work. As on the previous occasions, Osman Effendi and myself performed all operations in the open air under a big willow tree on the bank of the Tutchenitza, and in the shadow of an old Turkish mosque, where every evening at sundown an ancient priest, mounting a minaret, called the faithful to prayer.

Although we were greatly assisted by the magnificent physique of the patients, still their extraordinary reluctance to undergo operations perceptibly increased the average mortality. Three days after the battle, I saw a Turkish soldier crawling slowly along the street and stopping every minute. He was holding some object in his hand, and his appearance was so strange that I went over and had a look at him. I found that he had been shot in the abdomen, and about two feet of the small intestine had prolapsed, and was protruding through the wound. It was so altered in appearance by exposure that it looked exactly like a bit of tarred rope. Two of this man's comrades had been wounded, and had died in the hospital—a fact which had made him believe that the hospital treatment was responsible for the fatal termination of their wounds, and he resolutely refused to allow me to touch him with an instrument. The intestine was not strangulated; and if he had allowed me to open up the wound, wash it, and replace the intestine, he would probably have recovered. As it was, he lived for fifteen days in that pitiable condition.

The stoicism of the men was truly remarkable. A soldier was brought to me to be examined one day, and I found that he had been skylarking with a comrade, who had "jobbed" him in the stomach with his bayonet. The surgeon who first saw him could detect only a very small wound in the stomach, and he put a bit of plaster over the place and sent the man away. In a few hours' time the patient became very bad, and I was asked to see him. I asked him at once if he had vomited any blood; and when he replied in the affirmative, I knew that the wall of the abdomen had been perforated, and that his fate was sealed. He was quite cheerful, but he died at the end of twenty-four hours.

As the greater part of the fighting had been done from behind parapets or breastworks, the majority of the wounded were shot through the head or chest, and a large percentage of these wounds necessarily proved fatal. There was an infinite variety in the nature of the wounds. One man came under my hands who received six wounds from one bullet. The ball struck him on the outside of the right arm between the elbow and the shoulder, passed through the arm, through the fleshy portions of the chest, and through the left arm as well, leaving six distinct bullet-holes, all of which I washed and plugged. He made a rapid recovery, and after a few weeks in the hospital went back to the trenches.

Not a single wounded Russian came into my hands after the battle. The Russians always carried their wounded with them when they retired; and after the crowning episode of the battle, when I reached the Kavanlik redoubt as soon as Tewfik Bey had recaptured it, there was not a single living Russian left there. When the final assault was delivered, a Russian captain and eighteen men elected to see it out to the bitter end. Those brave men continued fighting to the last, and were all bayoneted by the Turkish troops who poured, victorious at last, over the parapet. It can readily be imagined that fighting of this sanguinary character left few wounded Russians for us to deal with.

The staff at the principal operating hospital included, besides Osman Effendi and myself, Weinberger, Kustler, Gebhardt, Kronberg, Waldemann, and Rookh. We had also a lot of *jarra bashis* with a rudimentary idea of surgery to assist us. Each man brought to us for an operation had to wait his turn, and such was the pressure of the work that many of the poor fellows were kept there for four or five days before we could attend to them. Still, at this period a large percentage recovered from their wounds, owing principally to the fact that the accommodation was not overcrowded and that we had few cases of septic disease. We were able to give them a liberal diet, as we had plenty of broth, milk, rice, and biscuits. These biscuits when soaked and steamed proved most useful.

Osman Pasha has been liberally accused of inhuman neglect towards the wounded; but those accusations have been made against him by people who had no opportunity of forming an accurate judgment, and who mistook his inflexible determination to get the wounded away from Plevna for cruelty and want of consideration for their sufferings. I had many opportunities of observing the *muchir* during my stay in Plevna, and I can definitely refute these charges of neglect and apathy in the presence of anguish. Unsparing of his troops in battle, Osman Pasha never forgot his wounded men when the fighting was over. At this period, after the third battle, he constantly visited the hospitals, encouraging the wounded by his presence and by his kindly words. He let it be understood, too, that all those members of the medical staff who worked well would be decorated; and it is only bare justice to say that all of them cheerfully performed long hours of very hard work on insufficient food and with little or no sleep during the trying days and nights that followed upon our greatest victory.

When the brunt of the work was over, I went back to my quarters, and Czetwertinski and Victor Lauri went with me—Czetwertinski because he was very delicate, and Lauri because he had no servant of his own, and did not know where else to go. About four days after the battle, Czetwertinski, who was in touch with the headquarters staff, heard that Osman Pasha was looking for someone who would endeavour to run the gauntlet of the Russians, posted all round Plevna, and carry his despatches to Constantinople. The gallant young Pole brought me the news, and asked me if I would join him in an attempt to get through with the papers. We sat up most of the night talking the matter over, and Czetwertinski carefully explained to me that, while we should certainly be hanged if we fell into the hands of the Russians, we should be rewarded with the highest decorations if we were successful in the attempt.

We agreed to offer our services as despatch-carriers to Osman Pasha, and next morning Czetwertinski waited on the commander-in-chief and formally represented our decision. Osman Pasha thanked us warmly, but declined our offer, preferring to entrust the task to a Circassian, who, being more intimately acquainted with the country, would stand a better chance of getting through the enemy's lines.

Gay, the *Daily Telegraph* correspondent, however, was extremely anxious to get away. He had shut himself up in his own room as soon as the battle was over, and had been writing all day and all night ever since, preparing a glowing description of the stirring events which had taken place. He had completed a fine budget of work, and was naturally burning to get it into his paper; for it meant a great journalistic coup for the *Telegraph*, as Gay was the only correspondent with the Turkish army, though Forbes, MacGahan, and many others were with the Russians. The first step was to engage a guide, and Gay selected a smart young Circassian, who willingly undertook the job for the munificent reward of three thousand *piastres*, which he was promised as soon as Sofia was reached. Sitting in his room in Plevna, Gay wound up his despatch for the *Daily Telegraph* by describing his plans for getting it to Sofia.

> Today, September 15, the cannonade goes forward languidly, nor is it at all likely that it will end so long as the Russians have a gun or a man anywhere near us. But it is comparatively

harmless, so far as affecting the Turkish position goes, and will some day, when Osman Pasha is reinforced, as he shortly will be, come to an untimely end. For my own part I am about to endeavour tonight to break the blockade which surrounds Plevna. For two days I have sought for Circassians who would undertake the task of piloting me over the mountains in the dark and failed.

Last evening Osman Pasha found a one-eyed chieftain, who with a comrade has engaged to conduct me if the feat is at all practicable, and according to present arrangements I am to start tonight about the time it begins to get dark. Mr. Victor Lauri too is anxious to go with me; and a Turkish officer also desires to be one of the party, which will thus consist of two Circassians, a Turkish sergeant, and my servant, an Ionian lad, a Greek groom, Mr. Lauri, the Turkish officer, and myself—in all a party of eight well armed. At the moment of my writing the Circassians and the Greek are out on a voyage of exploration, with a view to seeing whether there is the possibility of our accomplishing the task, in which case they will be back by evening ready to pilot us.

As the risk is great, the Circassians are to be amply rewarded directly Sofia is reached, that is, if the work be faithfully done, and upon their report now all rests. For myself I am determined to go if they will take me. What the result will be time alone can show. But if you get this letter safely, I shall have run the gauntlet, and will then telegraph you the history of our risky ride across country.

As a matter of fact Gay did not start on that night. Czetwertinski and I went out with him to the outposts to see him off; but it was plain that the psychological moment was not yet. It was a bright moonlight night, and we could see the Russian vedettes sitting on their horses all round us. A cat could not have got through the lines without being seen, let alone a man on horseback; and the captain in command of our outpost absolutely refused to allow the attempt to be made, pointing out that it meant certain capture and death for all the party.

On the following night, however, Gay and his escort got away. We heard afterwards that they had a lively time of it, for they were chased by Cossacks, and fired on repeatedly by startled Russian sentries. It was only through the speed and bottom of their horses that they reached Orkhanieh in safety, and thence made their way to Sofia. Gay had a quarrel with Lauri before he went, and the result was that the little German artist stayed behind with me.

CHAPTER 10

The Investment of Plevna

Amid the recollection of all those scenes of bloodshed, the memory of the little German artist's yearning for the unattainable stands out clear and distinct. It was connected with a German sausage; but in order to make the matter plain, it is necessary to point out that Gay and Lauri had expended about thirty pounds in equipping a private commissariat department before they came to Plevna. In Constantinople they had bought provisions of all kinds: English kippered herrings, American canned beef, potted vegetables of strange and fearful hues, portable meat lozenges, and last, but not least, a magnificent German sausage—not one of those insignificant cylinders of suspicious ingredients which are exposed for sale in the piping times of peace, but a sausage which was constructed, so to speak, on a war footing.

It was about four feet long and one foot six inches in circumference, and it was enclosed in a metal case of the kind generally used to carry maps and charts. This noble specimen of *wurst* was the apple of little Lauri's artistic eye. But, alas! I was ignorant of this. Before Gay went away, being incensed with Lauri over some trivial dispute, he presented me with the remains of the commissariat, which, it appeared, had been bought with his money, and which included the famous sausage. He also gave me several other things, including a capital bell tent, which, I am sorry to say, was afterwards stolen from me.

However, when I got this sausage Lauri was away, camping, I fancy, in one of the redoubts, and I at once invited every good fellow that I knew in the place to come to the banquet. We had two meals off it, and then—where, oh, where was that triumph of the sausage-maker's art? "Where," asks that inspired bard Hans Breitmann, "is dat little cloud that fringed the mountain brow?" We procured some *raki*, the pungent Turkish spirit which burns a hole in the membrane of the throat as it passes down, and we had dinner. Then we procured some more *raki*, and we had supper. After that we looked round for the sausage; but it was gone—"*gone where the woodbine twineth.*" Lauri came back to my quarters next day, and behaved with contumely when invited to sit down to our usual fare of boiled beans and rice.

He consigned every individual boiled bean in Turkey to a place where it would soon become unpleasantly scorched, and then he mourned for the sausage, which he believed Gay had eaten in the silence of the night all by himself. "If only he had left me my peautiful sausage!" he wailed, while I said never a word, but only winked at Czetwertinski. When Lauri had continued every day for a week making lamentation over the loss of that satisfying yard and a quarter of food, I broke the news gently to him that we had eaten it in his absence. Contrary to my expectation, he was not seized with an apoplectic attack, and at last even became reconciled again to the "*verdammte poiled peans.*"

One day when I rode up to the headquarters camp at about two o'clock in the afternoon, I found the whole place in a simmer of suppressed excitement, and addressed myself to Tewfik Pasha, who had been promoted to that rank after the battle, in order to ascertain the cause of the commotion. He told me that the Russians had sent forward a *parlementaire* to invite Osman Pasha or some officer representing him to meet a Russian general at a certain place and discuss a matter of interest to both. I asked what the subject of discussion was to be, and Tewfik replied that he did not know. He also told me that Osman Pasha wished to go himself, but that his staff were endeavouring to dissuade him, pointing out to him that he would impair his dignity by consenting to meet any officer of lower grade than the commander-in-chief of the Russian Army, who at this time was Prince Charles of Roumania.

As I sat on my horse at the headquarters camp I saw that Osman Pasha was ready to start. His best horse, a magnificent chestnut charger with a saddlecloth heavily embroidered with gold, was champing the bit in front of the *muchir's* tent, and presently Osman Pasha emerged, dressed in his full State uniform, and actually wearing, what I should never have expected to see in Plevna at that grim period, a pair of white kid gloves. It was arranged that if he went he should be accompanied by Tewfik Pasha.

At the last moment, however, Osman Pasha yielded to the advice of his staff, and decided to remain behind; so Tewfik Pasha and

Czetwertinski went forward with a small escort. They rode out about a mile and a half from Plevna, where they met two Russian officers, and after an elaborate exchange of polite courtesies the business of the conference was broached. It appeared that during the attack on the Grivitza redoubt and the subsequent night attack on the Bash Tabiya many hundreds of men had been killed; and as the Grivitza redoubt remained in the hands of the Russians, and the Bash redoubt, only one hundred and eighty yards away, was still held by the Turks, the corpses both of Turks and Russians which lay between the two works had been left unburied, with the result that the stench had become almost unbearable, and was a serious annoyance to the defenders of both forts.

The Russian officers politely pointed out that a removal of the nuisance would be as welcome to them as it would be to the Turks, and courteously offered to send out a burial party and inter all the bodies lying between the Grivitza and the Bash redoubts, if the occupants of the latter work would incommode themselves so far as to abstain from potting at the military gravediggers while they were pursuing their melancholy occupation. Tewfik Pasha and Czetwertinski begged that the Russian officers would excuse them for a moment while they considered the subject, and then, after a brief consultation in Turkish, Czetwertinski as spokesman took up his parable in reply. It was with feelings of the most profound regret, he explained, that Tewfik Pasha was obliged to deny himself the pleasure of accepting the generous offer of the Russians.

Certainly the odour from the ill fated corpses, both of the Turks and of their so gallant and courageous assailants, was decidedly offensive; but it would not be fair to allow the Russians to incur the whole of the annoyance which would attach to the burial of so many patriots who had fallen on the field of honour. In effect he would propose as an alternative that if the Russians would inconvenience themselves to the extent of sending out a party of men to bury all the corpses within ninety yards of their redoubt, the Turks on their side would feel it a pleasure and an honour to bury all the bodies within a similar distance of the work which they occupied. Thus the labour would be equally divided and the interment carried out most satisfactorily.

The wily Tewfik had seen at a glance the object of the Russians in proposing this generous action. If they had been allowed to advance one hundred and twenty yards from their redoubt on the pretence of burying the bodies, they would surmount the crest of the hill, and would be able to see into Plevna, besides securing most valuable observations as to the position of the various defences. Hence his polite reply.

The Russian officers were overwhelmed of course with admiration for the generous proposal made by Tewfik Pasha, but were desolated at their inability to accept it. After further parleying in the same strain it was plain that the *parlementaires* would be unable to come to terms, so the Russians produced a flask of excellent brandy which they pressed upon their visitors. Tewfik Pasha did not drink, but Czetwertinski politely drained a glass to the health of his entertainers, and all sat down for a few minutes' pleasant chat about the weather and the crops, the latest story from the clubs, and the legs of the last new ballet-dancer at the Paris opera-house. Then Tewfik Pasha took out his watch, and thought that it was really time to be going; so the Russian officers bowed, and wished their visitors *au revoir*, while Tewfik Pasha and Czetwertinski with their escort of a couple of troopers trotted back towards the Turkish lines. It is pleasant to reflect that the disagreeable necessities of war cannot blunt the exquisite politeness of true diplomacy.

Day by day the Russians, who were beginning to recover their lost *morale*, worked up closer and closer towards our entrenchments. Taught by the example of their adversaries, they began to make a more extensive use of the entrenching spade which had already revolutionized the art of warfare; and seeing the completeness with which the Turks protected themselves by means of the shield which they carried with them, the Russians too rapidly adopted the same practice.

One morning the Russian outposts were so close to our lines that they could see our men laying out fresh lines of shelter trenches, and working parties commencing their tasks with a will. Skobeleff accompanied by his staff, was examining these works, and, feeling irritated by the tenacity of the Turks, he ordered a gun to be brought up to the outposts. The gun was placed in position, and fired several rounds of case shot at the working parties, killing a couple of men and wounding three others. Our fellows replied energetically, and the workers presently returned to their burrowing with fresh zest.

Day and night a desultory bombardment continued. During the night the Russians used to fire from ten to twenty shells into the town, and at intervals during the day also the shells arrived, knocking down a few houses and killing a good many men, more Bulgarians, however, than Turks.

Very shortly after the battle we found that the 4th division of the Roumanian Army was entrenched about six hundred yards to the east of the Bash Tabiya. Owing to the terrible stench caused by the dead bodies which lay unburied, we had to change the entire garrison of the Bash Tabiya, numbering four thousand men in all, every forty-eight hours; and as the approach to the Bash Tabiya was exposed for about thirty yards to the fire of the Russians, the operation of relieving the guard was always exciting.

I often paid a visit to the Bash Tabiya in the afternoon to have a cup of coffee and a cigarette with old Sadik Pasha, who was in command, and these afternoon calls were always attended with a certain amount of risk. The fellows in the Grivitza redoubt used to keep a look out for visitors; but the range was over eight hundred yards, and I used to skip across those thirty yards of exposed space, dodging like a strong blue rock before the barrels of the pigeon-shooter, and always coming through safely. It did not take me more than three seconds to cover the distance, and before they could sight their rifles I was across.

At about three o'clock every afternoon Ahmet brought my horse down to the hospital, and I went for a ride out to the redoubts, and paid my respects to one or other of the commanders. One day a Turkish major in one of them consulted me about an eruption on his chin. He was mightily concerned about it, and I promised to bring him some ointment to allay the unpleasant symptoms. As a matter of fact, I believe it was barber's itch that he had. Accordingly I rode out on the following day with the ointment to the redoubt, which was commanded by a Russian redoubt built on the slope of a hill about a thousand yards away. As I got up to our redoubt there were three soldiers sitting on the rear wall smoking cigarettes, and I called to one of them to come and hold my horse.

The one who came was a magnificently built fellow. He was in great good humour, laughing and chatting with his comrades, and he came out of the redoubt and held my bridle while I walked into the work. As I did so the officer in command of the Russian redoubt, seeing a horseman approaching the work opposite to him, thought that it would be good fun to have a shot at him; so he let drive at me with three field-guns. I saw the three puffs of smoke together as I walked into the redoubt. One shell buried itself in the front wall of the redoubt without exploding, another burst in the redoubt, and the third passed over the redoubt and exploded just behind it.

The casing of the shell that exploded inside wounded a man in the heel, taking half the boot off and cutting the heel to the bone. He was a black soldier, a Nubian. I was looking after him, when someone called out to me to come outside; and the first thing I saw was my horse quietly grazing about fifty yards at the rear of the redoubt. The man who had been holding him had been cut in two by the third shell. He was quite dead. I went back into the redoubt, and dressed the Nubian's heel. Then the Turkish major and I had coffee and cigarettes together, and I gave him the ointment for his chin, whereat he was much gratified. We were so much accustomed to whole hecatombs of victims in those days, that we were callous to a single casualty.

We were beginning to get a little short of food in Plevna; and though I was not very particular about my cuisine and got on fairly well on boiled beans and rice, I felt sorry for poor Czetwertinski, who had been very bad with dysentery, and for whom I prescribed nourishing food in vain, for there was no one to make up the prescription. However, one morning I noticed a fine flock of geese in the yard of a Bulgarian house between my place and the hospital, so I approached the proprietor with an eye to purchase. He was a sour-tempered fellow; and though I offered him a *medjidie* apiece for the geese, he declined to trade. When I got home again that night and sat down to more boiled beans, I casually mentioned to Ahmet that there were a nice lot of geese in a Bulgarian house not far away.

Next night all the geese were in our yard. I did not inquire too closely the motive which impelled the toothsome birds to seek for change of scene; but it flashed across me that Ahmet and his mate Faizi were young and strong, and also that they were Circassians. We ate four of the geese in our house, and gave the rest away to my brother surgeons. There were a dozen of them originally, and I sent the Bulgarian goose-farmer a couple of Turkish *liras* for them, so that he did not do so badly after all out of his forced sale.

Although big engagements seemed at an end for the present, and the Russians evidently intended to starve us out, instead of attempting to take Plevna by assault, still we had plenty of casual skirmishes to keep us in form and remind us that we were not at a picnic. Towards the end of September, Mustapha Bey was ordered to go out with a squadron of cavalry across the Vid and reconnoitre the Sofia road, to see what sort of a force the Russians had placed there. I was a great favourite with old Mustapha, and he made an application to Osman Pasha that I should be allowed to accompany the column.

Permission was readily granted, and one beautiful morning I found myself cantering out of Plevna, with Mustapha Bey and Czetwertinski at the head of a troop of four hundred regular cavalry and three hundred Circassians. We rode out to the foot of the Janik Bair Colline below Opanetz, and from that point we could see the village of Dolni-Netropol, about a mile away.

As we were riding towards that village the troop suddenly halted, and Czetwertinski declared that he could make out a regiment of infantry drawn up about three-quarters of a mile away. We held a consultation, and Czetwertinski said that he could see a battery of Russian artillery in position as well. I had a great reputation for being sharp-sighted in those days, and was generally the first to see the enemy; but I fancied that what Czetwertinski saw was really a herd of the small black cattle of the country.

"Wait here a moment while I go on and have a look," I shouted; and sticking the spurs into my horse, I galloped forward by myself.

When I had gone about two hundred yards, I caught sight of a Russian vedette, galloping for his life towards Netropol. The Circassians saw him too, and in a second they were after him like greyhounds coursing a hare. The whole troop followed them; but before we had gone a furlong we heard the sharp crack of the rifles, and the *piff-paff* of the bullets striking the ground all round us.

Old Mustapha was taken by surprise, and was quite disconcerted for the moment; but we galloped on to the next ridge, and we found that the Circassians had thrown themselves on the ground at the top of the ridge in skirmishing order, and were busily blazing at a Russian cavalry regiment about five hundred yards away. We all took up the same order, lying down and firing away as fast as we could pull our triggers at the dense masses of the enemy scarcely a quarter of a mile away. I was on the extreme right, and I kept at it with my Winchester, vaguely wondering how long that sort of thing could last before we were driven back by the vastly outnumbering Russian force.

The fusillade only lasted about ten minutes; but during that time no fewer than thirteen Russian horses came galloping towards us riderless, showing that we had emptied that number of saddles at least. The Russians were giving us volley after volley; but they had not got the range, and our casualties were few.

I saw a very fine roan charger, which had lost his rider, come galloping towards us; and I started out to catch him, reckoning that he would do capitally for an extra mount, and to give my own horse a spell. Circassians, however, are keen judges of a horse, and a fellow on my left started out at the same time as I did and with the same object. It was a curious experience to be dodging bullets between the two lines; but the prize was worth the risk. However, when the roan saw the Circassian and myself running up with outstretched arms to stop him, he took fright, and, wheeling round, galloped back to his own lines, sending the earth flying behind him in all directions. The Circassian and I, looking rather sheepish, bolted back to the cover of the friendly ridge, which we both reached in safety. We only had two casualties so far. One man was shot through the thigh and another through the shoulder. I treated them both on the spot; but the man who was wounded in the shoulder died almost immediately.

The Russians brought up their infantry and artillery, and we retired as hard as we could upon the village of Netropol with the enemy in hot pursuit. We were only a handful, and things were looking pretty serious, when, to my great relief, I heard the boom of answering artillery and caught the sound of shells screaming overhead. I found that we were under the protection of our own guns, which commanded the whole of the plain, and had opened on the advancing Russians. We exchanged a few shots in the main street of Netropol, a dirty little Bulgarian village from which the population had fled; and at one time the Russians were so close to us that we fired our revolvers at them. We retreated towards our own lines, and the Russians dispersed under the fire of our artillery.

As we were riding back to Plevna, we looked down towards the Sofia road about a mile away, and saw a long train of *arabas* winding along like an enormous snake towards Plevna. This was the great train of provisions and supplies of all sorts that Hakki Pasha brought up from Sofia and Orkhanieh, opening up communication again with Plevna, and forcing a passage through the Russian opposition with reinforcements of six thousand fresh troops. The train of *arabas* was more than a mile long, and the extent of the convoy may be gauged from the fact that there were about three hundred waggons full of ammunition, rations, drugs, and medical stores.

As we were watching the train winding along the road, a trooper came galloping up and told Mustapha Bey that a couple of Russian regiments had swooped down upon the tail end of the convoy, shot a few men, and captured thirty waggons full of stores. We were ordered to go in pursuit, and away we went at a gallop, with the object of intercepting the Russian cutting-out party and recapturing the precious supplies. On the way we surprised a squadron of about sixty Russian cavalry who were camping in a maize-field. They had dismounted, and were resting when we came suddenly upon them; but they had time to mount and gallop off, many of them leaving their carbines behind in their hurry. As the cutting-out party had rejoined their main body, it was hopeless for us to attempt to recapture the waggons, and we had to return reluctantly to Plevna. It was a fairly exciting day's work, taking it all through, and when I got back I had spent fourteen hours continuously in the saddle.

We settled down to the routine of camp life afresh, with the prospect of a long winter siege before us, and I was much disheartened to find that our stock of medical supplies was already almost exhausted, and that there was no chance of replenishing them. The stock of drugs, bandages, and other appliances intended for our hospitals was unfortunately contained in the thirty waggons which the Russians carried off.

Although the prospect was gloomy enough, the troops continued in excellent spirits, and some of the daily incidents of the siege were decidedly humorous. Two days after the Netropol expedition I was riding out towards the Lovtcha road with Czetwertinski, when we came upon a party of about a dozen Turks jabbering away in a great state of excitement. They had got something with them, and from a distance I thought that they had caught a hare, but when we rode up we found that it was a Russian hussar. He spoke to Czetwertinski in Russian and told his story. It seemed that he was with his company when he got some vodka, and imbibed so freely that he speedily became drunk and went to sleep. When he woke up, he had not the faintest idea where he was, and, missing his company, walked right into our outposts, where the men on duty collared him.

He was still very drunk when we saw him, and he regarded his adventure as a capital joke. The Turks had treated him very well, and he was smoking cigarettes which they had given him, surveying his captors with the fatuous smile of semi-inebriety, while they in their turn laughed heartily over their strange find. In due course he was escorted into Plevna, and lodged in durance as a prisoner of war. I never heard what became of him afterwards; but he was doubtless more comfortable than in the Russian trenches.

We were in hopes that we should be able to get our wounded men away from Plevna now that the road had been opened, and Osman Pasha sent orders to the medical quarters for us to select all the men who were able to travel. However, before we could get them ready the

Russians barred the road again with a strong force, and once more we were in a state of siege. During the two days that the road was open, however, I sent Czetwertinski away invalided to Constantinople, and with him the German artist Victor Lauri. It was a very good thing for Czetwertinski that he left Plevna when he did, for as a Russian subject it would have gone hard with him when the Russians finally took the town. When the war was over, Czetwertinski met Skobeleff at San Stefano and lunched with him. Over the coffee and cigars the conversation naturally turned upon the recent experiences of both, and Czetwertinski ventured to ask his host with a smile what would have happened if they had met earlier.

"Oh!" said Skobeleff pleasantly, "we knew that you were in Plevna all the time, and we were always on the lookout for you. If I had happened to come across you there, I should have had you shot of course."

Kronberg was one of the most companionable of my medical colleagues. He was a regular daredevil, always ready for any adventure; and one afternoon he and I decided to go and pay a visit to the Bash Tabiya, the second redoubt opposite Grivitza which commanded the main Grivitza redoubt, at this time in the hands of the Russians. We rode up the slope of the Janik Bair, tied our horses to a tree under cover from the enemy's fire, and advanced cautiously over the exposed ground. We had to run the gauntlet as usual for about thirty yards; and though it did not take us more than three or four seconds, several bullets whistled past us from the Russian works. They used to watch the exposed space with field-glasses, and never missed an opportunity of having a "pot" at any one who showed himself either there or above the parapets of the redoubt or trenches.

Our men of course used to return the compliment from the Bash Tabiya. When Kronberg and I had safely passed this dangerous Tom Tiddler's ground, we struck the trenches in which my regiment was encamped, facing north, and I went to call on my colonel. I found him living like a prehistoric troglodyte in a neatly dug hole in the ground about four hundred yards from the redoubt. The hole was connected by a trench with the redoubt, so that the colonel could go forward and come back without drawing the fire of the enemy's rifles. It was about seven feet deep, and comfortably furnished with Turkish rugs and brightly coloured praying-mats to keep out the damp.

After a cup of coffee and a chat, I walked along the connecting trench, which was about six feet deep, and wide enough to allow the men to move about freely. In the clay inner walls tiers of bunks had been hollowed out like sleeping-berths on board ship, and the "watch below" were lying asleep, wrapped in their great-coats and looking like mummies, while the watch on deck kept their eyes open for squalls. Steps were constructed to enable the firing parties to aim over the parapet, and taking off my *fez* so as not to attract fire I cautiously peered over the parapet. I took up a rifle and had a few shots without seeing the result, and then I walked on through the trench and entered the redoubt. The first sight that met my eyes was a gruesome one, for the bodies of ten men who had been killed that day were lying at the entrance awaiting burial.

On my way to Sadik Pasha's abode I saw a Turkish soldier wearing a very fine pair of Russian high boots that had evidently belonged to a Russian officer, and without inquiring too closely how they had been procured I proceeded to do a deal. My own boots were thin patent leather riding-boots, which looked very nice, but were quite unsuitable for walking; so I persuaded the Turk to accept them, together with three *piastres*, or sixpence, in return for the more useful if less ornamental pair. The faithful servant of the Prophet was delighted with his bargain, and strutted about in my fashionable Bond Street patent leathers admiring himself, while I, for my part, had changed my nationality by stepping literally into the boots of a Russian.

Old Sadik Pasha gave me a warm welcome. I found him squatting on his haunches, with a praying-mat under him, looking the picture of contented cheerfulness. As the weather was pretty hot, he had rigged an awning over the top of his subterranean domicile to keep the sun off, and Kronberg and I squatted down beside him to hear all the news.

It was like dropping in to see a man at his club—with one or two slight differences. Sadik Pasha ordered coffee for three; and though we were six feet underground, the Roumanians in the Grivitza redoubt must have divined instinctively that we were having refreshments, for they decided to serve dessert. Finding it impossible to do much with the ordinary shells, they had pressed a mortar into the service, and just as the man was coming with the coffee they fired another projectile from this ingenious engine of warfare. Now the specific charm of the mortar is that it throws a shell with a very high trajectory, so that the projectile can soar like a hawk into the heavens and swoop down perpendicularly upon its prey.

With all their ingenuity the Turks had not succeeded in devising a protection from this mode of annoyance; and as the Turkish soldier was coming along like a well drilled waiter with a tray on his arm containing three cups of coffee, the mortar-shell exploded in the redoubt. No one was killed, but a fragment of the casing knocked the tray and the cups and saucers into smithereens, and Sadik Pasha had to order "The same again, please." This time the coffee reached the consumer without any interruption in transit; and I was in the act of drinking mine when another shell exploded in the redoubt about ten feet distant from where we were sitting, and made a hole in the ground big enough to bury a man in. I was so startled that I poured the greater part of my coffee over my breeches instead of into my mouth, and old Sadik Pasha chuckled mightily over my want of *sang-froid*. He gave me a cordial invitation to come and stop with him for a week, assuring me that I would soon get used to little accidents like that.

I was too polite to tell Sadik Pasha that, much as I liked his company, the smell round his house was so unpleasant that I felt obliged to decline his invitation. Owing to the inability of the *parlementaires* to come to terms at the conference which I have already described, the bodies of the Turks and Russians lying between Sadik's redoubt and the Grivitza work remained unburied, and the stench was so terrible that Kronberg was actually sick while we were calling on our hardy little entertainer, and I myself was very nearly guilty of the same solecism.

Owing to the vigilance of *nos amis les ennemis*, who saluted us so warmly on our arrival at the redoubt, Kronberg and I prolonged our call until it was dusk, and amused ourselves as well as we could in the redoubt. Occasionally we elevated a *fez* on a bayonet, and drew the fire of a dozen Roumanian rifles at once. Then we returned the compliment with much *empressement*. In this pleasant interchange of civilities the day wore to a close; and when it was dark we said *au revoir* to Sadik Pasha, slipped out at the back, found our horses, and rode into the town again.

Kronberg was, as I have said, a capital fellow, plucky as a lion and generous to a fault. He hated the Bulgarians bitterly, but never allowed his detestation of them as a class to outweigh his sense of justice. There was a Bulgarian of some rank and standing in Plevna whom Osman Pasha suspected of allowing his Russophile inclinations to go too far. In fact, the *muchir* believed that the man was a Russian spy, and he gave orders to have him shot.

Kronberg and Rookh were quartered in this Bulgarian's house;

and when the sentence was made known, the man's wife went to them in a terrible state of grief and anxiety, imploring them on her knees to save her husband, and swearing with the most solemn protestations that he was absolutely innocent. Kronberg and Rookh were of the same opinion; and knowing that I had a little influence with the headquarters staff, they came to me and asked me to see Osman Pasha on the subject, and ask him to reconsider his decision. Osman Pasha listened to my representations very courteously, and I was so far successful that he consented to the man being simply locked up instead of being shot. The Bulgarian's life was spared, and he was sent down as a prisoner to Constantinople when the road was opened up by Chefket Pasha.

It was at this period that my hospital work, which had previously proceeded on regulated lines, with a hopeful measure of success attending my efforts, began to degenerate into a desperate, single-handed struggle against wounds, want, filth, disease, and death.

I was sent to take charge of a large building which had been converted into a hospital, and was already overcrowded with the most pitiable cases. The building stood in several acres of ground on the bank of the Tutchenitza, and about a quarter of a mile from the town, up stream. It had previously been occupied by a wealthy Turk, and consisted really of two large houses, one behind the other, and connected by a passage. The house in the rear had been the *harem*, while the one in front had been occupied by the old Turk and the male members of the household. There was a small well kept garden leading up to the central entrance, and a picket fence with a gate shut it off from the road. There were two large rooms, one on each side of the front door, and two more behind the staircase, with others upstairs and in the building attached at the rear.

Altogether there must have been about twelve large rooms, high, fairly well ventilated, and whitewashed; but more than half of them had no beds, and the forms of the tortured soldiers were huddled together in their clothes on the bare boards. When I went there first, I had two hundred and fifty men to look after, and the task appeared such a hopeless one that my heart sank within me.

We had a hundred beds in the hospital, and a small supply of extra mattresses and blankets; but those were soon apportioned, and for the other unfortunates nothing remained but to lie huddled up on the floor in the clothes in which they had been shot. They lay on the floor of the passages as well as in the rooms, and were packed so closely that it was most difficult to pick one's way through the hospital without treading on them. In one room, fifteen feet by fifteen feet, I had sixteen men, all hideously wounded, dying hard on the hard boards. The bare, whitewashed walls were splashed with blood, which had turned to rusty dark brown stains, and the horrors of the place can only be faintly hinted at.

I was the only medical man on duty in that hospital, with a couple of *jarra bashis*, or dispensers, to assist in dressing, and a squad of Turkish soldiers as hospital nurses. I had chloroform, it is true, but no other drugs of any kind; for the first supply of medicines, as I have explained before, fell into the hands of the Russians when they captured the tail waggons of the convoy. Worse than all, I saw with dismay that the stock of antiseptic dressings was giving out, and that unless it could be replenished the fearful scourge of hospital gangrene was already threatening us closely.

In the large room in which sixty men were lying, some on stretcher-beds, some on mattresses, and many on the floor, the boards were covered with blood and filth like a shambles. Round many of the sufferers pools of pus had formed on the floor, and the smell was terrible. Here, where these brave men were dying, the atmosphere was intolerable, stifling, asphyxiating. As their eyes roamed round that house of suffering instinctively searching for relief, they rested at intervals on small glass windows set high up in the staring whitewashed wall. Through the latticed panes they could see small squares of far blue sky, and now and then there flitted past one of the white doves that Moslems regard as sacred, on its way to the willows on the bank of the Tutchenitza.

Presently the antiseptic dressings were exhausted altogether, and I had to fall back upon coloured prints from the bazaars for bandages, and to plug the wounds with plain cotton-wool, of which we had a large supply. This was non-absorbent, and naturally when treated in this way the wounds became frightfully repulsive. It was impossible to keep the tissues healthy, and all I could do was to go round on my hands and knees from one man to another, literally scraping the maggots out of the wounds either with my finger or an instrument. The unfortunate men were saturated with blood and pus from their wounds, and covered with maggots which lodged in the festering tissues. Often and often, as I went round the "wards"—save the mark—plodding on almost in despair against the dreadful odds, I have taken the plugging of cotton-wool out of a gaping wound, and found underneath it a nest of maggots, feeding on the flesh of the still living man, who would thank me with a look for temporarily relieving him of the torture.

In one small ward with five beds in it, I had five men who were the finest specimens of humanity that I ever saw in my life. I became greatly attached to them, as they did also to me; and it was pathetic to see their gratitude for the most trifling service. One of them, with his strong aquiline face and piercing eyes, reminded me very much of a statue of Dante which I had seen in the market-place of Verona. My patient had been shot through the thigh. The bone had been dreadfully smashed, and the whole leg was a mass of gangrened flesh. If I could have operated, I might have saved his life; but without antiseptic dressings, and without the possibility of subsequent careful nursing, an operation was out of the question, and I had to watch him suffering day by day dying literally by inches.

In the next bed was an Asiatic Turk, whose wound was a peculiar one. A rifle-bullet had struck the top of his skull, and cut a groove longitudinally from front to back through it. I could do but little for the man, except to keep the wound as clean as possible, and the poor fellow suffered great pain. He used to be continually telling me of his wife and children, in some distant Anatolian village, which he knew he would never see again, and he was very grateful for a sympathetic listener. I was always afraid of brain trouble developing, and after about a week of suffering he became delirious through inflammation of the membranes of the brain, and died at last in fearful convulsions.

Next to him was a man who had been hit in the shoulder by a piece of a shell. The bone was smashed to pieces, and several days after the battle I took a piece of iron as large as a hen's egg from a great hole near the man's armpit. I asked him to let me amputate the arm at the shoulder joint; but he would not let it be done, and he was still alive some weeks afterwards when I finally left Plevna. The fourth man had been shot in the thigh, and the wound had no chance of healing without proper dressing. I used to squeeze out about a pint of matter from it every day. The fifth patient had been shot in the clavicle, and had a huge ragged wound in the shoulder. I used to stuff it with cotton-wool, and try to keep the maggots from collecting in the cavity; but when I took out the plug of wool, there were always maggots underneath it. Four out of the five were dead before I left the town.

In the large room, which contained sixty men, though the space would not properly accommodate more than twenty, I had several cases of blood-poisoning due to the colours "running" in the cheap prints which I was obliged to use for bandages. The dyes got into the wounds, and *pyæmia* carried off the men like rotting sheep. The food up to this period was still fairly good, and we had plenty of good water.

Chapter 11

The Horrors of the Hospital

One very peculiar case came under my notice in the principal ward. It was that of a man who had been struck by a spent bullet over the region of the liver. The wound had not penetrated the flesh, and there was nothing but a small, sloughing sore over the liver to indicate the spot where the man had been hit. Two days afterwards he developed acute jaundice, and died in three days. I could not understand it at the time, but it struck me afterwards that the blow from the bullet had ruptured the liver.

To add to the horrors of the general situation, confluent small-pox made its appearance among the wounded; and as I had no means of isolating the patients, it quickly spread. Then several cases of typhoid fever broke out, owing to the insanitary conditions; but strangely enough the disease did not spread, and the mortality from it was small. Imagine the miseries of an unhappy man, who, while suffering from a smashed thigh which prevented him from even moving to resist the maggots that assailed him, was then smitten with small-pox or typhoid fever!

Little by little the septic troubles increased, and at last the crown of misery was reached when hospital gangrene made its appearance. Few civilian medical men now practising have ever seen hospital gangrene; but the records of the terrible mischief which it produced in the days before the discovery of the antiseptic treatment are still extant. The patients who took the hospital gangrene usually suffered considerably, while they rotted away before my eyes, and I was powerless to help them.

The men also got covered with body lice; and as I spent fourteen hours a day as a rule lifting them up, washing them, and dressing their wounds, the noxious insects attacked me too, and during the whole of my subsequent stay in Plevna I was never absolutely free from them. I had only two flannel shirts, and one of these was boiled every day by my servant; but in spite of all precautions, I could never keep free from the insect pests.

Every morning when I went to the hospital the first thing that met my eyes as I opened the little wicket-gate leading into the garden was the row of corpses of the men who had died during the previous night. They were put out there to wait for the burial parties, and the sight never failed to make a profound impression on me. As I walked past them up the path the sight of those dead faces fascinated me; and when I found among them men who were my special favourites, and who had told me the stories of their simple, uneventful lives, and of their wives and children waiting for them in distant parts of the Turkish Empire, a feeling of overpowering depression came over me. I was so utterly helpless to save them, and I was fighting such a hopeless battle, that once or twice I sat down in the hospital and cried like a child. As fast as the men died fresh ones were brought in, and often I found that twenty old faces had gone during the night and that the same number of new ones awaited me in the morning. Skirmishes were always going on between the outposts, and the intermittent bombardment claimed a daily quota of victims, a considerable proportion of whom were sent to me for treatment.

It was at this period that I was wounded for the first and last time out of all the scores of occasions that I have been under fire. It was a mere flesh wound, little more indeed than a scratch; but as I was in a very low state of health from continuous overwork and under-feeding, the flesh wound set up a local condition which still further reduced my strength, and contributed eventually to my leaving Plevna for a short rest. As I was unable to get back again, owing to the Russians closing the road, I was prevented from witnessing the last pathetic scene of all, when Osman Pasha's heroic defence was exhausted, and he had to surrender to the invader.

A chance shot from a Russian field-gun did it for me, during the desultory firing that went on languidly from day to day between the opposing redoubts. I was riding out one morning to visit Sadik Pasha, and was cantering leisurely across to the Bash Tabiya, when I heard the scream of a shell, and recognized instinctively that it was coming my way. One got so used to estimating the course of shells from constant practice that one could pretty well tell by the sound where a particular shell was likely to fall. My charger too was a perfect old war-hardened veteran, and he took no more notice of a shell exploding five yards in front of his nose than if it had been a custard-apple.

When I heard the whistle of the shell, I stuck the spurs in and tried to get out of the way in time; but I did not succeed, and when it exploded a bit of the casing took me in the back of the neck with a sharp, burning shock that felt as if I had been struck with a piece of red-hot iron. When I put my hand up to the place, I drew it back covered with blood; but I quickly discovered that it was a mere surface wound, and when I got back to town and bandaged it, I found that it did not in the least interfere with the performance of my medical duties. However, an abscess formed on the place, and troubled me a good deal.

I was very much overworked. Neither food nor rest was plentiful. I never saw a compatriot, and I spent all my waking hours in the midst of horrible sufferings which I was powerless to alleviate. It was no wonder, under these circumstances, that I became despondent; and after this lapse of time I may as well confess that the thought occurred to me whether it would not be better to blow my brains out than go on in the misery any longer. But when I looked round on those magnificent men—more long-suffering, patient, and courageous men I have never seen in my life—I banished the dark thought, and went back to the work with all the spirit I could muster.

Sometimes even now when I lie awake at night I see myself again dressed in a blood-stained shirt and pair of trousers, as I picked my way among the huddled forms with their ashen faces bound up in those fantastic bandages of coloured print. I see the pools of curdled blood on the floor, the staring whitewashed walls, and the little squares of blue sky through the latticed windows. I hear the stifled moans and I catch the delirious murmurs of that Anatolian Turk as in his death-throes, like Falstaff "*he babbled o' green fields.*"

Although we had no female nurses, still I found that the Turkish women, whenever they had an opportunity, attended to the wounded with the devotion of a Florence Nightingale. There was a small outbuilding in the grounds that surrounded the hospital, and this also was filled with wounded. One day I found two Turkish women there, and learned that they were frequent visitors, bringing milk and broth to the wounded. When I saw them, they were moving silently about in their long white robes, with only the eyes showing through their thick *yashmaks*. One exceptionally hideous case in the outbuilding received attention from them. The man had been struck on the side of the face by a shell, which carried away the whole of his upper and lower jaws. Only his eyes remained, looking plaintively out above the mangled mass that had once been a human face. The Turkish women could just see by the roots of the tongue the position of the gullet, and they kept the unfortunate wretch alive for four days by pouring milk down his throat.

One evening, as I was leaving the hospital almost heart-broken, three men were brought in, and I went back to attend to them. One man had both his legs taken off by a shell from a heavy siege-gun, and was blanched from loss of blood; the second had been struck by a shell, which had carried away arm and shoulder together; the third was shot through the lungs by a rifle-bullet. Next morning, when I returned to the hospital, I saw the three men lying out dead on the path as soon as I opened the gate. Some idea of the hopelessness of my position may be gathered by the medical reader, when he learns that I had forty-seven compound comminuted fractures under my hands at one time, and all were suppurating, while I had no appliances of any kind for dressing them properly.

This was the state of affairs when Chefket Pasha opened up the road from Sofia again with a relief column bringing up under his escort a supply of medical stores and a party of English doctors who desired to volunteer their services. The head of the medical party was Dr. Bond Moore; and very picturesque he looked when he arrived in his Circassian dress. With him was Dr. Mackellar, who had gained a reputation in the Franco-Prussian war, and was a well known authority on gunshot wounds. Then there was Mr. David Christie Murray, who was at that time a war correspondent, but was introduced to me as a medical student, and in that capacity had an opportunity of inspecting my hospital, which he afterwards described very graphically in the *Scotsman*.

A man named Smith, who was in the Indian Civil Service, and who had come up for the sake of the adventure, was another member of the party, which also included my old friend George Stoker, now a Harley Street physician. Last, but not least, there was Captain Morisot, a charming fellow, who was afterwards with me at Erzeroum.

The visitors hunted me up when they arrived, and we had a great supper at my quarters. It was an intense relief to meet some of my own countrymen at last, and I was so glad to see them that I distributed all my curios among them, presenting to these strangers the crosses in bronze and gold, the lockets, and the other trinkets that had belonged to Russian owners before they were sold in the Plevna bazaars as grim treasure-trove of the battlefield.

Dr. Mackellar was an old friend, for I had met him before the war when I was in Vienna; and I was delighted also to meet George Stoker, who was one of my fellow passengers when I came down the Danube. It is difficult for anyone who has never been placed in such a position to form an idea of the delightful sensation which I experienced at meeting with English-speaking men again after a period of seventeen months spent out of the hearing of my mother tongue. Imagine the feelings of an Englishman when he first catches sight of the white cliffs of Dover after long travelling in foreign lands; or think of the sensations of an Australian returning after a couple of years in Europe when he sees the lights at Port Phillip Heads or the entrance to Sydney Harbour again. My feelings were similar when I dropped my Turkish and picked up my half-forgotten English once more in the presence of men of my own race, whose cheerful talk dispelled the gloomy thoughts which my daily struggle against the ever increasing forces of suffering and disease had engendered.

The wound on the back of my neck was very painful, and the large abscess which had formed on it had still further reduced my system. Dr. Mackellar lanced it for me the first night he was in Plevna, and this gave me great relief.

George Stoker had a bad attack of dysentery when he arrived, and he arranged to stop at my place so that I could look after him more easily. I opened up negotiations with my little fair-haired Bulgarian boy, who managed, with a good deal of trouble, to get me some milk, and thus I was enabled to provide proper diet for the invalid.

On the morning after the arrival of the English medical party, Dr. Bond Moore, with Mr. Harvey, a man of English parentage, who was born in the Levant and spoke Turkish like a Turk, together with Dr. Mackellar, waited upon Osman Pasha in his tent. Dr. Bond Moore explained to Osman Pasha through Mr. Harvey that they had been sent out by the Stafford House Committee, a large national organization in London which had collected £50,000 for the purpose of relieving the sufferings caused by the war in Turkey. They desired to undertake the care of the wounded Turks then in Plevna.

Now Osman Pasha was essentially a man of action. Though there was plenty of the *fortiter in re* about him, there was little of the *suaviter in modo*; and Bond Moore and Mackellar, who did not know him as well as I did, jumped to the conclusion that he was intentionally discourteous in his reception of them and in his reply to their representations. He pointed out to them that of the four thousand wounded men who were then in the hospitals, more than two-thirds would be sent away to Sofia on the following day, now that the road had been opened up by Chefket Pasha. This determination on his part, he explained, was dictated by consideration for the wounded as well as for the rest of the troops in Plevna.

They would receive better treatment at Sofia, they would leave more rations for the fighting men, and there would again be room in the hospitals available for the wounded men who might be expected after future engagements. Probably, continued Osman, not more than four hundred wounded men would be left in the hospitals when the ambulance train went away, and meanwhile the medical staff at his disposal was quite strong enough to cope with the work. He also had another powerful reason for sending away the wounded in the overcrowding of the hospitals, which was causing terrible devastation by septic disease; and we knew that if the congested wards were relieved, we might get the upper hand of the gangrene and *pyæmia* which were doing all the damage.

Naturally enough Bond Moore and Mackellar were staggered to find that, after travelling all the way from England and incurring a good many hardships on the way, they were not to be allowed to do the work for which they had been sent. They represented to Osman Pasha the danger of sending away on a long and terrible journey wounded men who were quite unfit to travel; and Bond Moore, as the spokesman, entered a vigorous protest against the "gross inhumanity" of the course proposed by the Turkish commander-in-chief. Osman Pasha, however, was inexorable; and always a brusque and stern man at the best, he became still more forbidding in his manner when the English doctors reiterated their protests. The deputation left the tent in high dudgeon at what they regarded as the discourtesy of their reception, and were thoroughly disappointed after reaching Plevna in safety to be peremptorily ordered to quit it at once.

As a further protest, Dr. Mackellar waited upon Hassib Bey, our principal medical officer, and I was present at the interview, in which the English surgeon told the old Turk that it was a disgrace to humanity to send the wounded away by carts in the condition in which they were. The conversation was carried on in French, and Dr. Mackellar spoke very strongly, declaring that it was a barbarous and brutal thing to send the wounded men away, many of whom he considered, as a surgeon of large experience, to be quite unfit to travel. I felt quite sorry for poor old Hassib Bey, especially as I myself, with a full comprehension of the whole position, was thoroughly in accord with Osman Pasha's view.

It was perfectly plain to me that the wisest course was to despatch the wounded men from out the crowded hospitals into the fresh air and away to Sofia. No doubt a percentage of them would die on the road from the actual hardship of travel; but if they were left in Plevna, a far larger proportion would inevitably die of septic diseases, while the congested condition of the hospitals would be still further aggravated, and slow starvation would add shortly to the sufferings of the unfortunates. The proof of the wisdom of Osman Pasha's action was very manifest afterwards; for though he was starved out eventually, he could not have held the town nearly as long as he did if he had not seized the opportunity when the road was open to send the wounded away.

Hassib Bey listened deprecatingly to Dr. Mackellar's spirited protest; but the fiat had gone forth from headquarters, and he was powerless to accede to his visitor's request even if he had the inclination.

Dr. Bond Moore sent in a formal written protest to Osman Pasha, who vouchsafed no reply, and the Stafford House surgeons spent the rest of the day examining my hospital. In connection with this incident of the expulsion of the Stafford House doctors from Plevna, I may reproduce the report on the subject, which I afterwards sent to Mr. V. B. Kennett, the Stafford House commissioner. My report, which was published in the *Times* of November 15, 1877, ran as follows:

> At your request I write to you a short account of the state of Plevna on the occasion of the visit of Dr. Bond Moore, Stafford House section, and the circumstances attending the evacuation of the wounded. When Drs. Bond Moore and Mackellar arrived in Plevna, we had in our hospitals there between four and five thousand wounded, probably three thousand five hundred of them having received their wounds between September 5 and October 12, the remainder being the graver cases of our former fighting which were considered too serious to send on to Sofia.
>
> We have always received orders after any heavy fighting to send off all who were not too gravely wounded to Sofia, and so we have by this means never had more than five or six hundred in our hospitals. But unfortunately, during the hard fighting in

September, we were completely surrounded by the Russians, and were actually, so to speak, in a state of siege, so that we had the accumulation of nearly a month's fighting in addition to the graver cases of our earlier battles. Such was the state of affairs when Chefket Pasha relieved Plevna, and when Drs. Moore and Mackellar arrived and kindly offered to form hospitals in Plevna.

On presenting themselves to Osman they were received quite courteously. He told them he was very glad to see them, but that if they were sent in the real cause of humanity, and to assist his wounded, he much preferred them leaving for Sofia and establishing themselves there; if, however, they wished to remain and see the fighting, they were perfectly welcome to do so, but if they did they would have very little work to do, as he was sending nearly all the wounded to Sofia, and for those who were remaining he had a sufficient staff of surgeons. His reasons for sending away the wounded must appear most obvious to anyone knowing the circumstances of the case.

I believe that it is always one of the first considerations of a general, after a battle, to send off as soon as possible all wounded who are in a state to travel, in order to make room for further fighting. In addition to this main consideration, I must state that our accommodation was very insufficient, that many of our hospitals consisted of houses without windows, and we were fearfully overcrowded, often having thirty men in a room only large enough for ten. Then, again, we had no beds, and could not procure them as there was no wood to make them of. Another great consideration was that we had not sufficient nor proper food, having only the bare necessaries of life, such as biscuits and meat.

From a sanitary point of view, it was also extremely desirable to remove them as quickly as possible, thereby lessening the chances of an epidemic, which is always liable to break out when such a large population is confined in a small area. It was, I believe, in 1866 that a very serious epidemic of cholera broke out in Plevna. Of the four thousand five hundred wounded I believe that all but two hundred and fifty were sent off, the wounds of those remaining being of the very gravest character. Most of the wounds of those sent away were very slight, being flesh wounds caused by bullets, which would be perfectly healed in from twenty to thirty days.

I believe in all about sixty or seventy cases of fracture were sent off; in most of them union had already occurred, and in those in which it had not I am opinion that they stood a better chance of recovery by their removal from a hospital impregnated with septic germs into a purer atmosphere and where they could have more attention paid to them. Dr. George Stoker took with him in his ambulance to Orkhanieh forty cases, but it must be remembered that these were the very gravest. Three of them died on the way; but as they were cases out of my own hospital I can speak about them with confidence, and can say that in the most favourable circumstances recovery would have been impossible.

Osman Pasha also acted with foresight from a military point of view; for had he not sent off his wounded, and had Stafford House and the Red Crescent retained them in hospitals established there, what would be their position at present now that Plevna is again surrounded by the Russians? It must be a matter of satisfaction to Osman Pasha to have sent off as many of the non-combatant population as possible, for it must be a great drain on one's commissariat to have to feed four or five thousand non-combatants in a place like Plevna where provisions are so difficult to procure. I may add that I consider I am in a position to speak with authority on such a subject, as I have been for fifteen months in the Turkish service, and for the last five have been in Plevna.

When the medical men went round my hospital, they saw the horrors among which I had been working for the previous month, and then I took them out to our operating theatre under the blue sky on the banks of the Tutchenitza. Here Dr. Mackellar performed several operations, and showed us some brilliant surgery, including four disarticulations of the shoulder joint.

Next day we all rode out to the Krishin redoubt which Skobeleff had taken, and which was soon afterwards recaptured with fearful loss. I was able to point out the exact spot where the heaviest of the fighting had taken place to Dr. Bond Moore, Dr. Mackellar, and Mr. David Christie Murray, who were naturally interested in making a personal inspection of the scene of such a great historical fight.

As the four of us rode away in a southerly direction to the Ibrahim Bey redoubt, the Russian artillerymen saw us, and in a couple of seconds the Stafford House doctors and the war correspondent had an experience which struck them with all the force of the novel and the unexpected. The Russians fired six shells at us, and it certainly was a wonder that some of us were not killed, for the artillerymen had found the range by long practice at the redoubts, and their shells fell all round us. It was no novelty for me to hear the projectiles whizzing about, but I was surprised at the courage and coolness with which the visitors behaved, and luckily all four of us came out of it without a scratch.

That evening I thought the whole position over, and determined to apply for a short leave of absence, and take a trip down to Constantinople with the intention of returning to Plevna in a couple of weeks. I should not have dreamed of leaving the position so long as I could be of any real service there; but most of the wounded men were about to be sent away, and there would be nothing left for me to do. In addition to this, I was in a very bad state of health. I had a large suppurating cavity at the back of my neck from my wound, and my system had completely run down. My mother, whom I had not seen for years, was then in Europe, and I thought that it would be a capital opportunity to run down and see her. Moreover, my agreement with the Turkish Government was for only one year, and I had already been serving for seventeen months. It was these considerations, and not, as was afterwards stated in various newspapers, the refusal of Osman Pasha to avail himself of the assistance of the Stafford House doctors, that induced me to interview Hassib Bey and apply for leave of absence.

I asked him for leave of absence for two or three weeks, pointing out that nearly all the wounded would be sent away, and that there was no immediate likelihood of any more fighting before I returned. Hassib Bey said that he would give me leave with very great pleasure, and he voluntarily gave me a letter to the Seraskierat, in which he was good enough to express the very highest appreciation of my services. In fact, it was practically impossible for any man to get a higher testimonial than that which Hassib Bey gave me on the eve of my departure from Plevna. He suggested that I should ask Osman Pasha to ratify the leave of absence; and Tewfik Pasha having conducted me into Osman Pasha's presence, I repeated my application to him, assuring him that I would not think of leaving as long as there was any work for me to do. The *muchir* thanked me for my services, of which he expressed high appreciation, and hoped to see me back in Plevna.

If I could have foreseen that the road would be blocked again by the Russians, and that it would be impossible for me to return once I left the town, I would have stayed by the troops at all costs. I was devoted to the Turkish Army and the Turkish cause. I never spared myself in carrying out my duties, and I was bound by the strongest ties of attachment to my patients, as they were also, I felt and knew, to me. I positively loved the great, rough barbarians who bore their sufferings with such noble fortitude in my hospital, and during the whole of my time in Plevna I never had the slightest unpleasantness with a single one of them, and received always the greatest gratitude from them all.

At that time there was no Turk in Plevna more Turkish in sympathies than I was. I threw my whole heart and soul and all my energies into the Turkish cause, and no one could have gone through all that I had without being impressed with a feeling of the most profound admiration for the patience, courage, and heroic patriotism of the Turkish private soldier. Intending as I did to remain away for a couple of weeks at most, I felt that the parting was only temporary; and when I went to say goodbye to the colonel of my regiment, Suleiman Bey, he wished me a cheery *au revoir*, expecting to see me soon back again. I had quite an affecting farewell with dear old Hassib Bey, and I also went round and said goodbye to all my intimate friends and the men with whom I had been brought most closely into contact.

It was a great disappointment to me that I could not find the regimental barber, a little red-headed Turk, who used to shave me every Sunday, whether there was firing in progress or not, making me sit down on the ground and taking my head between his knees for the better performance of his task. Anxious as I was to make him a little present in recognition of his skill and punctuality, I was unable to find him. Like his brethren of the craft in other countries, he was a most loquacious conversationalist, and I got all the gossip of the trenches during the ten minutes that I was under his hands every Sunday.

My Circassian servant Ahmet had to go back to the ranks, much to his disgust, when I went away, and from that time forward his lot was by no means such a happy one as before. Instead of leisurely cooking my *pilaf*, grooming my horse, and occasionally raiding the country for hay, poultry, eggs, or anything else that he could get for his own benefit as well as mine, the poor fellow had to take his place in the wet trenches, with no bed but a hole scooped in the clay, and little to expect in the way of breakfast except a bullet.

Dr. Stoker had about twenty smooth-running ambulance waggons specially built for the conveyance of wounded men, and having loaded these up with the most dangerous cases he set out on the long journey to Sofia. Having no further use for a horse, I sold mine to Dr. Mackellar, and took my passage in one of the ambulance waggons. Then the night before I left Plevna the other fellows gave us a great send off and we had a splendid supper at the house of Dr. Robert, who, I regret to say, became hopelessly intoxicated, and insisted on yelling patriotic songs in half a dozen languages, while he thumped his piano until the yellow-faced Viennese housekeeper hauled him off in wrath and turned us all out. Poor Robert! Long before this we had eaten all his zoological specimens, his tame deer as well as his poultry; but he forgave us all. I never saw him again.

Old Mustapha Bey was quite concerned when I told him that I was going away. I had won the goodwill of this crusty old colonel of a regiment of cavalry some weeks before by the promise of a gift of some real Scotch whisky, which the old chap had read of but never tasted. He was an inveterate toper when he got the chance, being in this respect quite a rarity in the Ottoman army, and would drink *raki* or anything else with a fine, generous disregard of quality as long as the quantity was there. My friend Mr. Wrench, who was then the British consul in Constantinople, and who has lately, (as at time of first publication), died, promised to send me up a case of real Scotch whisky, and it came up in the previous train of *arabas*. At least the case came up all right, but of the dozen bottles only two remained for the disappointed consignee—myself. Of course we had a general jollification, and the last drop of genuine Glenlivet had vanished down the capacious gullet of an Austrian medico before I remembered with a pang of regret my promise to Mustapha Bey.

Fortunately he had never tasted whisky, so there was still a possibility of keeping faith with him, at any rate in appearance. I confided my predicament to my comrades, and we brewed a special *cuvée réservée* for the Turk. The basis, I recollect, consisted of a decoction of prunes boiled with some of the wine of the country, which was heavily loaded with kerosene or some other mineral oil, and brought to the right amber hue by the addition of a little harmless colouring matter. This salubrious beverage I filtered through a sponge, bottled in one of the empty whisky bottles, and sent to Mustapha Bey with my compliments.

When I next met him, he was smacking his lips with retrospective gusto, declaring that he had never tasted anything so delicious in his life. Poor old fellow! I felt quite guilty when I went to say goodbye to him, especially when he added at the last, "Be sure when you come back to bring me up another bottle of Scotch whisky."

Next morning I went away in one of the smoothly running ambulance cars brought up by Dr. Stoker. I had a pair of horses, and drove them down to Telish, where we stayed the first night. It was a mercy that we were able to get on in front of the long line of about three hundred *arabas*, each drawn by two small white oxen and laden with wounded. The carts creaked along at about two miles an hour, and as we passed them the groans and cries which the excruciating agony forced from the unfortunate sufferers were most painful to hear. Some of the men had fractures which remained unset, and the torture produced by the broken ends of bone jarring together as the waggon jolted and bumped over the rough road can be left to the imagination. Most of the men, however, bore their dreadful sufferings with a grim silence that was as painful as the cries.

Oh that ghastly journey of wounded men to Sofia! And here and there a cart would stop while the driver lifted out a dead man from among his still living fellow travellers, and laid him down by the side of the road, at rest at last from the fearful jolting of the *araba*. There was no time to dig a grave, so the body was left there to soak in the rain and bleach in the sun, along the white road that wound from Plevna to Orkhanieh. I have no means of knowing accurately what proportion of the wounded died on the road, but I should estimate it at about 7 *per cent*. Had they been left behind at Plevna, probably at least 50 *per cent*, would have been swept away by septic disease and slow starvation.

At Telish, where we spent the first night, I found Hakki Pasha in command, and was very kindly treated by him. This was the scene of a severe fight about a fortnight after we passed through.

After three days' travelling we reached Orkhanieh, our first stopping-place of any considerable size; and here a number of the wounded who could go no farther were placed in the hospital. At Orkhanieh the hospital arrangements were a welcome change from those at Plevna. I met a man named Temple Bey there, an Englishman, who had been in the Turkish service for a great number of years. There were several English surgeons, and suitable houses had been turned into hospitals. I met a man named Roy, and another named Gill, now a well known practitioner at Welshpool; a man named Pinkerton, working at the hospitals in Orkhanieh; and there I said goodbye to my friend Dr. Mackellar, who remained behind to perform some operations, and stayed there for a considerable time. When I was leaving him, he kindly gave me a letter to Baron Munday, an Austrian doctor, who was an enthusiast in the cause of philanthropy, and who afterwards showed me great kindness in Constantinople.

At Sofia I met Lady Strangford, who had a well equipped hospital, worked by three or four English doctors and several English nurses. There were fifty or sixty beds in it, and the contrast between this hospital and the dreadful place that I had left behind at Plevna was as startling as the difference between an "*Inferno*" and a "*Paradiso.*" Lady Strangford gave me a letter to the Baroness von Rosen, who had another hospital at Adrianople, and I spent a couple of pleasant days with that enthusiastic lady. Going on to Ichtiman, I met there Fano Bey, who was the second military officer in charge of the hospitals at Widdin; and as he arrived late at night, I was glad of the opportunity of repaying some of his past kindnesses by giving up my room to him. Next day we went on to Tatar Bazardjik, which was the terminus of the railway from Constantinople; and there, in the company of half a dozen jolly war correspondents, I shook off the last traces of the depression engendered by the horrors of my hospital work in Plevna.

CHAPTER 12

From Constantinople to Erzeroum

In Constantinople I put up again at Misserie's Hotel. During the fifteen months that had elapsed since I last saw that comfortable hostelry I had lived a whole lifetime, and coming back to it again, a war-worn veteran of twenty-three, the French cooking and the soft beds after many a dinner of raw maize cobs and many a sleep on the bare earth appealed to my feelings in the most convincing manner possible.

At this time the eyes of the world were turned towards Plevna, and I found, somewhat to my astonishment, that my name was already fairly well known in Stamboul. Everyone was anxious to hear something of the famous victories that had just been won from an eyewitness, and I had to fight my battles over again in the club and the café, the bureau and the *boudoir*, for the benefit of hundreds of patriotic inquirers all eager for the latest news. Among others I met General Sir Collingwood Dickson, an old Crimea man, who was intensely interested in the operations against the enemy, whose grey coats he had seen in front of him some three and twenty years before at Alma and at Inkermann. It was wonderful to see the warrior's eyes flashing with the battle-light again, as I told him the story of the Krishin redoubts—how Skobeleff took them and held them for one desperate day and night, and how, after many repulses, the Ottoman troops at five o'clock on the following afternoon poured over the parapets in a mighty, irresistible wave and swept the Russians back to the Green Hills once more.

Taking Osman Pasha's letter with me, I paid a visit to the Seraskierat, and, having presented my introduction, was welcomed most warmly by the officers of the War Office, who thanked me on behalf of the Turkish Government for my services. Up to this time the Ottoman troops had been making a very good fight of it on the whole, in spite of the losses at the Shipka Pass and on the Lom; and the brilliant victories which Osman Pasha had been winning encouraged the officers of the Seraskierat to hope for further successes. It is perhaps outside my purpose here to criticise in detail the conduct of the operations by the Turkish Government; but I cannot help referring to the opinion which was very generally expressed outside that the mismanagement and divided control at headquarters were entirely responsible for the headway which the enemy had made up to the present, and that if the brilliant qualities of the Turkish forces in the field had been supported by a more rational and consistent policy at Constantinople the peaked caps of the Russians would never have been seen before Stamboul.

My mother, whom I was very anxious to see, was in England at this time, and I had written to her upon my arrival in Constantinople. While I waited to get a reply from her, I had plenty of time to look about me and see the change which had taken place in the daily life of the Turkish capital since my previous visit. Upon the outbreak of a war the adventurers of all nations seem to emerge from their hiding-places, and flock to the scene of action for the profit, the pleasure, or the excitement that they can pick up. The carcase, in fact, was there, and one could see the eagles gathering together from every quarter.

I met a good many Englishmen of the roving, daredevil class that has done so much to build up our own empire, and here in default of an outlet among Christian nations they were trying all they knew to get into the Turkish army. Many of them had a special axe to grind of some sort. They had inventions, new weapons, or improved clothing, or equipment which they desired to sell to the Turkish Government. For instance, there was a man called Harris, who had a scheme for blowing up the bridge across the Danube at Sistova with torpedoes, and was very anxious that I should join him in his absurd scheme. His idea was to send down the river a small fleet of torpedoes which would destroy the bridge as soon as they came into contact with it.

How the destruction of the bridge could hinder the advance of the Russians or alter the course of the campaign he loftily declined to explain, and my stupidity was such that I missed this unique opportunity of securing fame and fortune at a blow. Another man whom I met belonged to a species which is fairly well distributed—more's the pity—over the outlying portions especially of the British Empire. He was gentlemanly, well dressed, and by no means presuming. He talked well, and evidently knew the world. One would take him to be about thirty-five years of age, though the lines in his forehead and round the mouth and the streaks of grey in his hair showed that he had lived all the time. He took a tremendous interest in the fighting round Plevna, and he invited me to dinner with him one evening. Let us call him Smith, although that was not his name. Well, I had a very excellent dinner; and when it was over I had to pay for it myself, as also for Mr. Smith's own well selected repast and bottle of Château Léoville. Over the cigars afterwards he casually asked me to lend him five pounds; but I found, to my regret, that I had not got the money on me.

If there were plenty of adventurers in Constantinople just then, there were also plenty of sterling, good fellows always ready to do one a good turn without any ulterior object. I made a delightful acquaintance, for instance, when I met Charles Austin, a Fellow of St. John's, Oxford, who had gone out to Constantinople to act as special correspondent for the *Times*. Another capital fellow was Frank Ives Scudamore, whom everyone in Constantinople knew. He was the head of the British post-office there; and when I told him that I had spent twenty pounds of my own money in telegraphing to the *Standard* from Widdin when their own correspondent went away, Scudamore paid me the money out of his own pocket, telling me that he would get it from the paper. His son was acting as the correspondent for some London paper too, and I saw a good deal of him. The names of the Englishmen whom I met in the town at that exciting time would fill many pages; but I can mention a few of them.

There was Colonel Valentine Baker, for instance (Baker Pasha), who was accounted one of the finest cavalry officers in Europe, and was engaged in reorganizing the *gendarmerie*. He had picked out a lot of retired English officers for positions, and among them I met Colonel Swire, Colonel Norton, Colonel Alix, and a fire-eating, devil-may-care Irishman named Briscoe, who had been in the Guards, and who was the life and soul of the club. An exceptionally interesting old chap was General Berdan, the inventor of the Russian rifle that bore his name. I looked at the harmless, gentle old chap with considerable awe when I recollected the awful scenes in my hospital and the deadly evidences of the hard-hitting Berdan bullets.

There were several fellows who had failed in examinations at Sandhurst or Woolwich, and were now hunting for glory where they fancied that a good seat on horseback would be more serviceable than trigonometry and a fair shot with the revolver would be more valuable than the most intimate acquaintance with the differential calculus. A Sir Peter Something-or-other, who was trying to sell uniforms to the Turkish Government, completes the list of my personal club acquaintances.

During the few days that I was at Constantinople, Valentine Baker organized a delightful picnic to the Gulf of Ismet, where the British fleet were lying, and he invited me to join the party. We went up the Gulf of Ismet in a small steamer, and at Prinkapo we took on board an addition to our party including several ladies.

After a few hours' steaming, we came in sight of the ships of the British squadron riding at anchor on the blue waters of the gulf; and fighting though I had been under the Turkish flag, I felt a thrill of pride as our little launch passed under the stern of the mighty *Téméraire* and I saw the dear old ensign flying over me again. Those were stirring times in international politics, for word had been passed round in high diplomatic circles as well as on the stages of the London music-halls that "the Russians shall not have Constantinople," and the presence of the *Achilles*, the *Alexandra*, the *Téméraire*, and the other ships of Admiral Hornby's squadron almost within shell fire of Stamboul showed that Great Britain had made up her mind definitely upon this point.

We lunched with Commodore Hewitt on board the *Achilles*, and after lunch we had plenty of time to examine the equipment of that splendid fighting machine. As I watched the ladies in their white dresses tripping along the snowy decks and peering down the sights of the great, silent, burnished guns that pointed out towards Stamboul, I thought of those other guns that I had left behind at Plevna, grim, powder-blackened, blood-bespattered veterans, that continued their deadly work until, broken and dismounted, with their gun crews lying round them, they were silenced at last in the Krishin redoubts.

We had a delightful day with the squadron, and in the evening we steamed back to the city of many minarets, upon which the eyes of Europe were day by day directed. At Prinkapo I met a man called Pearse, a brother Australian. He was the first graduate in law from the Adelaide University. He had a big practice at the bar in the English court at Constantinople, and we had much to tell each other of our adventures since we crossed the line.

My friend Mr. Wrench, the British consul at Constantinople, was extremely kind to me, and I ventured to approach him upon a somewhat delicate question. Much as I admired the character of the Turkish troops and their soldierly qualities in the field, I could not be blind to one conspicuous defect in Turkish official nature. It was plain from the first that the executive had a rooted dislike to paying over a single *piastre* to anyone for services rendered. The pay of the troops was months in arrear, and my own little bill was mounting up to a quite portentous figure. Perhaps it occurred to the paymaster of the forces that it would be folly to hand over good money to a man who might have his pockets carried away together with his legs by a convenient shell at any moment. At any rate the fact remained that I was owed about £70 by the Turkish Government at this time; and as I had no hopes of recovering my medical fees by my own unaided efforts, I laid the matter before Mr. Wrench.

Mr. Wrench had lived long in Constantinople, and was intimately acquainted with all the devious approaches to the ear of officialdom. I do not know how many cups of coffee he was obliged to drink, nor how many artfully worded compliments he paid to solemn old *pashas* sitting cross-legged on their divans; but I do know that in a remarkably short time, considering the length and tortuosity of the negotiations which he must have gone through, he was able to announce to me that the arrears of my salary of £200 a year would be paid on application. When I put in my claim for £70, they brought me the whole amount in silver coin, and I had to get a small hand-cart to remove my money, which consisted of about half a hundredweight of Turkish *medjidies*. It was certainly the heaviest fee that I have ever received for professional services.

In order to be more in the swim, so that I could hear prompt news of all that was going on at the seat of war, I left Misserie's Hotel, and took up my quarters at the club in the Grande Rue de Pera. This was a very comfortable and very cosmopolitan *caravanserai*, and the members included the leading section of the foreign element in Constantinople. Here I met again many of my old acquaintances, among them being the Hon. Randolph Stewart, the Queen's Messenger, who had come down the Danube with me when I first entered Turkish territory.

I found plenty of congenial spirits in the club, and devoted a day or two to well deserved relaxation, which was readily obtainable in Constantinople. In the evenings we used to go the round of the *cafés chantants*, and always found lots of fun there. One night a French girl came forward on the stage, and sang a song about Plevna, which was rapturously applauded. While the song was going on somebody spotted me in the audience, and I was accorded a demonstration which, although it was highly flattering, was nevertheless decidedly embarrassing.

While I was amusing myself with these frivolities, the most momentous events were occurring at the theatre of war. In Asiatic Turkey the Russians were making rapid headway, and I learned from Mr. Barrington Kennett, the head of the Stafford House Relief Committee, who was then in Constantinople, that the condition of the Turkish garrison of Erzeroum was deplorable. Medical aid was urgently required there, and Mr. Barrington Kennett offered me an engagement at once to take charge of the ambulance work at Erzeroum for the Stafford House Committee. I was offered far better terms than I was getting from the Turks, and a free hand to do what I liked at Erzeroum; but I determined not to desert my old friends at Plevna, and made up my mind to get back there as soon as I had seen my mother. Mr. Barrington Kennett asked me to reserve my final decision, and when I left him the offer was still open.

On the very same day something occurred which compelled me to change my plans. Sir Collingwood Dickson sent me a telegram asking me to call upon him at once in the summer residence of the British Embassy at Therapia, and in an interview which I had with him there he told me that news had just been received of terrible fighting at Gorny Dübnik and Telish. The Russian Guards had been brought up, and after a desperate battle at Telish in which the Russians lost four thousand men the Turkish forces sustained a complete defeat. As a result of this victory the Russians were in possession of all the approaches to Plevna, and communication with Osman Pasha's army was absolutely cut off. I listened to this news with dismay, for it was clear now that I could not get back to Plevna; and that night as I lay in bed at the club I made up my mind to accept the offer of the Stafford House Committee and go to Erzeroum.

Before I was up in the morning Mr. Barrington Kennett came into my room and told me that he had received a telegram from Erzeroum giving the news of a sanguinary battle close to that place. Mukhtar Pasha had suffered a terrible defeat, and the condition in Erzeroum was desperate. The town was full of wounded men, and supplies of all kinds were urgently needed. Mr. Kennett asked me to start that day at twelve o'clock as there was a steamer going, and he offered to give me any one I liked to go with me, suggesting that I should take a dragoman and Captain Morisot, whom I had already met at Plevna, as a companion. Mr. Stoney, who also belonged to the Stafford House Committee, and who had treated me with the greatest kindness, also urged me to accept the offer; and the upshot of it all was that I told

Mr. Kennett that I would be ready to start by the steamer at twelve o'clock.

Steamers, however, suffer from unpunctuality in Turkey as well as elsewhere, and at the last moment we found that the boat would not start until next morning. Baron Munday heard of this, and gave a grand farewell dinner to me at the club that night, when about a dozen of us sat down to a regular banquet, and drank each other's healths in bumpers of champagne. In those old fighting days a farewell dinner to any one was a thing to wonder at; for it was always a shade of odds that a fever or a rifle-bullet would claim a good many of the guests before they could meet again, and the more risky the prospects of the future the more lively was the certain pleasure of the present. Late that night, or rather early next morning, they saw me down to the quay where the Messageries boat was lying, and I went on board, lugging with me a bag containing three hundred English sovereigns—perhaps the only coins on earth that will fetch their face value anywhere. With me there went Dr. Woods, an adventurous spark from the north of Ireland, who was deputed to act with me, Captain Morisot, and Mr. Harvey.

A fine old Frenchman commanded the little Messageries steamer, and by his manner and language he seemed a regular old aristocrat, who had not always been running a small "tramp" boat on the Black Sea. Although far from Paris, he had not forgotten the principles of gastronomy, and the cuisine on board that perambulating little tub was simply perfect. I had never lived so well in my life. We had a delightful passage up the Black Sea, calling in at the different ports on the north side, Sinope, Samsoun, and finally Trebizond, where we disembarked for the overland journey to Erzeroum.

Trebizond is a beautiful town built on a table-land at the top of high cliffs looking down over the Black Sea. There was a very good Greek hotel there, and we put up for the night in it. As soon as possible we called on Mr. Biliotti,[1] the English consul at Trebizond, and he gave us a message to push on to Erzeroum as quickly as possible, as Mukhtar Pasha was in urgent need of medical officers and stores.

With Mr. Biliotti we met Captain McCalmont, who was on the staff of Sir Arnold Kemball, the British Military *Attaché* in Asiatic Turkey. All the preliminaries for our journey had been settled by the indefatigable Mr. Biliotti; and as we had two *dragomen*, I left one of them,

---

1. Later Sir Alfred Biliotti, H.B.M. consul in Crete, who distinguished himself by his exertions on behalf of the inhabitants during the disturbances in 1897.

a man named Williams, behind us to bring on the heavy packages, the bandages, drugs, stimulants, and other medical stores, while we pushed forward with the other.

When we left Trebizond, our party consisted of Dr. Woods, Captain Morisot, Harvey, and myself. We started early in the morning for our long ride to Erzeroum through the wild and picturesque country which ethnologists and philologists have alike decided upon as the cradle of the human race, and where biblical legend, agreeing with the conclusions of science, has placed the primitive Garden of Eden. The road that we travelled was a splendid one, macadamized nearly all the way, and built in that solid and enduring form that men gave to their highways before the railways came to compete with them. It was this road that Xenophon travelled with his legions over two thousand years ago when they made their famous return march to Greece.

Readers of that dead-and-gone Greek captain's diary will remember his explicit description of the journey, and his continually recurring remark that they came after a stage of so many "*parasangs*" to "a populous town, well watered, and situated on a river." Since Xenophon's day most of those populous towns have disappeared, and nothing is left but the beetling cliffs that frowned down upon the homeward marching Greeks, and the sea that ripples as fresh and blue today as when the hoplites and the bowmen saw it gleaming at last before them and ran forward with the glad, exulting cry, "*Thalassa, Thalassa!*"

The road is still divided into posts or stages, and we travelled from stage to stage with fresh post-horses. It was tiring work riding these rough and badly broken brutes, and Dr. Woods, who was an indifferent horseman, suffered very severely; but the excitement of the journey and the wildness of the scenery kept us up.

Our first day's journey was very picturesque, for the road wound along the side of a deep ravine for many miles, and then curled along the flanks of the hills that rose above us beautifully clad with hazel trees. We passed through a part of the district of Lazistan, and were much struck by the magnificent type of men that we saw there, tall, straight, muscular fellows, lithe and hardy as the mountain ash. Perhaps it is true that this country is the real cradle of the human race, and that from there the tide of migration flowed westward over Europe, sending one tributary stream down into Greece, and another down into Italy, and passing onwards in ever increasing volume, until it spread population, not only through Western Europe, but away, as industrious archæologists have whispered, conning their strange finds among the Incas of Peru and Mexico, to the great Western continent that lay beyond the fabled inland of Atlantis.

At any rate those who hold to this theory might find support for it in the magnificent physique of the present population of this primeval country. At times, when a sick man is sent back to breathe the air of his native place after a lifetime spent in some distant city, he gathers new health and strength in some mysterious way. So tired humanity, sick and undersized in Western Europe, regains its pristine vigour and development among the mountains and ravines where it first saw the light.

Not only were these men of Lazistan very fine fellows themselves, but we saw that they possessed some magnificent dogs, powerfully built, shaggy coated animals, with enormous muscular strength. These dogs were greatly prized by their owners; and though I tried hard to secure one by purchase, I failed. They are used to guard the flocks of their masters, and many a fierce duel has been fought at night between a grey old wolf, impelled by hunger to attack the sheep, and the grim custodian of the flock. In the winter all the mountains in Lazistan are covered with snow for months, and the white covering of those lonely grassy slopes is often stained by the traces of these battles *à outrance*.

After completing our first day's journey, we came in the evening to a small village, where we put up at a filthy little *khan*, and made ourselves as comfortable as we could. We had brought plenty of food with us, and our principal discomfort was as usual occasioned by the fleas, which were as pertinacious as those which Thackeray has depicted as pulling the Kickleburys out of bed during their famous excursion up the Rhine.

On the second day we were able to push on a good deal faster as the road was more level, and in the evening we came to the small township of Ghumish Khané, which was chiefly known to fame owing to the existence of some very old silver mines in the neighbourhood. To an Australian like myself it did not look at all like a mining township. Where were the familiar poppet heads, the heaps of *mullock*, and the diligently *fossicked alluvial*? There was no roar of stampers, no monotonous gurgle of pumps, and there was not one decent bush shanty in the place. We had seen enough of the comforts of a *khan* on the previous night, so like wise men we went straight to the *hammam*, or Turkish bath, with which even the smallest Turkish township is always provided. Here we enjoyed the refreshing luxury of being well steamed; and *backsheesh*, in the shape of a few *piastres* to the man in charge, procured for us permission to sleep on the divans provided for patrons of the establishment. We had supper and spent the night in the *hammam*.

Leaving Ghumish Khané next morning, we rode on through a narrow valley between two ranges of hills covered with hazel trees and other light scrub. In this valley, which was about seven miles long by half a mile wide, we found magnificent groves of pear trees fringing the road on either side. When we passed through in the middle of autumn, the fruit was just ripe, and the great juicy pears almost knocked against our faces as we rode on under the trees with the branches interlacing overhead. We telegraphed to the *kaimakan* at Baiburt, our next stopping-place, before leaving Ghumish Khané, in order that accommodation might be prepared for us; and when we reached Baiburt in the evening, we were agreeably surprised to find it an extremely beautiful town. Baiburt, like all the towns in that country, is a place of grey antiquity.

It sleeps on in the present, dreaming of the past and of all the wars that have raged about it since the first men of Baiburt built themselves defences against the robbers of the hills hundreds, if not thousands, of years ago. It was taken by the Russians in 1828, after the massacres in the Ægean Sea had roused England, France, and Russia to take joint action against the Turks, and had whetted the thirst for blood once more by precipitating Navarino. Looking at the majestic ruins of this town of Baiburt and at the traces of their presence, left there by the Russian cannoneers, one thought of the causes that had brought about these ruins; one thought of the Greek struggle for independence, and of the massacres at Chios and the adjacent islands; one thought of Byron singing of "The Isles of Greece," with his passionate appeal against "Turkish force and Latin fraud," and of Béranger stirring all Europe with the lament of the heroic Ipsariotes, "*Les rois chrétiens ne nous vengeront pas.*"

After leaving Baiburt we got among the mountains again, and rode along a track hewn out of the side of the hills that almost overhung us, a road that reminded one in places of the magnificent solitudes of the Julier Pass in Switzerland, and at times brought back the softer beauties of the track from Hobart to the Huon River in Tasmania.

On either side of the road grew groves of giant rhododendrons, making splashes of rich colour amid the green; and here and there the ruined castles, built by Genoese merchant princes to protect their commerce from the robbers of the hills, loomed in lonely state above us. Along this road in the Middle Ages came the greater part of the trade from Persia; and as the long caravan, laden with silks and spices, with fabrics from the Persian looms and precious stones from the Persian mines, made its way slowly towards the markets of Europe, it was no wonder that the brigands descended from their native fastnesses and risked a fight with the well armed escort that rode beside the treasures.

Inspired by a desire to get a nearer look at these romantic old ruins, I climbed up to the ridge upon which one of these castles was poised like an eagle's nest between earth and heaven; but I regretted my curiosity very quickly, for it was only with the utmost difficulty and most frantic clutching at convenient shrubs that I reached the road again with a wild glissade in which everything was forgotten except the instinctive desire to keep myself right side uppermost.

Towards evening we passed through a gloomy gorge where the cliffs rose perpendicularly on each side; and the air, never warmed by the sun's rays, was bitterly cold. Soon after emerging from this we came to a village whose name I have forgotten, and rode at once to the *konak*, or town hall, where we had a rest and a meal. Here I learnt that Sir Arnold Kemball was at Purnekapan, at the end of the next stage, and that he had with him Lieutenant Dugald of the royal navy as an *attaché*.

Having sent a telegram to Lieutenant Dugald notifying our approach, we resumed our journey, travelling over a pass which rose to a height of between six and seven thousand feet; and at the summit we halted for an hour at a place called the Kopdagh, from which there was a superb view over hills and valleys and distant mountain-peaks. Far away in front of us was the silver line of a river, the very name of which sent a thrill through our hearts. It was "that great river, the River Euphrates"; and as we looked down over the plain we realized, almost with a gasp of astonishment, that we were gazing at the legendary site of the Garden of Eden.

At Purnekapan I called on Sir Arnold Kemball, whom I had met previously at Nish during the Servian war. Sir Arnold Kemball had stirring news for us. He had just received a telegram from Erzeroum announcing that the Russians had delivered a terrific assault, and that the town had fallen into their hands.

Next morning we pushed on as fast as we could, crossed the Euphrates at midday, and at five o'clock in the afternoon we reached

Erzeroum. As we entered the town we naturally expected to find the Russians in possession of the town; but we could see no trace of the well known uniforms, and gradually it dawned upon us that Sir Arnold Kemball had been misinformed when he told us that the long expected Russian assault had already been delivered.

We went straight to the British Consulate, and called upon Mr. Zohrab, our consul, who gave us a most cordial reception, and informed us of the position in the town, which was certainly serious. About a week before our arrival a desperate attack had been made by the Russians, who had taken one of the forts, and the Turks lost two thousand men in killed and wounded. Consequently the hospital resources were taxed to the utmost, although in addition to the Turkish medical staff there were several English doctors in Erzeroum before we got there.

Lord Blantyre had sent up a number of English doctors at his own expense; but the total strength of the medical staff had been depleted by various accidents. Dr. Casson and Dr. Buckle, for instance, had been taken prisoners, and were then in the hands of the Russians; Dr. Guppy had died of typhoid fever about a week before we got there; and the available surgeons were Charles Fetherstonhaugh, James Denniston, whom I had known before in Edinburgh, and John Pinkerton. We took up our quarters with these three, in the great bare house where they lived without any except a table and a couple of benches. There were no beds, so we slept on the floor; and our by no means luxurious meals were cooked for us by an Armenian named David whose son Siropé, commonly called Jonathan, acted as waiter and general factotum.

As soon as we were installed we had time to look round, and my first impression of Erzeroum was a very favourable one. I found that we had come to a very picturesque town, lying under the lee of a range of mountains which rose to a height of six thousand feet, the town itself being about four thousand feet above the sea level. A remarkable feature about the place was the entire absence of timber, which I noticed at once with the apprehension of an old campaigner who knew the value of a supply of fuel and the horrible discomfort of being without it. I found that the nearest timber was seventy miles away, where the great forest of Soghanli Dagh was situated. There were very few trees in the town, and the mountains were great masses of bare rock, without a trace of vegetation to hide their cold nakedness. Under these circumstances the inhabitants relied for fuel principally on dried camel's dung, which was a most precarious source of supply.

Erzeroum was surrounded by a great wall, strengthened by forts at intervals, and also by a moat and drawbridge. It was a very important town, because nearly all the trade from Teheran went through it; and it had a population of forty thousand inhabitants, most of whom were Armenians. The houses were strongly built of stone, with flat roofs, which were used by the inmates as promenades during the warm evenings; and the bright colours affected by the Turkish women in their dress lent colour and animation to the scene. The town contained several handsome Armenian churches, the inner walls of which were decorated with beautiful blue tiles; and the *konak*, or town hall, was a very handsome structure. The water supply was chiefly drawn from wells, and there was besides a small stream that came down from the mountains, while the Euphrates was only four miles away.

Mr. Zohrab, who was to all intents and purposes an Englishman, and had an English wife and two sons, introduced all of us newcomers to Mukhtar Pasha, the commander-in-chief, who welcomed us most kindly, and thanked us for coming. We found that Fetherstonhaugh, Denniston, and Pinkerton were in charge of a large hospital, which was known as Lord Blantyre's Hospital; and I arranged to take over from the Turks a large hospital which had been organized in the Yeni Khan. Pinkerton agreed to come over to me, as the other two could get through all the work at Lord Blantyre's Hospital; so Pinkerton, Woods, and myself, with Harvey and Captain Morisot as assistants, were installed in the Yeni Khan, and took over all the staff of assistants, servants, and *jarra bashis* that had been employed under the Turks. There were two of these *jarra bashis;* and one of them, a Turkish sergeant, who had been trained as a dresser, was one of the hardest and most conscientious workers as well as one of the best fellows that I met in Turkey.

I agreed to pay all those whom I took over wages at the rate of half what they received from the Turkish Government in addition to their ordinary pay; and as they could never look forward with any degree of certainty to receiving their money from the Turks, they had an additional incentive to faithful service, and I was enabled to secure a direct control over them by holding the power of the purse. I also took on a Hungarian surgeon, named Schmidt, to assist us. He was given a room in the hospital, and was made the house surgeon; so that in cases of hæmorrhage there was always a competent person ready to arrest it until one of us could come up.

We soon had everything ship-shape in the old *khan*, which was converted into a well equipped hospital, containing at the outset three hundred beds. It was very different from the awful building that I had left behind in Plevna. The main ward of our Stafford House Hospital was a hundred feet long, with a width of sixty-five feet and a height of thirty feet. It was ventilated and lighted by means of large glass skylights, and warmed by two large stoves. This ward contained ninety-eight beds, and there was another large one containing sixty-two beds, while smaller rooms, opening off these large ones, provided accommodation for six or eight patients each, the total number of patients when I took over control being three hundred. We had an operating-room, a storeroom, and all the necessary offices.

In the main wards the scene was almost picturesque, if any hospital ever could be picturesque; for the place was scrupulously clean, and the beds were dressed with Persian quilts, bright with the most gorgeous colours. As the midday sunbeams poured in through the skylights overhead, they lit up the scarlets and the greens, the cobalt blues and lemon yellows, the deep crimson of the rose, the pink of the geranium, and the purple of the violet, until the whole place looked like an immense garden full of flowers. But against this background of brilliant colours the white, drawn faces of the wounded soldiers stood out in pitiful contrast, and the gay hues only threw into still stronger relief the ghastly sufferings.

At first we had no cases of sickness, and none but wounded men to treat. Our death-rate was low—in the first week we only had six deaths out of three hundred patients, and we sent thirty men out cured to rejoin their regiments. After the hideous experiences in Plevna, this state of things was a blessed relief, and we became quite light-hearted. But before I left Erzeroum I had seen sufferings and horrors before which the sufferings and horrors of the Plevna hospital paled into insignificance.

The first sign of coming trouble was the discovery one morning of a case of genuine typhus and several cases of typhoid. These we sent away at once to the medical central hospital, as we took over our hospital with the stipulation that we were to treat only wounded cases. But that solitary case of typhus worried me a good deal, and it seemed to presage with dreadful certainty the mischief that was to come.

Chapter 13

A Beleaguered City

As we went round the hospital wards, now that fever had made its appearance, needless to say that we examined each patient anxiously, and every day we found three or four more cases of typhus among the wounded men. These we weeded out, and placed in a room specially prepared to receive them, for on account of the severity of their wounds we could not send them away to the central hospital.

Early in December the weather got very bad. There was a heavy fall of snow, and the hospitals were filled with sick, until altogether there were about four thousand sick and wounded in the town. Captain Morisot and Mr. Harvey were most valuable assistants; but in the first week of December Mr. Harvey, who was wanted at Constantinople, had to leave, much to our regret. Williams, our dragoman, who had been delayed on the road by the bad weather, came up with the stores, and took his place, turning out a very useful assistant.

Pyæmia began to make great ravages, and the intense cold increased the sufferings of the wounded. I amputated a man's arm at the shoulder joint, and hoped to pull him through; but the weather beat me, for he took pleurisy, and went off in a day.

Pinkerton, Woods, and myself lived in the great, bare Armenian house with Fetherstonhaugh and Denniston. Every morning we went off to our respective hospitals, returned home to lunch, and then went back in the afternoon to work again. Wood for fuel cost us two pence per pound, and rations were poor and scarce; but we pegged away doggedly, and Mr. Zohrab was very good to us. He had a splendid house amply provisioned for the winter, and he was most hospitable in his invitations to dinner; while his wife, who was a charming Englishwoman, was always cheering us up, and his two sons often gave us a hand at the hospital.

An ominous silence was maintained by our Russian besiegers, and we found that they had withdrawn the greater number of the troops from Erzeroum in order to carry out the assault on Kars. Typhus, *pyæmia*, pneumonia, and the bitter, deadening cold were working for the Russians, and slew as many of the defenders of Erzeroum daily as would have fallen under the heaviest shell fire. Woods became ill; and as there was evidently heavy work before us, I sent him down to Constantinople, thus reducing the strength of our little medical garrison by one.

Snow began to fall heavily, and soon the streets were covered to a depth of several feet. At night the thermometer dropped to forty degrees below freezing-point, and the soldiers in the open suffered severely. Every morning five or six men were found frozen to death on outpost duty, lying in the snow with their eyes closed and their rifles clasped in their arms.

Meanwhile General Melikoff was making preparations for his great attack on Kars, and at last the long expected assault was delivered, and the Russians with their strange, untranslatable cry of "*Nichivo*," which is the ultimate expression of a reckless bravery that refuses to count any cost, swept in upon the Turkish batteries, and took the town.

Melikoff could not accommodate his numerous wounded prisoners with quarters, so he conceived the brilliant idea of sending them on to us; and, presenting each man who could walk with a blanket and a few *piastres*, he despatched the men on their journey from Kars to Erzeroum. What a march was that! The snow lay thickly on the frozen ground, and for league after league the legion of the wounded dragged themselves along, staining the snow with their blood as they "blazed" their pathway from Kars to Erzeroum. Hundreds dropped dead on that terrible march, and Mukhtar Pasha told me that out of two thousand men who left Kars only three hundred and seventeen reached Erzeroum. About fifty of the survivors came to our hospital, and one of them told me that he left with a party of thirty, only ten of whom came through alive, and of these ten no fewer than seven lost all their toes from frostbite.

Some typical cases of frostbite were grotesque in their ghastliness. Fancy the experience of two men who came to us for treatment after dragging their wounded bodies over the hundred and eighty miles of snow that separated Kars from Erzeroum. Their hands had been frostbitten early in the march, and for the last week nothing was left but the skeleton of each hand from the wrist to the finger-tips. Every particle of flesh had rotted off, and the bones were black with decomposition. They came to me holding out their blackened skeleton hands feebly and pitifully before them, and I lopped off the maimed remnants at the wrists. Both these men died from the effects of that terrible march, which not even the lurid imagination of a Dante could easily rival.

We in our turn had to send out some of our lightly wounded men to relieve the congested hospitals and to diminish the chances of an epidemic. On Christmas Day we sent away sixty-six, most of whom were wounded in the hands or arms, and they started to march to Baiburt. We were able to give them warm jerseys, under-clothing, long stockings, and woollen comforters, thanks to the generosity of Lord Blantyre; and three days later we sent out another thirty, each of whom got ten *piastres* from Lord Blantyre's fund in addition to the clothes. All of the men reached Baiburt safely.

The hospitals were soon so crowded that typhus and typhoid fever raged with added violence, and hospital gangrene, that I had seen before in Plevna, once more made its dreaded appearance. We had eight cases in our hospital, and lost three of them. *Pyæmia* and frostbite were the other chief causes of mortality.

Pinkerton and I, with Morisot and Williams to help us, managed our three hundred beds fairly well; but it was a great blow to us when Williams took the fever, and was added to the sick list. When Pinkerton and myself met Fetherstonhaugh and Denniston in the evenings at dinner, we used to look at each other curiously, wondering which would be the first. It was Fetherstonhaugh. He was attacked by a kind of remittent fever, but tried to shake it off and went about his work as usual. One night, when the rest of us were at dinner, Fetherstonhaugh came into the dining-room, and remarked that there were three men with their throats cut in his room. We rushed in, but found nothing, and came to the conclusion that it was time Fetherstonhaugh left off work, so we sent him down to Trebizond.

That was the last that I saw of him for a long, long time; but the curious agency that for want of a better name we call coincidence brought us together again after many years in a strange way. It happened in Melbourne, when I had settled down to steady work at my practice, and had almost forgotten the stirring days in Asia Minor, except for a few rare glimpses when memory lifted the veil. I was engaged one day at the Supreme Court as a professional witness in some case; and when I stepped out of the box, it occurred to me that I knew the face of a man who was sitting below me in the body of the court.

"Hullo, Ryan, how are you?" he said.

I looked again, and recognized Denniston, who told me that he had come out from England on a trip, and had just strolled into the court out of idle curiosity. As he was talking to me, I looked through the door leading into the passage, and saw another face that I recognized.

"I wonder what has become of Charlie Fetherstonhaugh?" said Denniston.

"Look behind you. There he is," I replied, as Charlie Fetherstonhaugh himself came up, sound and hearty, having left the three men with their throats cut behind him in the hospital at Erzeroum. He too had dropped from the clouds, and strolled into the court by mere chance. So we had dinner together that evening, and great was the jollification thereat.

At our Stafford House Hospital in Erzeroum we had a continual stream of fresh cases, for the cavalry were continually making dashes against the Russians, and small affairs between outposts came off nearly every day; so that as fast as one lot of patients died or were discharged cured, a second lot were brought in. Cases of frostbite became very numerous, and many a time I had to lop off a man's feet or hands the flesh of which was simply rotting on the bones. Rations too were getting scarce, and as there was not enough food for every one the prisoners in the gaol were the first to suffer.

The interior of that Erzeroum gaol was a sight not soon to be forgotten. Crowded together in a state of indescribable filth, the prisoners fought with the ferocity of wild beasts for the few handfuls of raw grain that the guard threw to them occasionally. Still, we continued to get beef tea and mutton broth for our wounded, and I made a point of going round the wards and administering it myself to those who needed it.

It was in connection with a matter of rations that I remember Edmund O'Donovan especially. O'Donovan was one of the wildest, most brilliant, and original geniuses who ever left Ireland to follow up the avocation of a war correspondent. He came to dinner with us one night, and his wit and versatility made a great impression upon me. The next time that I saw him was in response to an urgent request that I should call upon him and get him out of a scrape. His adventure was so thoroughly characteristic that I may be excused for narrating it.

O'Donovan, it seemed, with the warm-hearted generosity of his race, had invited half a dozen Circassian officers to dine with him, and had prepared an appetizing banquet for them. Among the dishes was an *entrée* so savoury, so succulent, so entirely satisfying to the palate of an epicure, that the Circassians, like the simple children of nature that they were, sent back their plates again and again for more. There was something new and strange yet delightful withal about that *entrée*. The meat was white and delicate and tender, the gravy was of a luscious brown, and in a fit of absence of mind the Circassian officers loaded up the whole cargo, while they laughed politely at O'Donovan's best Dublin stories, which were chiefly remarkable for having points where one never expected them.

Then O'Donovan expressed a hope that they had enjoyed the dinner, and the Circassians were most effusive in their thanks. Really they had never eaten anything like that *entrée* before, and would their host mind telling them the recipe?

"Begorra, I can tell ye that aisy enough," spluttered O'Donovan, with a mighty laugh. "Ye've been atin' the natest slip of a pig I've ever seen out of Connaught, and beautifully cooked he was too." Then he explained to them in Turkish more clearly, and these good Mussulmen burst into eruption. What a shindy there was at that dinner-table! The Circassians could not have been quicker if they had been at Donnybrook Fair, and they rushed at their host with the first weapons that came handy. O'Donovan did very well with the bottles for a minute or two, and afterwards with the leg of a chair; but they were too many for him, and when the table was upset and the lamps put out there was a fairly lively five minutes round the wreck of the dinner-table and of the empty dish that had once contained a sucking-pig *à l'Irlandaise*.

The Moslem Circassians, full to repletion with the flesh of the accursed creature, fought under a disadvantage; and when O'Donovan's servants rushed in and took their master's part, the issue was no longer in doubt. Although the revolvers were going freely, only one man was hurt, and it appeared that O'Donovan had shot him in the arm. The affair created a great deal of excitement at the time, and the Circassians vowed vengeance for the insult; but we managed to pacify them eventually, and there were so many other things requiring attention that the trouble soon blew over.

This was not the only occasion that O'Donovan got into a scrape, for not long afterwards, while promenading on the roof of his house, the idea occurred to him that a little revolver practice might improve his aim. Drawing his six-shooter, he proceeded to blaze away at a dog that was gnawing a bone in the middle of the street; but like another famous character in fiction, he "missed the blue-bottle and floored the Mogul." In other words, a bullet which went wide of the dog found its billet in a fleshy part of the body of a very stout Turkish woman, who on receiving this flank attack fled in great disorder screaming loudly.

O'Donovan sent for me to help him out of this difficulty too, and we had to give the woman £10 to square her. The erratic marksman was then the war correspondent of the *Daily News*; but I never saw an account of this incident in his graphic descriptive sketches. He left Erzeroum in December, and afterwards, when the army of Hicks Pasha was cut to pieces in Egypt, O'Donovan met a soldier's death.

At this time we lost the services of Mr. Zohrab, the consul; for after the fall of Kars, Lord Derby, desiring to avoid any complications in the event of the Russians occupying Erzeroum, instructed the British consul to retire at once to Constantinople. Mr. Zohrab and his wife and sons accordingly left the town, much to our regret, for they had been very helpful to us. When he went, however, he handed over to us his house, which was fully provisioned, amply supplied with fuel, and provided with a well stocked cellar. We took possession at once, and after the poor kind of way in which we had been living our new quarters were most luxurious.

Although we personally were much better off than before, yet the condition of the bulk of the people in the town was getting steadily worse every day. Stores of every kind were getting scarce, and Kurd Ismael Pasha, who replaced Mukhtar Pasha as commander-in-chief when that officer was ordered to Constantinople, had a difficult task in administration. Towards the end of December it became necessary to relieve the town of a portion of the population, and an expedition consisting of four hundred men and two hundred women and children was ordered to start for Erzinghan, a town which was supposed to be five days' journey distant from Erzeroum.

This march rivalled in its horrors the march of the wounded men from Kars; for before the expedition had gone a day's journey from Erzeroum a fearful snowstorm swept down upon the hapless creatures, and when the miserable remnant had dragged themselves back to their starting-point it was found that of the two hundred women and children not a single soul remained. All died where they fell, including the wife of the colonel commanding the expedition, and were buried under the drifting heaps of snow that the wind piled high over the uncoffined remains. Of the soldiers who got back to Erzeroum the greater number perished from frostbite, dysentery, and exposure. It was an awful holocaust.

In spite of fever and dysentery, gunshot wounds in horrible variety and septic disease in every hospital, so strangely is the Anglo-Saxon mind constituted that we decided to "enjoy ourselves" at Christmas, although the Russians were practically knocking at our gates. My previous Christmas dinner consisted of a handful of maize cobs eaten in solitude on the ice-bound road to Orkhanieh. During the intervening year I had lived and worked and suffered much—and almost to my own astonishment I was still alive. So here at Erzeroum I proposed to have a Christmas festivity, and Pinkerton, Denniston, and Woods eagerly accepted the suggestion. We decided to invite all the European doctors in the town, and to give them a real English Christmas dinner, for which great preparations had to be made.

When we took over Mr. Zohrab's house, we also assumed a right title and interest in the services of two sturdy henchmen. One was old Tom Rennison, who had been *dragoman* for General Williams during the siege of Erzeroum thirty years before, and the other was an Armenian named Vachin. Tom Rennison, veteran campaigner as he was, had never seen mince-pies made, so to speak, under fire; and Vachin knew more about the preparation of *pilaf* than plum pudding. Consequently not only the arrangement of the *menu*, but the actual work of cooking it, devolved upon the medical staff; and I am sorry to say that, though by this time there were few things in surgery which we would not attempt, from disarticulation of a thumb to amputation of a thigh, nevertheless in the science of cooking we were painfully unlearned. Lister was an open book to us; but the dark sayings of Brillat-Savarin were as obscure as the Rig-Vedas.

Pinkerton, Woods, and myself held a consultation over the plum pudding, which was intended to beget envy and jealousy in the hearts of the Austrian and Hungarian doctors, and to be a dazzling example of the superiority of Anglo-Saxon cooking over the unsubstantial kickshaws of continental cuisines. I noticed that Vachin, who was always an ill disposed fellow, looked undisguisedly contemptuous of our preparations, and that old Tom Rennison was obviously fluctuating between the extremes of hope and fear. It is not easy to recollect exactly what was in that pudding. Denniston had heard that suet was an ingredient of supreme importance, so the yellow fat was cut from the joint of beef which had been moving about the yard only two days before as the sirloin of Mr. Zohrab's best heifer.

We found plenty of currants and raisins among the stores; but there was no candied peel, and the spices which had been imported from Teheran somehow smelt quite unlike the unconvincing substance that we remembered to have seen in our youth at the suburban grocer's. We had plenty of flour of course, and we mixed our *chef-d'œuvre* in a big brown pot. It was a viscous, œdematous mass, of the consistency of soft india-rubber, when we had done mixing it, and it resembled nothing so much as a bucketful of Zante currants which had fallen by accident into a glue-pot. The other fellows made some very discouraging remarks; but I tied up the ghastly mixture in half a clean sheet, and sat up all night on Christmas Eve boiling it in the iron pot.

On Christmas night we had a grand banquet, and about twenty other European doctors came in answer to our invitations to receive our hospitality. We explained to them at some length that we were going to give them a real English dinner, which was a treat that they had probably never enjoyed before, and very likely might never enjoy again.

Certainly the beef was a little tough, as the hapless heifer had only been sacrificed on the previous day, and then there was no horse-radish and very little gravy; but the geese were first-rate. Like everything else in Asia Minor, they were evidently of great antiquity. Probably they had seen the former siege of Erzeroum; but age, which weakens most other things, had strengthened their limbs and steeled their muscles, until to disintegrate the closely knitted tissues was a veritable feat of strength, and one swallowed a mouthful with the comfortable glow of satisfaction that follows the surmounting of a desperate difficulty. Of the mince-pies I cannot speak with certainty, for Woods had taken complete control over the manufacture of these delicious delicacies, and, much as I respected my colleague, I was suspicious of his ingredients.

I can testify, however, from the simple experience of lifting one up from the dish that the mince-pies were solid and weighty additions to the *menu*. I waited with some anxiety for the pudding, and the happiness that the artist feels in a work completed came over me as I saw old Tom Rennison bearing in the dish containing the pudding, surrounded by leaping tongues of blue flame from the burning brandy. Up to this period the Hungarian doctors had been politely complimentary, and had accepted slabs of heifer's flesh as hard as boot leather and chunks of goose that would have made excellent ammunition for siege artillery as typical dishes of a correct English dinner.

By dint of washing the food down with plenty of wine and many tumblers of brandy-and-water, they struggled along gamely through the first courses; but when they received their portions of the plum pudding they distinctly jibbed. With the flames playing round its charred, excoriated surface, it certainly had a diabolical look, and it held together with a glutinous consistency that for an appreciable number of seconds defied the attack even of a carving-knife. The Hungarian doctors viewed their plates with an alarmed suspicion that was too genuine to be concealed, and I must confess that when I got a spoonful of my masterpiece into my mouth the taste did not compensate in the least for the difficulty of detaching the fragment from the surrounding bed-rock. That was the first and last time that I cooked a plum pudding.

In spite of these little drawbacks, however, we all thoroughly enjoyed our Christmas dinner, and we made a fair hole in Mr. Zohrab's cellar, which was well stocked with wines and spirits and also with beer and porter. The dawn was coming up over the snow on the distant hills when we separated, laughing, singing, and wishing each other a Merry Christmas and a Happy New Year.

Within a fortnight nearly every one of us was down with typhus, and within a month more than half of our number were dead.

The first of the English doctors to catch the fever was poor Pinkerton. He was always terribly frightened of it, and used to carry quantities of camphor about in his pockets as a disinfectant; but with the epidemic raging as it was, any attempt at personal disinfection for a medical man attending the cases was practically hopeless. Pinkerton was always talking about his dread of getting typhus, and saying that if he caught it he would never get over it. This made Denniston and myself very anxious about him; for though he was a splendidly built, handsome fellow, with an excellent constitution, his apprehensions laid him open to attack more readily, and would certainly decrease his chance of recovery if the fever got its clutch upon him. Wrought up to a state of high nervous tension by continually moving among the sick and the dying, it was not to be wondered at that we attached significance to the veriest trifles, and both Denniston and myself recollected with dismay that every one of our patients who had had a presentiment of death up to that time had died.

On the last day of the old year Pinkerton became ill, and we put him to bed. He was very despondent, and I could see at once that he had an attack of the most malignant typhus. He was a very bad patient, and would take neither his medicine nor his nourishment without a great deal of trouble. Our number was now reduced to two, and Denniston and myself looked at each other every morning with questioning gaze. Fortunately Denniston had had malignant typhus in his student days at Glasgow, and was not likely to take it again, while I felt that if I could only pull through we might still be able to keep on the two hospitals. After three or four days Pinkerton fell into a semi-comatose condition, from which he never emerged, but lay in bed moaning feebly, and talking incoherently at intervals of fighting and of operations and of places and people whose names were unfamiliar to me.

How clearly those dreadful days come back! We had the ever present, bitter, numbing cold, and the ceaseless work in the hospital as one passed from bed to bed, from the moaning wounded to the poor wretches who were being consumed by the fires of fever, and thence to the ghastly mutilated creatures who had lost hands, feet, ears, and even noses by frostbite. Then there was in addition the anxiety about Pinkerton, and the fear that one or both of us two survivors would succumb to the strain, and thus leave the bulk of the sick and wounded without medical succour. In addition to it all was the nervous strain of waiting for the expected Russian attack, which would have been gladly welcomed as a relief from the intolerable tension.

During these early days of January, 1878, the mortality in Erzeroum was something appalling. Out of a total number of about seventeen thousand troops in the town, there were on one day no fewer than three hundred and two deaths, and the daily death-rate frequently rose to two hundred! The weak, emaciated survivors had hardly strength left to dig graves for their dead comrades in the hard and frozen ground. At last they gave up even the pretence of digging, and the bodies were simply carted out about a mile from the main thoroughfares of the town, and left in the snow just inside the city walls.

Of course all conveyances were placed on runners while the snow was on the ground, and the little sleighs which served as dead-carts passed our house every morning at about ten o'clock with their mournful loads collected from the various hospitals. The bodies of the dead soldiers were stripped of their clothing and wrapped in clean white sheets according to the Moslem custom. Each little sleigh contained ten or twelve bodies, and as I looked out in the morning I could see the burial parties going out on duty. The white-sheeted corpses were packed closely together; and as the sleighs had no tailboards and

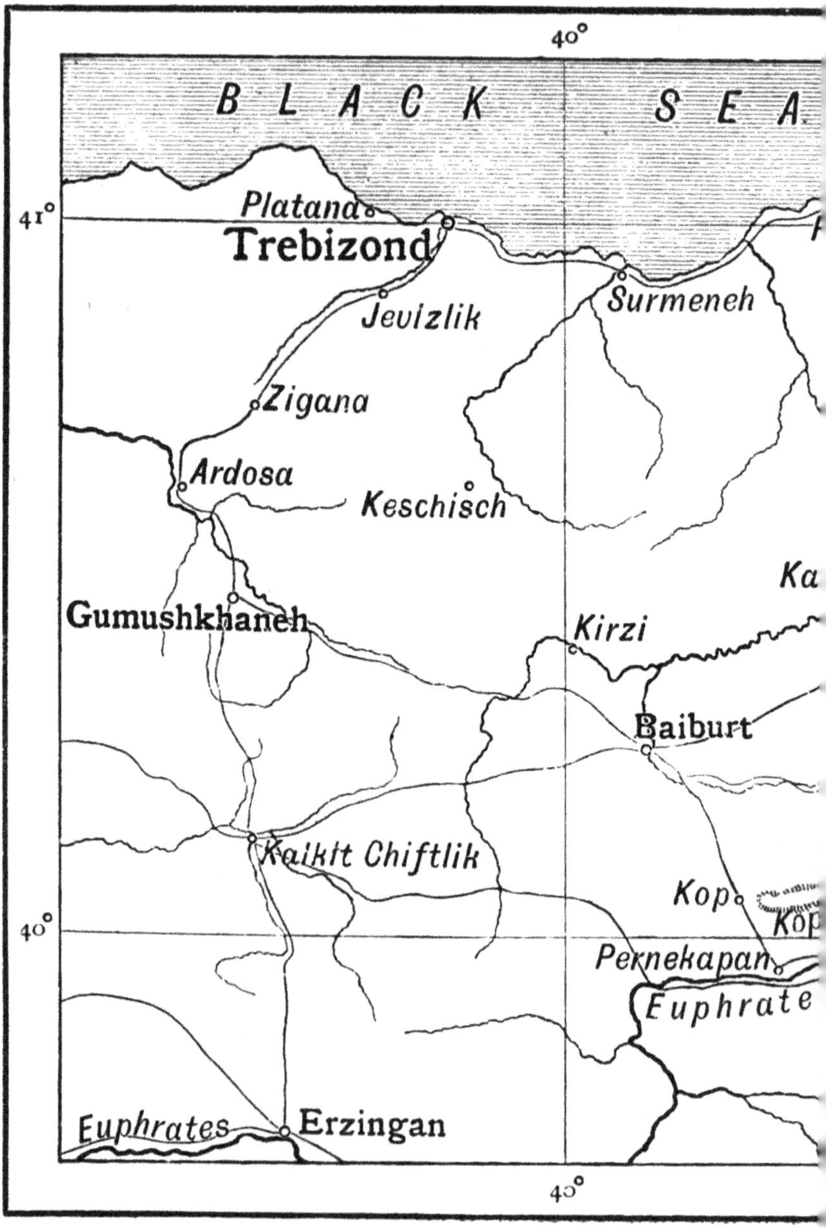
40°
BLACK SEA
41°
Platana
Trebizond
Surmeneh
Jevizlik
Zigana
Ardosa
Keschisch
Ka
Gumushkhaneh
Kirzi
Baiburt
Kalkit Chiftlik
Kop
40°
Pernekapan
Euphrate
Euphrates
Erzingan
40°

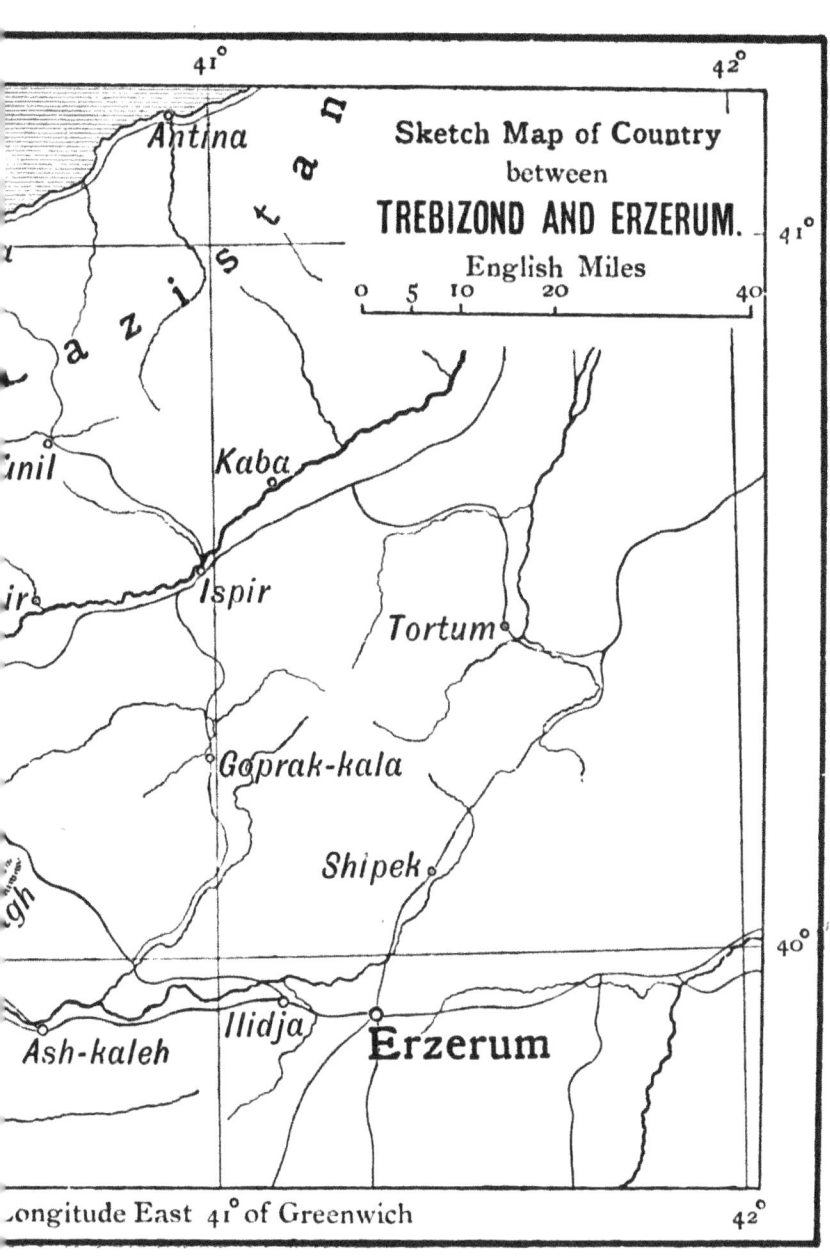

were very small, the naked feet of the corpses projected out at the back in a horribly grotesque fashion. As the little vehicles, which were dragged by the fatigue squads, glided in ghostly silence over the frozen snow a long howl in the distance broke the stillness. This was taken up by another, and another, and another, until the voices of fully fifteen hundred famished dogs came through the crisp, clear wintry air with terrible significance, chilling the marrow of the listener as he watched the long procession of helpless, white-sheeted corpses moving slowly over the white-sheeted ground.

A Parsee's obsequies, when the filthy vultures flap their wings and gather to the feast, must be an eerie sight; a Gussein's funeral in the Ganges, where the great flat-nosed alligators swarm expectantly, must stir even the sluggish imagination of the impassive Hindoo. But surely no man ever had more dreadful burial rites than were celebrated daily over hundreds of the dead inside the walls of Erzeroum, where the famished dogs disputed the possession of the poor mutilated remnants with sickening ferocity, and where the only prayers over the bodies of the dead were the muttered growls of the worrying pack. There is a short passage in "The Siege of Corinth" which exactly describes the grisly scene. Lord Byron wrote of Alp the renegade as he paced under the walls of Corinth these lines:

> And he saw the lean dogs beneath the wall
> Hold o'er the dead their carnival,
> Gorging and growling o'er carcase and limb.
> They were too busy to bark at him.
> From a Tartar's skull they had stripped the flesh
> As ye peel the fig when its fruit is fresh,
> And their white tusks crunched o'er the whiter skull
> As it slipped through their jaws when their edge grew dull,
> As they lazily mumbled the bones of the dead
> When they scarce could rise from the spot where they fed.

In this passage the poet has described with more detail than one cares to give in a plain narrative the scene which was enacted every morning in the early part of that month of January within the walls of Erzeroum.

It was about January 8 that I took the fever, which was by this time ravaging both the civil and military population. At first I tried to shake it off, and continued to walk about with aching head and quaking limbs in the hope that it might not have got a fair hold of me. On the second day I became quite stupid, though I still refused to go to bed, and on the evening of that day Pinkerton died.

Next morning we buried him. Wood was so difficult to get, that we were put to great straits to make a coffin for him; but at last we contrived one out of an old packing-case. Pinkerton was a very tall man, and the flimsy coffin was hardly big enough for the body. There was scarcely enough wood to make the lid fit properly. When we were making the preparations for the burial, I was myself nearly delirious with typhus, and almost the last thing that I can remember before going off altogether was the sight of the miserable coffin with a gaping crevice in the top, through which the end of poor Pinkerton's silky fair beard was protruding.

Denniston notified Hakki Bey, the civil governor, of our loss; and an escort of soldiers came down and buried our comrade by the side of Dr. Guppy, who had died on duty in the same place before we arrived there. The burial service was read by the Rev. Mr. Cole, an American missionary, who was in Erzeroum, accompanied by his wife and family and by a young American lady, also engaged in missionary work among the Armenians. Then the soldiers fired a volley over the grave, and the career of the fine young army surgeon was closed.

When I was put to bed, the whole strength of the medical and assisting staff of the two English hospitals, Lord Blantyre's Hospital and that of the Stafford House Committee, was reduced to one man, namely, Dr. Denniston. Guppy and Pinkerton were dead, and Williams, Morisot, and myself were down with typhus. Under these circumstances, Denniston was left with the two hospitals full of patients to look after as well as us three at home, and he rose to the occasion most heroically.

Of course at that time I was unconscious of everything, but I found out afterwards what happened. Denniston handed the English hospital back to the Turkish administration which had managed it before our arrival, and he secured an assistant from the French consul to help him with the other one and with us. He told me afterwards that I made a very good patient, but I doubt it. I can just remember him coming in to see me one day and giving me a pill, which, though I was almost delirious, I made a great pretence of swallowing, but really kept it under my tongue and spat it out as soon as he had left the room!

The American missionary, Mr. Cole, used to come and sit with me sometimes. I had known him before I was ill, and admired his character greatly. He seemed to me to be a very fine type of man and a true

Christian. In Erzeroum at that time the healing of souls was attended with as much danger as the healing of bodies, and there were martyrs in both causes. Mr. Cole lost one of his children from typhus, and the bright, winning, and enthusiastic young American lady who was working as a missionary in conjunction with him and Mrs. Cole also laid down her life in the noble service in which she had engaged.

During the day, while Denniston was away at the hospital fighting a desperate single-handed battle against wounds and disease of every kind, we patients at home had many kindly visitors. Morisot and Williams got over the worst of the illness sooner than I did; but for some time we all required watching.

I am sorry to say that during my illness I grievously erred against good taste, and quite forgot the esteem and regard which I venture to believe I had always hitherto shown towards ladies. The fact of the matter was that I had seen so few ladies in the past eighteen months that the sight of them irritated and annoyed my disordered brain exceedingly. So it came about that, when two sweet-faced French nuns, who had heard from Dr. Denniston of his desperate need for nurses, called in and visited me, I viewed their presence with the profoundest suspicion and distrust. I had been working for so long among great, strong, hairy-faced Turks that my delirious imagination failed to recognize these two young nuns, with their rustling skirts and their soft white hands, as fellow creatures at all, and I expressed such terror and alarm at their appearance that the poor things were obliged to fly.

In the *Ingoldsby Legends* there is a picture of François Xavier Auguste, the gay *mousquetaire*, sitting up in bed in an attitude of horror, while on chairs at each side of his pillow sit duplicate images of Sister Thérèse. I must have looked very much like that when the well meaning nuns came in to sit by me, and found my language and demeanour so terrifying that they had to decamp at once, leaving me to the less exciting ministrations of a dear old Capuchin monk called Father Basilio, who was sent to take their place. He used to sit up with me in the long night watches and humour all my fancies, kindly old soul that he was; but I think he never expected that I would pull through.

Though young in years, I was a veteran as far as horrors were concerned, and I can truthfully say that I was absolutely without fear of death. Possibly it was this that saved me, for I remember telling Denniston at the worst period of my illness that he need have no fear on my account, for I had not the slightest intention of "pegging out."

I was very bad for about twelve days, and the events of that time of illness impressed themselves on my brain in the vaguest and most indistinct manner. Still, it is interesting from the scientific point of view to note that impressions can be made even upon a semi-comatose brain which are sufficiently strong to be of subsequent use. The negatives on the convolutions of the brain were not very sharply outlined; but the will, like a skilful photographer, could retouch them afterwards until they made a perfect picture. This scientific fact I was able to demonstrate myself, to the great confusion of our Armenian *dragoman* Vachin.

It happened this way. When I recovered from the fever, I was helping Denniston to make an inventory of poor Pinkerton's personal effects, so that we could send them to his relatives, when we made the unpleasant discovery that a sum of £20 which he had in his possession was missing. Pinkerton used to carry the money in Turkish *liras* in the pocket of his trousers; and as I had been shifted into his room after his death because it was larger and airier than my own, his trousers were hanging on a nail on the wall right opposite my bed. We examined the pockets, but they were empty.

Then I began to think back and to think hard. Gradually there appeared before the eye of my mind the picture of a shadowy, misty, unsubstantial figure, that wobbled grievously from side to side as it walked, and seemed to turn round and round with the room, the bed, the chair, and the window, which all swung and oscillated like the engines of the little Messageries steamer that brought us up to Trebizond. What on earth was the captain of the Messageries steamer going to do! and how the little tub was rolling, to be sure! Was it the captain, though, or someone else? I fastened all the will power of my brain, healthy once more, upon the misty shadow cast upon its disordered surface during illness.

I saw the scene again, more distinctly now, and noted that the wobbling figure approached the wall exactly at the spot where the trousers hung on the nail opposite my bed. The engines seemed to be slowing down, little by little the room ceased to revolve, and at last the figure turned round towards my bed, and I saw the face. It was not the captain of the steamer, but it was Vachin, our dragoman, and he was deliberately counting out money from poor Pinkerton's trousers pocket.

All this came back to me with greater clearness the longer I thought over it; and at last I felt morally certain that Vachin was the thief, and that he had cynically taken the money before my eyes, knowing that

I was delirious, and confident that I would never recover to bear witness against him.

We taxed the Armenian with the theft; and when I told him that it was no use denying it, for I had seen him take the money, he confessed his guilt. A short consultation between Denniston and myself was followed by the despatch of a note to Hakki Bey, the civil governor; and as a punishment for misdeeds in the past and an incentive to virtue in the future, Vachin was consigned to the Erzeroum general prison pending the pleasure of the governor. We got back the £20 from him before he went, and for three weeks we left him in a place, from which the Black Hole of Calcutta would have been a pleasant change, to meditate upon the instability of human happiness. We sent him some blankets and also food at intervals, besides going up occasionally to see how he was getting on and whether he was truly repentant.

The condition of the unfortunate wretch, however, was so deplorable, and the interior of that prison, with its gangs of half-frozen, half-starved prisoners fighting fiercely among themselves for the scanty dole of raw grain and old rags that were thrown among them by the gaolers, was so distressing, that we relented, and procured a release for our thievish dragoman from Hakki Bey. On the night that he was discharged from prison he deserted to the Russians, and we never saw him again. And so farewell to Vachin.

CHAPTER 14

The Surrender of Erzeroum

When I rose from my sick-bed I was very thin and weak; but under Denniston's care I soon picked up my strength, and at last he allowed me to go out for a walk. It was the first week in February, and the snow was beginning to melt on the low ground; although beyond the valley in which Erzeroum stood it still lay thick upon the hills, and Kopdagh in the distance rose to a crystal spear-point of dazzling whiteness outlined sharply against the sky.

Contrasted with the serene purity of the mountain heights, the squalid horrors of Erzeroum in the valley struck home to the imagination with redoubled force. Here and there, as I paced through the streets with the unsteady gait and the frequent pauses of a man scarcely yet recovered from fever, I could see in the dirty, brownish, melting slush grim evidences of disease and death. The hordes of dogs which infested the town had dragged the bones of the dead men who had been abandoned to them into the very streets; and as the snow which hid the poor remains for a time began to melt, the bones reappeared in ghastly fashion. Close to the doorstep of our own quarters I saw a skull picked as clean as a piece of ivory; and before I had gone a hundred yards another pitiable sight met my eyes. It was the bone of a man's arm, from which the hand was missing, and the cleanness of the cut showed that it had been amputated during life. Probably it had been a case of frostbite.

On every side, as I walked on feebly and slowly, I saw these human remains peeping shamefacedly from the snow that would no longer cover them; and a few inquiries showed me that while I was raving with the fever and unconscious of all around me, terrible things had been happening in Erzeroum. The place had become a veritable pesthouse; and while the civil and military population had alike fallen under the scourge of typhus, by far the heaviest losses had occurred in the ranks of the medical staff. No fewer than twenty-seven doctors had been attacked by the disease; and the malignant form in which it appeared may be gauged from the fact that of these twenty-seven more than half had succumbed. Of the survivors I was one. I knew then—and have remembered it ever since—that I owed my life to the skill and care of that devoted surgeon James Denniston.

Looking round the fever-stricken town, I saw on every hand dead men lying in the snow, and living men, worn to shadows like myself, crawling feebly about the streets; while outside the gates the Russians were waiting grimly until the thaw should enable them to bring up their artillery and complete the work that sickness had begun. Then lifting my eyes to the mountains, I saw them rearing their unapproachable pinnacles to the sky, far above human suffering and weakness. The shadows of the clouds moved across the face of one great snow-field to the southward, but the ice-peak that pierced the blue above was iridescent in the sunlight. It seemed like an illustration of the words of that French poet who wrote:

En haut la cime,
En bas l'abîme.
. . .
En haut mystère,
En bas misère.

As I drew near our quarters again after my short walk, I saw a small crowd gathered near the door; and next minute I was shaking hands, with a heart too full for words, with my old friends Dr. Stoker and Dr. Stiven, who had come up from Constantinople on a mission of relief.

When I fell ill and Denniston was left alone, he managed to get a letter away to Constantinople through the Russian lines announcing the precarious position in Erzeroum, and Dr. Stoker and Dr. Stiven at once volunteered to come up as a rescue party. Reaching Trebizond on January 27, they pushed forward at once, preparations for the journey having been expedited by Mr. Biliotti; but they had to stop most of the first night at Jevislik to rest the post-horses, and here the hazardous nature of their undertaking was brought home to them. An early start was made next morning, and all that day these two heroic men pushed on with tired horses, a reluctant guide, and one hundred and fifty miles of snow and ice in front of them.

The road was excessively difficult, for the little pathway, about two feet wide, was frozen and slippery, and wound along the edge of a cliff about nine hundred feet high, while snowdrifts, which in some places were twenty feet deep, threatened to engulf them. Several times the baggage-horses fell, and the whole party had to halt and unpack and reload the animals; so that the march was much delayed, and it was two hours after dark before they reached the summit of the Zegana Pass, where they camped for the night. The next day they reached Ghumish Khané, and there for the first time since leaving Trebizond they got a relay of post-horses. A long struggle of eighteen hours brought the relief party from Ghumish Khané to Baiburt; and after procuring fresh horses with some difficulty, they pushed on to the Kop village at the foot of the worst pass on the whole road.

Here another misfortune befell them; for the guide, who had been showing an inclination to give in for several stages past, refused when they were half-way up the mountain to go a step farther, declaring that it was madness to attempt the pass in such weather, and that they were courting certain death from the avalanches that they could hear at intervals thundering down into the valley below.

Taking their lives in their hands, the two doctors left the guide to make his way back as best he could, and faced the rising path again, taking the pack-horses with them. Once the whole party were submerged in a snowdrift, but managed to get clear again; and after a great struggle of nine hours, they passed the Kopdagh, and arrived at a place called Purnekapan, where they learnt that they were close to the Russian outposts. At the top of the pass the snow lay so thick that, had it not been for the telegraph poles, the whole party must have lost their way and perished; but by dint of following the track thus marked out they were able to advance as far as Ashkaleh, where a Cossack guard was stationed.

Hoisting the British flag and also the ambulance flag, the intrepid doctors were escorted by the Cossacks to Ilidja, where they were well received by the Russian general Sistovitch; and after some delay, caused by the necessity of telegraphing to the Grand Duke Michael for permission, they were allowed to go on to Erzeroum, which they reached on February 3. Surely that hazardous relief march of seven whole days, undertaken voluntarily, and carried out with unswerving resolution in the face of every danger, should live in the annals of the medical profession as an example of the unflinching devotion of the two brave men who made it.

Stoker and Stiven told me that the news of my illness had been received in Constantinople with great regret, and they had orders if they found me alive on their arrival at Erzeroum to send me down to the capital at once to recuperate. They also brought me an invitation from Vice-Admiral Sir Edward Commerell, who was stationed in the Gulf of Ismet, to pay him a visit on board his ship for the purpose of regaining my health.

However, it went against the grain with me to think of leaving a sinking ship; and at last we arranged that Stiven should go back, taking Captain Morisot with him, and that Stoker should remain with Denniston and me to look after the hospitals. So we said goodbye to Stiven and Morisot, and devoted ourselves anew to the hospital work. During my illness the Stafford House Hospital, which had been handed back to the Turkish authorities, had been allowed to go to the bad very much; but after four or five days' hard work we soon had everything ship-shape again.

At this period the sickness in the city was at its worst, and the ravages of typhus and typhoid were fearful. We three English doctors had our hands full, and whenever we had an hour to spare from the military hospital our time was taken up in attending upon the poorer Armenians in the city. We could have earned large fees if we had chosen to attend the wealthier classes; but we thought it right to devote all our spare time to the poor people, who had no one else to look after them.

Among our patients was the Catholic Armenian archbishop of the place, a dear old fellow, who was most grateful to Denniston and myself for attending him. When he recovered he wanted us to take a fee, but we declined; and then he insisted on presenting us with the only article of value which he possessed. This was a bracelet which had been excavated from a subterranean village of great antiquity at the foot of Mount Ararat, and consisted of a large ring of bronze, ornamented with two serpents' heads. It was supposed to be about two thousand three hundred years old or thereabouts. We accepted this strange old ornament, which might have been fashioned by some cunning artificer whose father saw the sunlight flashing on the Athenian helmets at Marathon or watched the beak of a Greek galley come crashing through the Persian ship in which he laboured at the oar at Salamis.

The serpents on the old bronze bracelet had slumbered on in the subterranean village while centuries came and went and dynasties flitted past like shadows; but at last they were restored again to the light of day. Denniston and I regarded our new acquisition with curiosity not unmixed with awe. Then in our simple, unpoetical way we decided to toss up for it, and the spin of a Turkish *piastre*, minted so to speak but yesterday, gave Denniston possession of this souvenir of the times of mighty Xerxes.

As soon as it leaked out that archæological objects were regarded with interest by the English doctors, an extraordinary variety of ancient curiosities were pressed upon our notice; and owing to the precarious situation in the town, the owners were all ready to sacrifice their treasures at an alarming reduction. There was something pathetic in the eagerness of a few of these collectors to realize upon their treasures. I was offered an iron signet ring supposed to have belonged to an exalted personage in the time of Alexander the Great for the price of a few doses of quinine; and half a bottle of brandy would have purchased me a curious black stone bearing an inscription that would puzzle the antiquity experts at the British Museum. One day an Armenian named Magack, who held an official position in the British Consulate, brought me a gold coin stamped with a bull's head. He explained to me that it was coined in the reign of the second Persian king, and that it was worth £70 in London; but the evidence on one point seemed to me as inconclusive as on the other, and I declined to purchase it at the price of £30.

Although the snow had begun to melt in the streets, it was still bitterly cold, and we knew that the Russians were only waiting for a regular thaw in order to bring up their artillery. However, we were fortunately not called upon to undergo a bombardment; for with the fall of Kars and Plevna the war was virtually at an end both in Asia Minor and in Europe, and rumours of an armistice were already beginning to be put about.

At last one day I saw a couple of Russian cavalry officers in the town; and hurrying back to my quarters as fast as possible, I sent old Tom Rennison up to headquarters to find out what had happened. He brought back news that they were two *parlementaires*, who brought telegrams from Constantinople *viâ* St. Petersburg, notifying the commander-in-chief that the town would be occupied by Russian troops in accordance with the terms of an armistice.

When old Kurd Ismail Pasha heard this news, he wept tears of rage and tore his beard in a frenzy of grief. The troops also, in spite of their terrible losses by wounds and sickness, were very despondent at the prospect of the town being occupied by the enemy without another blow being struck in its defence. Lamentations, however, were useless; and two days later the gates were opened, and General Melikoff, surrounded by his staff, rode into Erzeroum, and took up his quarters in the town.

On the same night, just as Denniston, Stoker, and myself were sitting down to a good dinner in our comfortable quarters, four Russian doctors, who had come in with Melikoff, called at our house. They belonged to the Russian Red Cross Society, and explained that they did not know where to go for the night; so we sent their horses round to our stable, and we invited them to dine with us and stay the night—an invitation which they gladly accepted. We gave them a capital dinner, which they enjoyed very much; and the only thing that marred the complete success of the gathering was the difficulty under which conversational intercourse had to be carried on.

It was on this occasion that my deplorable deficiencies in the matter of conversational French actually endangered my life, which I had managed to preserve up till then, in spite of shot and shell, fever and frostbite. Neither Stoker nor Stiven had pursued his studies in the language of diplomacy much farther than the irregular verbs which tormented them in their fourth-form days at school; and my own French, painfully acquired during my early days in Australia, and never afterwards improved by practice, was distinctly of the Stratford-atte-Bow variety. Consequently the natural embarrassment of finding conversation for the enemy within our gates as well as dinner was increased by the difficulty which we experienced in achieving any remark which we considered it in good taste to utter. Drifting naturally to professional subjects, I made a reference to our colleagues Dr. Casson and Dr. Buckby, who were captured by Cossacks on their way from Kars to Erzeroum, after having been under fire with Mukhtar Pasha's troops at the fighting round Eolia-tepe and Nalban-tepe.

I wanted to say that I had heard that the Russians treated the two doctors who were taken prisoners with great kindness, and made things as pleasant as possible for them. What I did say, however, falling into the common schoolboy error of attempting to render an idiom in one language by a phrase of similar sound in another, was this. "*J'ai entendu,*" I remarked, with a smile intended to convey grateful appreciation of services rendered, but which was interpreted as a sinister and sardonic grimace denoting a deliberate intention to insult, "*que vous avez fait beaucoup de plaisanteries pour nos deux amis.*"

There was an awkward pause. It was just that sort of pause which occurs at a large dinner party when you inquire audibly from your neighbour the name of the hideously ugly woman who is sitting opposite, and he replies that it is his wife. Then the four Russian doctors began to jabber excitedly to each other, and one of them, jumping to his feet, hurled half a dozen rapid sentences at me, which I dimly felt denoted astonishment, anger, and a demand for satisfaction. It was very clear that I had put my foot in it somehow; but to correct my mistake I strove in vain. The more I said the less it pleased our guests, who loudly insisted upon a duel. This was a pretty go. Morisot, who would have been my best friend in this emergency, was unfortunately in Constantinople; but necessity sharpens one's wits wonderfully, and it flashed upon me in a moment that Magack, the owner of the gold coin with the bull's head that was stamped during the reign of the second Persian king, could speak French admirably.

Accordingly the invaluable numismatist was summoned in hot haste; and although I am sure that he never forgave me for not buying that bull's head, he condescended to explain to our guests the difficulty in which the defects of my education had landed me. The Russian doctors turned out to be very good fellows after all, and when they left us General Melikoff sent an *aide* to thank us for the hospitality which we had shown to them.

Captain Serge Pizareff was the name of the *aide-de-camp* who came to call on us, and a very pleasant young fellow he was. He told us that the Russians would make a formal entry into the town next day; and that if we liked to see the spectacle, he would send us horses and place himself at our disposal, an offer which, needless to say, we accepted.

There was one thing about Captain Serge Pizareff which struck me very favourably. He had been to England, and spoke English as well as most Englishmen. I argued from that circumstance that the Russian doctors must have dropped a hint as to our deficiencies in the matter of French; but I was prepared to overlook the humiliation for the sake of the convenience.

We got a capital view of the spectacle, thanks to the kindness of Captain Pizareff; for some Cossacks brought us horses in the morning, and we rode out to the large open space inside the walls where the demonstration was to take place. It was a most impressive demonstration. Outside the town a *corps d'armée* of sixty thousand Russian troops, belonging to all branches of the service, was stationed in the various villages. It was not deemed advisable to bring them all in at once; but detachments from every regiment, including cavalry, infantry, and artillery, were marched forward and brigaded outside the gates. Then at the word of command, while the bands played the regimental quicksteps, they came forward, with colours flying, and entered Erzeroum without striking a blow, across the ground where those same regiments had been swept by the fire from the redoubts along the walls a couple of months before, and had been hurled back in terrible disorder.

General Melikoff reviewed his troops in the great open space between the town and the redoubts which defended the walls. It was a crisp, clear, exhilarating day, and the hard, smooth surface of the glistening snow was still strong enough to bear the troops without sinking in, though here and there an officer's horse would put his foot through the solid crust into the soft powdery snow below and flounder back again, plunging and snorting.

We three Englishmen sat there on the Cossacks' shaggy, hardy little horses, and watched with mingled feelings the triumphant military display of the great Northern power which was celebrating the close of a victorious campaign. We guessed by a kind of instinct that England herself had come within measurable distance of war with the same great power; but we scarcely realized that the issue was still hanging in the balance, and that the steady hand of one man held the scales of war and peace. The treaty of San Stefano had just been signed. This document, which the *sultan* ratified on March 3, concluded the war between Russia and Turkey; but the Ottoman Government had to buy peace at a price. Not only was an indemnity of three hundred million roubles secured to Russia, but she also took large possessions in Asia Minor and enormous advantages in Europe.

While we sat on the horses of the Cossack irregulars listening to the huzzas of the Russian troops, Lord Beaconsfield, with the provisions of the treaty before him, was evolving the policy of England. It was not until May 15 that he returned to London with Lord Salisbury, after the Berlin Congress, bringing back "peace with honour."

As we dangled our feet in the big Cossack stirrups watching the Russian standards that made shadows on the snow as they waved lazily in the breeze, a British squadron was steaming to Besika Bay, and the Government of India was preparing to despatch a strong force of Indian troops to Malta. That was because Russia refused to submit the treaty of San Stefano to the other powers in accordance with the peremptory demand of Beaconsfield, and held on her course until the determined attitude assumed by England forced her to modify her claims in Europe.

Although we did not know all this at that time, yet we knew enough to realize that possibly we might see the Russian troops very shortly under quite different circumstances; and this reflection lent piquancy to the situation.

We watched the Russians as they marched in on parade and formed up in a great hollow square, with General Melikoff and the headquarters staff sitting on their horses inside it, and the imperial standards of yellow silk embroidered with the black eagles flaunting in the air.

Then at a given signal the massed bands of all the regiments struck up the Russian national anthem, and the huzzas of the soldiery were given with a goodwill that showed how welcome was the close of the campaign. Our troubles had been severe enough in Erzeroum; but the sufferings of the Russian army camped outside in the snow transcended anything that we had undergone, and General Melikoff told me himself that he had lost 40 *per cent.* of his army from typhus fever and exposure.

A cleric, or "pope," as he was called, who accompanied the troops in the capacity of an army chaplain, delivered an excited harangue, declaring that the Almighty had given the soldiers of the cross the victory over the infidels; and then the men were dismissed from parade, and allowed to go where they liked. Several carts full of wine were brought in, and the champions of Christendom embarked on a glorious carouse.

All the Turkish troops who were able to travel had been sent away to Erzinghan or Baiburt in order to make room for the Russian army; but we still had about two thousand men in hospital, and these it was impossible to remove, so that Stoker, Denniston, and myself had plenty of work before us. There was a great deal of sickness among the poorer Armenians in the town, and these unfortunate creatures were almost entirely dependent upon us for medical aid; so it may readily be guessed that we had our hands full.

On the day after the review General Melikoff invited Stoker, Denniston, and myself to call on him. Piloted by our excellent friend Captain Pizareff, who was the general's *aide-de-camp*, we found our way to headquarters, and were introduced to the Russian field-marshal in the big house which he had selected for his residence.

General Melikoff at that time was a man of striking appearance, and looked every inch a soldier. His tall, well knit figure, his aquiline nose, and dark, flashing eyes marked him out at once as a military leader. He received us with the greatest courtesy, and told us that he had heard how hard we had worked, not only in aid of the sick and wounded soldiers, but also in aid of the poverty-stricken civil population of the town. He assured us of his sympathy, and promised to do everything in his power to help us, asking us to make any suggestions with regard to improvements that might be desirable in conducting the sanitation of the city, and expressing his willingness to meet our views in every way. Encouraged by the kindly and considerate attitude of the general, I ventured to approach him by letter a few days afterwards, and once again my unfortunate deficiencies in the matter of French exposed me to treatment which I shall never believe was authorized by General Melikoff.

Hussein Effendi, the Turkish principal medical officer, was the original cause of the trouble; for he ordered the wounded to be removed from the English hospital and sent away when they were in such a weak condition that many of them died in consequence of this heartless treatment. We reported the matter to Hakki Bey, and Hussein Effendi was at once sent for; and having no satisfactory explanation to give of his conduct, was imprisoned. At the same time, remembering General Melikoff's injunction that I should let him know of anything that required seeing to in the hospitals, I wrote to him explaining the circumstances. The letter was really the joint production of Denniston, Stoker, and myself. We wrote it in the best French that we could muster; and as there was no cream-laid notepaper left in Erzeroum, we were obliged to use the only kind of stationery available, which happened to be a bit of blue foolscap. We surveyed our joint production with pardonable pride, and despatched it without delay to General Melikoff.

When next I saw the unfortunate letter, it was in the hands of the Russian consul, who had returned to Erzeroum with the army of occupation, having left the town in the first instance on the outbreak of hostilities. He was a tall man, with a very pale face and a thick black beard. His manners were in striking contrast to those of the Russian officers whom we had met, for he was an insolent fellow, who had not wit enough to conceal the signs that betokened an ignorant Jack-in-office unaccustomed to mix with men of the world or in polite society. This individual came to me next day, holding in his hand my letter to General Melikoff, which he flung in my face, remarking at the same time that it was not usual to write to a field-marshal of the

Russian army on a dirty bit of foolscap and in atrociously bad French. I was relieved to find from Captain Pizareff, whom I apprised of the circumstance, that such a message was never sent by General Melikoff. Probably the facts of the case were that Melikoff handed the letter to this uncouth personage with instructions to attend to the matter, and that the Jack-in-office, annoyed by the duty, vented his spite upon the writer.

We became very intimate with Captain Pizareff, and also made the acquaintance of a number of Russian officers, whom we invited round to our quarters in the evenings.

We found ourselves much sought after by the Russian officers; and, in fact, the English Consulate, where we lived, became to all intents and purposes a Russian club. It got to be quite the thing for them to drop in during the evening; and we occasionally gave little dinner parties, which were much appreciated. Our house, furnished as it was with Mr. Zohrab's excellent supply of provisions, and with his admirable and carefully selected stock of wines and liquors, was the only place in Erzeroum where a decent dinner was obtainable. An invitation to dine with us was very acceptable, as may be imagined, to these young Russian aristocrats, who had been half starving in the snow for several months past.

Most of those who came to us were friends of Pizareff, who practically lived at our place. He was a fine type of young fellow, with the frank and dashing manner of the born soldier, and with a nature widened and improved by travel. Like my other great friend, poor Czetwertinski, he was a brilliant horseman, and his charger was the envy of the regiment. This horse was an extremely handsome white stallion, which, as the advertisements say, was formerly the property of a gentleman, and had been parted with simply because the owner had no further use for him. The original owner happened to be a notorious brigand in Daghistan, who for a long time defied all efforts to capture him, but was taken at last and summarily hanged. Pizareff was offered enormous sums for this famous animal, which added to his undoubted worth as a charger something of the extrinsic sentimental value that might have attached to Dick Turpin's Black Bess.

Another charming man who used to come to our house was the colonel commanding the Orenburg Cossacks. We saw a great deal of him, and also of his adjutant, Captain Anisimoff, who spoke English like an Englishman, and looked exactly like a British naval officer. They all drank brandy at a rate that threatened to deplete our stock of this medical comfort in an alarming manner; and I remember that one evening a party of them polished off three bottles between them, which made me open my eyes, especially as brandy was worth two pounds a bottle in Erzeroum at that time. One of the party was a young Russian prince, whose name I have forgotten. He had never tasted brandy before, and was so proud of his achievement that he insisted upon sending a telegram to his father at St. Petersburg announcing that he had been drinking *eau-de-vie* in Erzeroum at the house of three English doctors—a highly important despatch from the seat of war.

About this time I received a telegram one day from Constantinople informing me that the *sultan* had been pleased to confer upon me the decoration of the fourth order of the *medjidie* in recognition of my services. Mere lad as I was, I felt very proud of my decoration, and Denniston, Stoker, and myself had a great consultation about the matter. They opined that there was only one course open to me, and that it was incumbent upon me to give a party in celebration of the event. As the guests would be all Russians, I felt bound in honour to do the thing properly, and determined to go outside Mr. Zohrab's cellar in order to provide materials befitting the occasion. Mr. Zohrab had forgotten to lay in a stock of champagne before he went, and it was clear that champagne was the only liquor which would meet the requirements of the case. Now I knew that there was no champagne in Erzeroum before the arrival of the Russians; but I guessed that the sutlers and purveyors who followed the Russian army would not have forgotten to bring the wine which is so much favoured in Russia.

Old Tom Rennison, a campaigner whose vast experience enabled him to live in luxury in places where a goat would starve, thought that he knew where to get some "fizz"; so I despatched him to bring in half a dozen bottles *coûte que coûte*. Still, it was a bit staggering to find that, when he brought back the required quantity, he also had a little bill of eighteen pounds to render for the half-dozen of Moet and Chandon which some enterprising purveyor had carted on a sledge over the snow from Tiflis, four hundred miles away.

About a dozen Russian officers came round to my party, and we made a great night of it. Denniston proposed my health in English, and I responded in the same language. Then Pizareff proposed it in French, and I made shift to reply in that tongue. Someone else made a few complimentary remarks in German, and several speeches were added in Russian. Before the evening was half over we were paying the most extravagant compliments to each other, and I have an indistinct recollection of trying somewhere about midnight to teach a big, fair-bearded captain "Auld lang syne," and to render "We twa ha' paid'lt i' the burn" into my own peculiar French, a task in which I was entirely unsuccessful.

We had quite a number of little dinner parties after this. One night General Komaroff, who afterwards commanded the Russians at the famous fight which goes down to history as the "Pendjeh incident," invited us to dine with him; and Stoker and I accepted, though Denniston was sick and obliged to stay at home. The general, who was then a young man, although he wore a beard and spectacles, treated us very hospitably, and had evidently spared no pains to make the entertainment a success. A regimental band stationed in the courtyard outside played English airs as a compliment to the visitors; and the *menu*, which began with a *zacuska* of caviar and anchovies, was a capital one. A small tumbler of raw absinthe was poured out for each guest to begin with; and as they insisted that I must drink mine in spite of all my protestations, I was nearly poisoned. Later on English bottled stout was served round gravely in wine glasses. How on earth it got to Erzeroum I could not make out, for the Russians do not drink stout; but it was evidently intended as a compliment to us, so I tossed mine down, much wondering.

Captain Pizareff, who lived in General Melikoff's house, asked me to go round and dine with him one night as the general was going out, and with great thoughtfulness my host sent round a Cossack with a spare horse for me. We had a capital dinner; but the only thing to drink was a big stone bottle full of Benedictine, which we finished between us. Pizareff was equal to the emergency. Late at night he sent me back to my own quarters with my Cossack guard doubled. I had a Cossack riding on each side of me to hold me on. They were jolly, good-humoured fellows, clad in heavy sheepskin overcoats; and they laughed immoderately every time I fell off my horse, which occurred three times during the journey of about a mile.

On each of these occasions, as I sat disconsolately in the frozen snow, a melancholy figure in a long overcoat, boots, and spurs, and a sword which insisted in getting between my legs, my Cossacks replaced my *fez* on my head, deftly disentangled me from my sword, and hoisted me once more into the saddle. In spite of the terrible stories that one hears about them sometimes, I shall always have a warm corner in my heart for Cossacks.

Although we got on capitally with the Russian officers, the rank and file of the army of occupation behaved very badly to the few unfortunate Turkish soldiers who were left behind to recover from their wounds when the bulk of the sufferers were sent away. Whenever the Russian linesmen came across these poor devils crawling about the streets, they would jeer them and mock them first, and then beat them cruelly. I have seen half a dozen Russians attack a couple of wretchedly weak and emaciated Turks who were painfully creeping along the street, and kick them brutally, leaving them half dead by the side of the road.

Once Denniston, Stoker, and myself had a narrow escape. We had gone for a walk by ourselves outside of the town proper towards the redoubts, when we came upon a party of Russian infantrymen who were undisguisedly hostile. One fellow came up to me, said something in Russian, and then hit me a crack over the head which annoyed me so much that I went for him with my fists. Denniston and Stoker sailed in at the others; but the soldiers had their side arms with them, and it would have fared badly with us but for the sudden appearance of a Russian captain, who saw the affair, and came running to our assistance, revolver in hand. He knocked down my assailant with the pistol-butt for a start, and discharged such a volley of remarks at the others that they slunk off like beaten curs. We were grateful for his timely intervention, without which we would probably have been killed outright; and we paid due attention to his warning that it was dangerous to come unprotected so far from the town.

The comfort in which we lived at the consulate had not escaped the envy of some of the Russians, and one man in particular was consumed with jealousy when he saw the fine house in which we were quartered. This was General Heymann, who commanded the Russian column of assault at Devoi Boyun, and showed conspicuous bravery during the engagement. In fact, he was generally spoken of afterwards as the hero of Devoi Boyun. It seemed that about twenty years before the war he had been in Erzeroum, and had occupied the house, which was afterwards turned into the English Consulate.

During the long months of discomfort while the army was encamped in the stinking little villages outside Erzeroum, General Heymann had buoyed himself up with the hope that as soon as the inevitable occupation arrived he would go back to his old quarters again; and when at last he got into the town, he was disgusted to find the house upon which he had set his heart in the occupation of some

English doctors. His first move was to send an *aide-de-camp* to us with a request that we would vacate the house, which we at once declined to do. Then the trouble began. Although the fascinating pursuit of "draw poker" is not practised to any great extent in Russia, still that *aide-de-camp* was fully conversant with one of its leading features, and he set himself to play the game of bluff with great vigour. He began to bluster in great style, hoping that I would throw up my hand at once; but I went one better every time.

At last he remarked that might was right, that the Russians were an army of occupation, and that if we did not go out of our house we would be turned out. I said that we certainly would not go unless turned out by force, and that as the Russian troops occupied the town under the terms of an armistice, and not as a consequence of a successful assault, they could not disturb us in our quarters. I closed the conversation by saying that if they turned Denniston, Stoker, and myself out of our house, I would telegraph to Lord Derby requesting him to make representations at St. Petersburg on the subject. Then I bowed out General Heymann's *aide-de-camp*. Next day, however, a communication arrived from the *konak* announcing that the general insisted that we should be turned out, and that the civil authorities of the town would be glad if we would leave quietly.

This was rather too much, and I went up to the *konak* next day, taking Tom Rennison as an interpreter. I was shown into a room where Hakki Bey, the civil governor, and a number of Turkish and Armenian officials were discussing the situation. Here I stood up and made a speech, which was interpreted as I went along by Tom Rennison. I told them that we had come out there to help their sick and wounded, that two of our number had already died in their cause, and that the rest of us had risked our lives for them over and over again.

"We have done all this for you," I said; "we have cared for your wounded, and eased their sufferings; we have tended your sick, and sent them food and wine from our own table; and now, you ungrateful beggars, you want to turn us out of our own house. Well, we won't go." They listened very courteously to my exordium, which was translated into Turkish by the faithful Rennison; and when it was finished, I could see that I had made an impression. Our eviction was no longer insisted upon, and General Heymann had to content himself with a large house immediately opposite our quarters.

Some little time after this the French consul, M. Jardin, approached us, and used his influence with us, asking us if possible to humour the old general by granting his wish. Finally we agreed to do so, and I wrote a letter to General Heymann, saying that as a personal compliment to His Excellency we would give him up the house. At the same time I warned him that there would be a risk attached to his occupancy, as we had had several cases of typhus in the house. He came over the same afternoon in great glee, bringing his dragoman with him to thank us, as he himself spoke nothing but Russian. He said that, being an old campaigner, he had no fear of typhus; and he marked his appreciation of the favour shown to him by presenting us with a box of four hundred cigars, which were most acceptable.

Next day he sent us twenty soldiers to remove our baggage to the house which he was giving up; and when the moving was accomplished he entered into possession of the consulate. He went to bed feeling poorly on the very day that he got into his new quarters, and four days afterwards he was dead of typhus. Denniston, Stoker, and I all attended the poor old fellow's funeral, wondering at the strange fate that had allowed him to live through many a hard-fought fight only to let him die in his bed when the campaign was over.

CHAPTER 15

The End of the War

While the Turks and Armenians in Erzeroum were dying by hundreds from typhus, the Russian soldiers also suffered severely; and as I went round the town, I found many of them lying sick and untended, not from any want of care on the part of the Russian doctors, but simply because the soldiers stole away and hid themselves when they fell ill.

Captain Pizareff would not believe it when I told him that his men were dying like sheep, and declared that it was impossible for such a thing to happen without the knowledge of the colonel of the regiment. In order to convince the *aide-de-camp*, I asked him to go with me and see the state of things with his own eyes.

Next morning I started out early to visit a poor Armenian woman whose child had been accidentally scalded, and I took Captain Pizareff with me. The woman lived in a miserable quarter of the town, inhabited only by the poorest people; and evidences of distress and semi-starvation were present on every hand. I found my patient easily enough; and after dressing the injuries of the scalded child, I took Pizareff on a tour of inspection down the street. The snow was piled high round the walls of the first dilapidated, tumble-down shanty that we entered; and at first, as we went inside out of the strong glare of the sun on the snow, we could hardly see at all.

A small latticed window near the roof admitted a few gleams of light; and as our eyes became accustomed to the semi-obscurity, we could make out three Russians lying on a heap of straw in a corner of the room. They were all down with typhus. One was lying on his back, with his eyes wide open, staring at the ceiling. As we entered he looked at us, and seemed to recognize Pizareff. He made a feeble effort to rise from the straw and lift his hand in the military salute;

but the strain was too much for him, and he fell back exhausted. The other two men were moaning and tossing from side to side, calling at intervals for water. An Armenian child about seven years old was playing with a dog in the snow which lay thickly in the yard at the back of the house. While I was looking at the men, the child came to the door, peered curiously in, and then returned unconcernedly to his game in the yard. The sight of sickness and death was not sufficiently novel to disturb the amusement of the moment.

In several other houses in the same street similar scenes were met with; and in one an Armenian family consisting of a father, mother, and three children were unconcernedly eating their dinner—a bowl of grain boiled into a kind of sticky porridge—while the corpse of a Russian soldier who had just died lay on the floor in the next room.

Captain Pizareff was petrified with astonishment, and reported the circumstances to General Melikoff at once. I sent word to the Russian Red Cross doctors, and they despatched a party of ambulance men to collect their sick and bring them into the hospitals. How it was possible for the absence of the men from roll call to remain unnoticed I cannot understand; but I heard afterwards that the colonel of the regiment to which these unfortunates belonged got into serious trouble over it.

Denniston, Stoker, and myself found plenty of work to do among the Russian sick as well as among our own men, and were glad to lend the Russian doctors our assistance. We found our Russian *confrères* capital fellows, and also excellent surgeons. They had worked on bravely while their army was outside Erzeroum and afterwards at Kars, though their resources were severely taxed by the number of the wounded at Devoi Boyun, as well as by the fevers and frostbite that decimated the troops during the long intervals between the different engagements.

They spoke of General Melikoff in terms of the highest admiration, praising his administrative ability as well as his military capacity; and I felt that their opinions were well founded, when I reflected upon the difficulties under which he had laboured, especially in the transport and commissariat department. On one occasion General Melikoff said to me himself, "I am prouder of having been able to feed my army than I am of any of my victories." When it is remembered that everything in the shape of supplies, including provisions and medical stores, had to be brought over the snow from Tiflis, four hundred miles away, it will be conceded that the general's pride in his achievement was justified. General Melikoff was most appreciative of our medical services on behalf of his troops, and told us on one occasion that he would recommend us for decorations at the hands of the Russian Government. However, during the anxious political times which ensued the Russian Government had something else to think about besides the services of three unknown English doctors in far away Erzeroum, and the decorations never came.

Gladly and willingly as I gave my services in the cause of humanity, it was nevertheless a real pleasure to find that they were appreciated by the Russian troops as well as by the Stafford House Committee, and also the Turkish Government. Captain Morisot, who returned to Erzeroum from Constantinople, brought me up, not only fresh supplies of money, but also the news that the Stafford House Committee had passed a special vote of thanks to myself and the other doctors of the Erzeroum section. The document setting forth this vote of thanks, signed by the Duke of Sutherland as chairman of the committee, is couched in most complimentary terms; and, needless to say, it forms one of my most cherished mementoes of the war. Similar special votes of thanks were accorded to Dr. Stiven and Dr. Beresford for their great bravery during the fighting at Rustchuk. I had already received the fourth order of the Medjidie, and to this the Turkish Government were afterwards pleased to add the fourth order of the Osmanli and also the Turkish war medal.

We were reinforced during March by the arrival of Dr. Roy and a party of doctors sent out by the Red Cross Society. They had undergone a good deal of hardship since they left Constantinople, and one of their number, a Dane named Price, had died. I shall always remember Roy through a remarkable incident of which I was informed by him some time after I had left Erzeroum. In my quarters I was accustomed to sleep on the floor on a mat, and even in a besieged town I had kept up the early habit of reading in bed. The usual military candlestick was a bayonet, which was stuck in the floor, with the candle jammed into the socket; but I found a more convenient receptacle in a Turkish conical shell, which I had picked up somewhere, and which made a capital candlestick when the brass cap at the end was unscrewed.

Into the orifice of the shell I stuck my candle every night, and read *Vanity Fair*—which I got out of Mr. Zohrab's capital library—for the first time. I never can think of Becky Sharp to this day without a shudder, not on account of her treatment of Rawdon Crawley or her dubious relationship with the Marquis of Steyne, but simply owing to the circumstances under which I first met her. She was certainly a risky acquaintance for me. A week or two after I left Erzeroum my candlestick fell into other hands, and one night it exploded, fortunately in an empty room, which it wrecked without damaging an one in the house. My first introduction to Becky Sharp was effected by the light of a candle stuck in the mouth of a live shell!

Powder was unnecessarily burnt more than once during our last month in Erzeroum. One night I was awakened by a terrific explosion, and almost before I could collect my senses a frantic knocking at the door showed that somebody wanted the doctor in a hurry. We all jumped into our clothes, and followed the guide to a place where an Armenian house had stood a few minutes before, but which when we reached the spot was a mere heap of wreckage. One of the few survivors explained what had happened. He told us that a lot of Armenians had got hold of some Turkish cartridges, and were endeavouring to convert the powder to their own use. Sixteen men were sitting in a circle on their haunches in the middle of a big room, busily pulling the bullets out of the cartridges and emptying the powder into a heap, which was gradually increasing in size in the centre, when the desire for a cigarette came upon one of them, and he struck a match.

The next instant the house was in the air, and ten of the Armenians were in paradise—or somewhere else. There was a good deal of confusion in the darkness; but I recollect finding myself down on my knees in a stable at the back of the house examining two of the sufferers who were still alive. One of them lay between the legs of a cow, and while he was in that position I dressed his injuries. The crowd had been very troublesome, and I had locked the door of the stable on the inside to keep them away, when I heard a tremendous hammering and someone demanding admittance. I called out that there was strictly no admittance; but in a very few minutes a file of soldiers burst the door in, and General Duhoffskoy, very angry at being kept out in the cold, stood before me. He was good enough to accept my apologies when I explained why I had locked the door, and also to thank me for attending to the sufferers.

General Duhoffskoy was appointed to act as a kind of chief commissioner of police at Erzeroum in addition to his military duties, and whenever there was any excitement in the town he was always on the spot. One night we had a very big fire; in fact, half the street seemed to be burning. There was plenty of water, however; and if it had not been for the crowd, there would have been no difficulty in extinguishing the flames. An Armenian crowd at a fire is very much like any other crowd, and the people indulged in sudden stampedes and all sorts of "alarums and excursions" to such a degree that the work of the soldier firemen was greatly hindered. General Duhoffskoy took in the situation at a glance, and at once announced that if the crowd did not disperse it would be blown to pieces, as one of the burning houses contained an enormous quantity of powder and other explosives. The effect was instantaneous, and the miscellaneous mass of Turks and Armenians melted away as if by magic.

Soon after the return of Captain Morisot, I received a telegram from the Stafford House Committee saying that we had done enough for honour and glory, and that we had better go back to Constantinople, as the Turkish administration was able to cope with all the hospital work that remained to be done in Erzeroum. I was instructed to place the balance of our medical stores at the disposal of the Turks before leaving, and accordingly I handed everything over to Hakki Bey, receiving a receipt, and also a grateful acknowledgment of our services to the Turkish troops, together with a special letter for presentation to the Seraskierat.

My last week in Erzeroum was a busy one, as we had to make extensive preparations for the journey to Trebizond, which was quite a formidable undertaking. I had collected a great deal of personal baggage during my travels, and our equipment was considerable; so I arranged with a Persian caravan which was going down to Trebizond for the conveyance of the heaviest of our impedimenta, retaining only my valuables and the curios which I had got together to take down under my own supervision with the caravan. There were many Persians in Erzeroum, and as a rule they got on very well with the Turks, though occasionally racial antipathy was responsible for those minor persecutions known as practical jokes, of which the Turks were very fond.

One day in the *hammam*, or Turkish bath, I met an old Persian, who was in a deplorable state of grief in consequence of the treatment which he had received from two young Turks. The Persians all grew very long beards, of which they were inordinately proud, and they were accustomed, after coming out of the bath, to dye them a fine rich brickdust colour with henna. One never saw a Persian with a white beard. Now this particular old Persian had carefully rubbed his beard with *henna*, in blissful ignorance of the fact that two mischievous young Turks had been to his *henna*-pot and had mixed a quantity of corrosive acid with the dye. The consequence was that when the Persian applied the dye the beard came away in pieces, and left the poor man beardless in his old age and disgraced.

On the day before we left Erzeroum I called on General Duhoffskoy, as the military governor of the town, in order to obtain from him a pass through the Russian lines and the necessary papers authorizing my departure. The general was a distinguished-looking man of about forty years of age, and he received me very courteously, expressing polite regret at my departure, and promising to facilitate my journey as far as possible. It struck me that I had never seen him in such good spirits before, and that there was a beam of sunshiny contentment in his face, which was an agreeable change from the rigid military look of his usually stern features. As I was inwardly wondering what could have happened to effect this change, the door opened, and a lady entered the room. "Permit me to present you to my wife, Dr. Ryan," said the general; and turning I bowed, there in remote, snow-clad, devastated Erzeroum, to one of the most beautiful women I have ever seen.

Princess Duhoffskoy, *née* Princess Galitzin, was then about twenty years of age, and to my youthful imagination, with her beautifully chiselled features, complexion of exquisite fairness, and large blue eyes that looked me frankly in the face, she seemed like a visitant from another world. For a year and a half almost the only specimens of womanhood that I had seen were squat and swarthy Bulgarian girls, frowsy Armenians, or Turkish women closely veiled in their yashmaks. It was no wonder that this lovely Russian, with her delicate, refined beauty and her frank and gracious manner, made a profound impression upon me, and set my heart beating quickly with mingled surprise and delight.

The general returned to his writing-table, and I was left to talk to this beauteous vision alone. I stammered a few remarks in execrable German; for though I spoke that language fairly fluently on ordinary occasions, my sensations drove my vocabulary out of my head, and I felt that for one in my position at any rate the resources of that grave and elephantine tongue were exasperatingly inadequate.

"Oh, Doctor Ryan, would you not prefer to speak English?" said the princess, to my intense astonishment, without the least trace of a foreign accent. Like many cultured Russians, she had learnt to speak English as well as French and German when a child; and she soon showed me that she could not only talk, but talk interestingly, in my own language. In her lips the Doric harshness of sound in spoken

English disappeared, and the well known words took on something of the smooth, musical cadence of the softer Italian. She told me that she had only reached Erzeroum on the previous day, after travelling four hundred miles across the snow from Tiflis to join her husband, and she chatted away pleasantly of the incidents which occurred on the way as if there was nothing unusual in a delicately nurtured lady going through the hardships necessitated by such a journey in a sleigh. She expressed great interest in my work among the wounded, and listened attentively while I spoke of the bravery of the Turkish troops and their fortitude under pain. When I told her of an Anatolian Turk who died in my hospital at Plevna with his wife's name on his lips, the beautiful eyes of this Russian princess filled with tears. "Poor fellow," she whispered softly; "I hope it is not wrong for us to pity the sufferings of the enemy."

Coffee was brought in, and I sat there for about two hours chatting with the princess, while the general continued writing at his table. Every now and then he looked up with a glance which seemed to say, "Not gone yet? I wonder how much longer this confounded Englishman is going to stay." At last I managed to tear myself away, and I said goodbye to this beautiful Russian lady, with many regrets that I had to leave Erzeroum next day. I never saw her again; but when I got back to the consulate, I selected about fifty standard English books from Mr. Zohrab's excellent library, packed them on a little sleigh, and despatched them to Princess Duhoffskoy with my card, presenting my compliments, and hoping that the books would lessen the tedium of her stay in such a dull place as Erzeroum. General Duhoffskoy is now the governor of a province in Siberia, where he resides with his beautiful wife, whose visit to Erzeroum was the one gleam of real sunshine that I had seen throughout that terrible winter.

Before we started for Trebizond, a slight difference of opinion arose between myself and my comrades, Denniston and Stoker, upon a matter affecting our joint interest. It did not in the least disturb the friendly relations existing between us, and I only mention the matter now because it was all my fault that my companions were induced to assent to incurring the responsibility and inconvenience of escorting another traveller to Trebizond—and that traveller a lady.

M. Jardin, the French consul, was a true Frenchman of the best type, agreeable, polite, and above all things always anxious to oblige a lady. Accordingly, when he came to me with a pathetic appeal on behalf of a charming Spanish widow, whose husband had been an apothecary attached to the medical staff I found the greatest difficulty in turning a deaf ear to him. He explained to me that the beautiful Spaniard was most anxious to get to Constantinople, where she had friends who would arrange for her passage back to her own country, and that he would take it as a personal favour to him if we would allow the lady to join our party.

I foresaw the inconvenience of taking a lady on an extremely rough journey, which had to be accomplished entirely on horseback, over mountain tracks and passes deep in snow; so at first I gave a polite refusal to the French consul's request. But M. Jardin would not be denied. He minimized the difficulties of the journey, which he assured us would be nothing to such courageous and experienced men as ourselves. He extolled us for the services which we had already rendered in the cause of humanity, and he urged us not to decline at the last moment to still further add to our laurels in this direction.

Finally he dwelt at great length upon the grace and beauty of this dark-eyed Spanish lady, whom none of us had ever seen, and he painted the despair with which she looked forward to the prospect of remaining widowed and alone in Erzeroum, perhaps to die, far from her country and from her own people. What could I say in answer to such an appeal? What could I do? There was nothing for it but to submit with some misgiving to the inevitable; and accordingly I informed M. Jardin that I would withdraw my own objections, and would consent to the arrangement if he could prevail upon Denniston and Stoker to agree also.

If M. Jardin had not been an exceedingly decorous as well as polite Frenchman, I feel sure he would have jumped with joy when I capitulated, and he went off forthwith to interview Denniston and Stoker. What occurred at that interview I cannot precisely say, because both my comrades were strangely reticent upon the subject. I conjecture, however, that M. Jardin praised their courage and their chivalry in a truly generous spirit, and I am convinced that he dwelt with all his astonishing eloquence upon the grace and loveliness of this poor Spanish beauty in distress. At any rate, Denniston and Stoker agreed to let her travel with us.

Just before we started, and when the pack-horses upon which we were to ride to Erzeroum were at the door, M. Jardin brought up his beautiful Spaniard and introduced her to us. I hope I shall not be considered impolite when I confess that our jaws all dropped simultaneously. No doubt the lady had been beautiful in her youth; but her particular style of beauty had not been proof against the devastating power of years, and I doubt whether any man in Erzeroum, except that very polite French consul, would have seen extraordinary loveliness in the lady who was handed over to our care at the very last moment. However, there was nothing for it but to hoist her upon a pack-saddle, to mount ourselves upon similar uncomfortable seats, and to start the melancholy procession.

We said goodbye with real regret to Pizareff, who had been a capital friend and a most charming and genial companion. Fully thirty or forty other Russian officers came to see us off, and we parted on the very best of terms. They told us laughingly that they intended to drop in upon the British army in India some day, and we assured them that we would be there to meet them when they came. Then we waved our last *adieux*, and turned the heads of those long-suffering pack-horses towards Trebizond.

Our party consisted of Denniston, Stoker, Morisot, myself, and Williams our trusty dragoman, while last, but not least, came the lady. We had hired twelve horses to carry ourselves and our baggage, contracting to pay the headman of the caravan four pounds per horse for the journey to Trebizond; and accordingly when we started we formed an important section of the whole caravan of about fifty horses which set out from Erzeroum. Besides the headman, who was a most forbidding-looking Persian, there were fifteen drivers who accompanied us; each, I think, dirtier, hungrier, and more truculent-looking than the other. We guessed when we started that the journey would not be exactly a pleasure excursion; but the reality far exceeded our anticipations, and the next time that anyone asks me to make an overland journey with a widow, a still small voice within will whisper, "Beware! Remember Erzeroum and the Spanish *doña*."

Riding on a pack-saddle, which consists of two plates of hard wood joined by hinges at the apex where it fits over the horse's spine, is not the most agreeable way of taking horse exercise; and the *doña*, who was necessarily riding *en cavalier*, began to give tongue before she had gone a hundred yards. We made a cushion out of an old sack filled with hay, and our incubus heaved a sigh of relief when we placed it between her ill used anatomy and the bare boards which she bestrode. Then the procession went forward again, the horses stepping out in single file on the first stage of the long journey of one hundred and eighty miles that lay between us and the sea.

We left Erzeroum on March 31, intending to catch the Messageries steamer *Simois*, which was due to leave Trebizond on April 10, and fancying that by giving ourselves ample time we would have three or four days in Trebizond to recruit before going on board. However, we reckoned without our host, or on this occasion, to speak more accurately, without our guest—the lady. She spoke every continental language except English with equal facility, and her vocabulary in each was surprisingly extensive.

Day and night for one consecutive fortnight her shrill falsetto voice poured forth a never failing stream of complaint and invective, abuse and lamentation in half a dozen languages. What she suffered no one knew except herself, although this was not her fault, to be sure, for she lost no opportunity of imparting the information, sometimes in Spanish, and when she had exhausted the resources of that noble language in the slang of half the capitals of Europe. We found too late that our *doña* had not been cast in the heroic mould. She had never learnt how beautiful it is to suffer—and be silent.

A few miles from Erzeroum we came to the village of Ilidja, which was occupied by the Russians; and there we halted for half an hour, and had a glass of wine with a party of jovial officers, who were keeping up their spirits as well as they could in the lonely, God-forsaken place. On a dunghill in the village we counted eleven dead Russians; so we guessed that the typhus was not confined to Erzeroum.

When we got to Purnekapan, we camped for the night in the town, intending to make an early start, so as to negotiate the Kopdagh Pass before the sun spoiled the road. An unexpected difficulty, however, presented itself, for our Persian headman refused to go on, declaring that it was necessary to rest his horses for a day. In vain did we cajole, threaten, or bully him. He had come under the spell of a fixed idea, and nothing that we could say seemed to have the slightest effect upon his diseased intelligence.

But at last I found a way to move him. There was a Turkish regiment in the village, and I sought an interview with the colonel, who had heard something about our work, and was very well disposed towards us. Tapping the butt of his revolver significantly, he suggested to the Persian that it was high time to start, and the hint was accepted with alacrity. However, all this had taken time, and before we left the foot of the mountain and began the ascent it was eleven o'clock, and the sun's rays were ruining the track.

It was as exciting a bit of mountaineering as I have ever gone through, and we had to strain every nerve to climb the pass. In many places the track was only a couple of feet wide, a winding path cut round the side of the mountain, with a cliff on one side and a precipice on the other. As we mounted slowly and cautiously up the path, every nerve was at tension and every sense on the alert. Now and then, as the Persian drivers shouted and urged the frightened horses with voice and whip to face the slippery rising ground, one of the animals would slip, and for a second or two one's heart was in one's mouth.

In spite of every effort we lost three pack-horses before we won the summit. A slip on the glassy surface, a couple of frightened plunges in the loose snow near the edge, and then the unfortunate creatures disappeared over the side, falling upon a lower spur four hundred feet beneath us. One of the horses that we lost in this way was loaded with my personal effects. The presents that I was taking back to my friends, some beautiful turquoises from the Tiflis mines, as well as the Russian furs, the Russian leather cigar-cases, and the other keepsakes that the warm-hearted officers in Erzeroum had given me, all vanished with that hapless pack-horse into some inaccessible ravine far below the Kopdagh peak.

However, all the Persian drivers came through safely, and there were no missing faces in our party when we reached the summit, nine thousand feet above the level of the sea. The widow was still with us, numbed with the cold, exhausted with fatigue, and half shaken to death on her pack-saddle, but voluble as ever, and, like the person in the Greek play, "full of groans and not devoid of tears."

Just as we neared the summit I saw a Turkish woman climbing slowly and painfully up the track; but when we got to the shelter-house erected on the crest of the mountain, I lost sight of her. As we resumed our march, I noticed tracks in the snow in front of us, and drew the attention of Williams the *dragoman* to the impressions which had evidently been made by a woman. The *dragoman* disappeared for ten minutes on a tour of exploration, and when he returned he brought back a strange piece of intelligence. A Turkish baby had been born in a shed near the shelter-house while we were there, and the mother, whom we had seen climbing the pass, was already walking off with her newborn infant to her own village five miles away across the snow. Surely the cares of maternity lie lightly on those hardy Turkish mothers in the mountains of Asia Minor.

As may be guessed, we found a good deal of difficulty in replenishing our commissariat during this eventful journey. The Turkish troops had pretty well swept the board; and if the villagers had not hidden away some of their scanty stock from the foraging parties, we should have come off very badly. We managed to get eggs occasionally *en route*, and onions were also obtainable. I used to stuff my pockets with these delicacies and munch them raw. I found them very sustaining, and I have no doubt that my companions when they ventured near me could testify that my diet was strong.

When we reached the village at the foot of the Kopdagh where we were to camp for the night, we were all ravenously hungry, and as I shot a keen glance round the village in search of supplies I espied a kid. It was a very nice-looking kid, and it frisked and gambolled most alluringly. I slipped off my pack-horse, and approached the kid in a friendly manner that disarmed suspicion. Then I grabbed it by the ear, drew my big clasp knife, and cut its throat on the spot. I skinned it and cleaned it with my own experienced hands, and Williams the *dragoman* made an excellent *ragoût*. I gave the owner of the kid a Turkish *lira* as compensation for his loss, which was truly our gain, for the kid was a succulent little creature, and tasted very much like venison.

We could not have travelled fast under the most favourable conditions, and hampered as we were by the Spanish widow our progress became very slow indeed. It was not an easy task, even for one accustomed to riding, to remain on the wooden pack-saddle when a rough horse was plunging about in the snow; but for the Spanish widow it was literally impossible—a fact which she demonstrated by falling off five times during the journey over the Kop. It always happened in the same way. The hind legs of her pack-horse would slip down in the loose snow up to the hocks, while the forefeet remained steady for just one second on a harder patch, so that the animal's back described an angle of forty-five degrees with the surface of the ground.

During that one second the widow seized the opportunity of slipping off backwards over the horse's tail; and so quickly did she accomplish the feat that the watchful Williams, whom I specially told off, much to his disgust, to look after her, only arrived in time to pick her up. The sight of that middle-aged, sallow-faced Spanish person, in short skirts and blue goggles, sitting helplessly in the snow while Williams patiently collected her once more, would have made us laugh heartily were it not for the "damnable iteration" of the occurrence.

The presence of the widow caused us much annoyance whenever we camped for the night, because sleeping accommodation was usually scanty, and we always had to find a room for the lady before we turned in ourselves. Once, when we reached the village where we were going to camp for the night, we found that there were only two sleeping-rooms available for the whole party, so that we had to give one to the widow, and camp—all five of us—in the other.

First we showed the lady to her apartment, and then we went to look at our own. It was not a cosy bedroom, with French bedsteads, dimity curtains on the windows, and roses creeping up the walls outside. On the contrary, it was a small, square room, that would have made an excellent dog-kennel. The floor was of mud, and in a corner there was a heap of dirty straw, on which lay two dead Turkish soldiers who had died of confluent smallpox. We put the bodies outside the house, and Denniston, Stoker, Morisot, and myself, with Williams the dragoman, all went to sleep on the straw.

As we travelled along day after day the glare on the snow was very trying to the eyes; and though we all wore blue goggles, we suffered a good deal of inconvenience, while our faces were dreadfully blistered by the sun. The Persian headman was always wanting to stop and rest his horses; so that what with perpetually working at him to keep him up to the mark, pacifying the Spanish widow, and foraging for our daily bread, we had plenty of occupation *en route*. All our drivers of course were eager to rob us whenever the opportunity offered; and in addition to the furs and turquoises which I had already lost through a pack-horse going over the precipice, I was also deprived of two very fine cats from the province of Van.

I had purchased these creatures, which were very much like Persian cats, in Erzeroum, and I had hired a pack-horse specially to carry them. They were transported in a wooden box fixed to the pack-saddle, and Williams fed them with milk whenever we halted at a village. A couple of days before we reached Trebizond, however, my beautiful cats disappeared; and the only consolation that was vouchsafed me for my bereavement was the vague lie of a Persian driver, who averred that they had escaped from their box during the night. Of course he had planted them somewhere for subsequent conversion into ill gotten *piastres*.

When we commenced to get down towards Trebizond, we left the snow behind us on the mountains, and entered a tract of well timbered country, which was looking its best in the first flush of the early spring. The sides of the hills were gorgeous with pink cyclamen, and with a beautiful blue bulb which I could not identify. At last we entered the avenue of pear trees which were laden with juicy fruit when I passed up to Erzeroum six months previously. When I retraced my steps to Trebizond with new companions, I found the pear trees in full bloom. Since I had seen them bending under the burden of the ripening fruitage, fire and sword and frost and fever had brought many hundreds of men to death before my eyes, and I myself had been down to the very borders of the Valley of the Shadow. But now the war was over, the winter was done, and the scent of the white pear blossoms that filled all the valley blended with the first faint fragrance of the breezes from the ever nearing waters of the Black Sea.

Trebizond at last!

CHAPTER 16

Conclusion

We had time to call on Mr. Biliotti again, and to thank him for all his kindness; and then we went on board the *Simois*, which was ready to cast off her moorings and head out for Constantinople. Our Spanish widow was consistent to the last. The real hardships of the journey had not improved her temper; and when we resolutely declined to pay her passage to Constantinople in the steamer, she cursed us up and down Trebizond, each and severally, with the comprehensive particularity that was devoted to the historic cursing of the Jackdaw of Rheims. She was indeed that rare—or somewhat rare—phenomenon, an ungrateful woman.

When we reached Constantinople the whole place was full of excitement, for the Russian army was at San Stefano, only a few miles away, and Pera was almost like a Russian town. Every day hundreds of Russians might be seen clanking up and down the streets in full uniform, when they came in on leave from San Stefano.

English philanthropy was displayed as generously at this stage as it had been throughout the entire course of the war, and English gold was freely spent on the relief of starving and fever-stricken refugees from the Turkish provinces as well as on the sick and wounded troops. We got into touch with the philanthropic scheme undertaken by the Baroness Burdett-Coutts, who had sent out a large sum of money for the relief of the refugees; and we also met Mr. William Ashmead-Bartlett, the administrator of the fund, who afterwards married the baroness. He was ill with typhoid fever contracted from some of the refugees, and was under treatment at the English hospital, where his brother (now Sir Ellis Ashmead-Bartlett) was looking after him. Denniston, Stoker, and I paid a visit of inspection to the temporary hospitals established with the money supplied by the Baroness Burdett-

Coutts, and furnished a report upon them.

It is to Sir Ellis Ashmead-Bartlett that I owe my first introduction to a very charming American lady, who has since become known to a wide circle through her career on the stage. When I first met her she was an extraordinarily pretty woman, and she and her husband were on their honeymoon trip. He was a very gentlemanly man, with a rather retiring disposition; while she was about twenty years of age, and a perfect model of youthful womanhood. Every glance of her brightly flashing eyes and every line of her finely moulded figure told of bounding life and vivacity. Sir Ellis Ashmead-Bartlett and I saw a good deal of her and her husband for a week or two.

We had lunch together often, and took part in several picnics up the Bosphorus, in that spring-time nineteen years ago, when the blue waters of the strait and the bright eyes of *La belle Americaine* laughed in harmony, while Europe was waiting with beating heart for the verdict—peace or war. I met the B—— P——s again on board the steamer which took me away from Constantinople. Then our paths in life divided, and I had almost forgotten the vivacious American lady, when one evening a year or two ago I dropped into the Princess's Theatre in Melbourne to see Sardou's great play *La Tosca*. In the actress who was playing the name part I recognized my acquaintance of the stirring times of the war. It was Mrs. B—— P——.

Osman Pasha, who had been a prisoner of war in Russia, had been sent back into Turkey at the cessation of hostilities, and I went up to call on him at the Seraskierat. He was never a very communicative man, and the mental strain which the magnificent defence of Plevna and ultimately the tragic fall of the town imposed upon him seemed to have deepened his natural reserve. However, he gave me a hearty welcome, and appeared to be much interested in my account of our doings in Erzeroum. I told him that if war broke out again on a larger scale than before, I would return to my old comrades; and I said that if I ever came back to Constantinople, I would like to bring him a little present from England. When I asked him what he would choose, he said that there was nothing which he would like so much as a real English saddle and bridle. Osman Pasha was a thorough soldier in his love for a first-class equipment, and I was sorry that I never had the opportunity of seeing him again to make him the present.

Dear old Hassib Bey, the principal medical officer in Plevna, was quite affected when he saw me again, and we had a great chat over old times.

Tewfik Pasha, who was the Skobeleff of the Turkish army, was living in a house at Galata, and I went to call on him there. When I entered the room, he was deeply moved, and embraced me warmly. Tewfik was always in the forefront of the battle while I was in Plevna; and when the memorable attack was delivered in which he recaptured the Krishin redoubts from Skobeleff, it was Tewfik who headed the column of assault and cheered the Turks on to victory. He seemed to bear a charmed life; for in spite of all the hot fighting that he had done, he had come through the campaign without a scratch. When I mentioned that he had been extraordinarily lucky in all his fighting, he motioned to his soldier servant who was in the room to take down a big military *paletot* which hung on the wall.

The man took down the overcoat which was the garment that Tewfik Pasha had worn all through the siege. It was fastened down the front with frogs instead of buttons, and was provided with ample skirts that would blow about in the wind when the coat was not fastened securely. At Tewfik's request I examined it, and counted no fewer than eleven different bullet-holes through the cloth. In some cases no doubt one bullet had made two holes; but it was evident that on a good many different occasions the gallant soldier who wore the garment was literally within an inch of death.

Captain Morisot and I were invited to go to dinner one day at San Stefano with a party of Russian officers; but, much to my disappointment, something interfered with the engagement, and I missed the only chance I ever had of meeting the famous Skobeleff, who was then quartered at the little port on the Dardanelles. I found Morisot a delightful companion; and now that we were not oppressed with hospital duties, I had plenty of time to enjoy his society. His career indeed was a most romantic and interesting one. He had been shut up in Metz with Bazaine during the Franco-Prussian war, seven years earlier; and when the much criticised marshal capitulated, Morisot became a prisoner of war with the rest of the garrison, and was sent away to Stettin on the Baltic.

Though the prisoners were carefully watched, Morisot, who spoke English like an Englishman, managed to arrange a plan of escape; and one dark night he and another French officer eluded the guards, and pulled out in a dingy to a small Scottish schooner, trading between Glasgow and Stettin. The skipper, who was a "braw mon fra Glasgie," and hated the Prooshians with a deep and deadly hatred, received Morisot and his companion with enthusiasm, and landed them after a fair passage at Copenhagen, where they were given quite an ovation. The Schleswig-Holstein affair was still fresh in the minds of the Danes, and they were delighted at the opportunity of doing honour to men who had drawn the sword against Germany. Morisot afterwards went to England; and when the Russo-Turkish campaign broke out, he hurried to Constantinople in search of further adventures. Animated as he was by the true spirit of a soldier of fortune, Morisot found a scope for his energies afterwards in the ideal field of military adventure. *"Ex Africa semper aliquid novi,"* wrote an old historian; and the dashing young Frenchman, recognizing the truth of the remark even in these days, went to the Cape.

A feeling was creeping over me that it was high time I had a rest after all the storm and stress of battle; and when a letter came to me one day from my mother, who was in England, I packed up my things on a sudden impulse and stepped on board the Messageries steamer *Gamboge*. Among my fellow passengers were Mr. and Mrs. B—— P——, who were bound on a trip through the Holy Land, and left us at Smyrna. I also met again Admiral Sir William Hewitt, who had entertained us on board his ship the *Achilles* before I went to Erzeroum. He and I occupied the same cabin on the voyage.

At Smyrna I found our old friend Mr. Zohrab with his wife. Mrs. Zohrab was a dear, kind, motherly Englishwoman; and when she saw me, the thought of the sufferings that we had all gone through in Erzeroum and the fate which had fallen upon so many of the people whom she knew quite overcame her. She flung her arms round my neck, and burst into tears. Of course Mr. Zohrab was very anxious to hear all that had happened to us since he left Erzeroum, and whether we were comfortable in the house that he was obliged to desert.

I told him that we did full justice to his provisions and his wines; and the expression of his face was quite pathetic when I described the delightful little dinner parties that we gave to the Russian officers out of his ample stores. Poor old Zohrab! He listened with much the same feelings that Ulysses might have had when the island princes, overbold, were feasting on his substance and the steam of the roasting beef (which the poet avers is dear to the gods) rose up in his lordly halls.

Recollections of Osman Pasha's ball at Widdin came back to me when I met at Smyrna Zara Dilber Effendi, the skilful entertainer who arranged all the details of that never to be forgotten function. He and I spent the afternoon together, and had much to tell each other. The sight of this polished and dignified gentleman carried me back to my first experiences in Turkey, and his face was almost the last that I saw before I went on board ship again, and said goodbye for ever to that strange empire where the glow of romance and chivalry and the pure flame of passionate patriotism shone among the gathering shadows that have since almost obscured the "light of other days."

When I reached London, I found all England ringing with the tidings of the fighting, and there were plenty of evidences of the interest taken in the political situation. The music-halls, where one may touch the pulse of popular feeling, were crowded every night with audiences who tumultuously applauded the patriotic ditties that were encored over and over again, especially the famous song which set forth that "The Russians shall not have Constantino-o-ple."

I happened one night to stroll into the newly built "Canterbury Theatre of Varieties," which, by means of the novelty of a sliding roof, combined with a programme illustrating scenes in the campaign which was just concluded, drew big crowds nightly. One of the items on the programme was a realistic scene depicting the taking of the Grivitza redoubt by the Russians, and I watched the gallant "supers" with mingled feelings as they charged home upon the cardboard bayonets. The scene was capitally done, and there was a prodigious expenditure of ammunition, which the audience applauded mightily. After the performance I sent my card round to Mr. Villiers, who was the proprietor of the show, intimating that I would like to see him.

A tall, rather good-looking man, in the elaborate evening dress of a prosperous theatrical manager, and wearing an enormous diamond in his shirt front, made his appearance, and listened quietly while I complimented him upon the realism of the entertainment. I told him that it was really a very creditable show, but that there were one or two points in which it might be improved, and that, as I was the only Englishman in Plevna during the attack, I could give him some hints which would make the representation more accurate historically, while at the same time not impairing the spectacular effect. Mr. Villiers, who, by the way, was the uncle of my friend Fred Villiers, the war correspondent, did not seem very enthusiastic. In fact, his demeanour was distinctly discouraging. I felt that he had something to say, and waited anxiously for his answer.

"Well, sir," he remarked, looking me straight in the face while he twiddled his heavy gold watch-chain, "I am not going to say that I don't believe you; but you are the eleventh man who has come round here with exactly the same story." I was crushed, and bowed myself out from the presence of the potentate, almost wondering whether I really ever had been to Plevna.

That there were plenty of impostors about, and that Mr. Villiers had ample ground for being suspicious of casual strangers professing to have Turkish military experience, I soon discovered for myself. I happened to be travelling up to Scotland a couple of days afterwards, when a gentlemanly looking individual got into the smoking carriage with me, and we fell to chatting upon the current topics of the day. The stranger began to interest me vastly, when he turned the conversation dexterously into a discussion of the Russo-Turkish campaign, and informed me that, though an Englishman, he had served in the artillery under Osman Pasha, and had been present in Plevna during the siege.

I let him go on for fully a quarter of an hour recounting his apocryphal exploits, and then I thought it was time to speak. "Well, sir," I said, "it is a most extraordinary thing to think that you could have told that story to any other man in England except myself, and he might have believed you." I gave him my name, and told him that I knew all the artillery officers in Plevna, and that he certainly was not one of them. Never was an unfortunate *raconteur* so nonplussed. He threw up the sponge at once, and admitted that his story was a fabrication suggested to him by the fact that he had once made a holiday trip in Turkey.

And now the close of the book is reached; but before the last word is written, I should like to express my profound admiration for the soldierly qualities of the rank and file of the Turkish Army, with whom I lived on terms of intimate companionship for nearly two years. Courageous in misfortune, uncomplaining under the most awful suffering, good-humoured in every situation, the Turkish troops, both officers and men, showed throughout all the campaign the temper of true heroes. I need hardly say that for me it is deeply painful to think that the men whom I almost idealized, the men with whom I fought and suffered, with whom I tasted the glory of victory and the bitterness of defeat, should lie under the accusation of the atrocities which we must believe have been committed in 1896, not only in Armenia, but also in Constantinople. Yet through the black cloud that hangs over the Turkish Empire today, (as at time of first publication), I can still discern the distant stars; for I can look back with honest pride to the high sense of honour, the dauntless courage, the loyalty and true patriotism of those who were my comrades in arms in the earlier and brighter days.

The Third Battle of Plevna
By William V. Herbert

The unique race in July, 1877, for the sleepy Bulgarian townlet, hitherto obscure, known by name only to scholars or travellers, now famous for all time, had been won by the Turks by a short head.

Osman with his small corps, hurrying from the west, had arrived on the 19th of July a few hours before Schilder-Schuldner with his division came up from the north-east.

On the following day the first Battle of Plevna was fought, resulting in a disastrous defeat for the soldiers of the *Czar*. Ten days later the Russians, with two corps, renewed their attack, and General Krüidener's forces received the best beating that army ever had. The Russian retreat resolved itself into a flight of the most disorderly description, but a rally was made with admirable promptitude. Then six weeks were spent in virtual inactivity on both sides, broken only by some fighting around Lovdcha, and by Osman's futile sortie in the direction of Pelishat on the 31st of August. The Turks had utilised this period of tranquillity for constructing the system of redoubts and trenches which constituted the stronghold of Plevna, and which General Todleben, the defender of Sebastopol, has characterised as an impregnable fortress.

Meanwhile, reinforcements had reached both belligerents. In the beginning of September the Turkish army of defence counted forty-six battalions of infantry, nineteen squadrons of regular and five of irregular cavalry, with seventy-two guns—altogether 30,000 men, under the command of Osman Pasha, whose chief-of-staff was Tahir Pasha. The Russian-Roumanian Army of assault consisted of one hundred and seven battalions of infantry, ninety-one squadrons of cavalry (including Cossacks), with four hundred and forty-four guns—a total of 95,000, 30,000 of whom were Roumanians; its nominal leader was Prince (now King) Charles of Roumania, who was, however, a mere figurehead, and had no real command over any but his own (the Roumanian) troops, the actual principal being his chief-of-staff. General Sotow. Both the *Czar* and the Grand-duke Nicholas, the Russian commander-in-chief, watched the third Battle of Plevna from one of the hills beyond Radischevo, and had invited a brilliant staff of foreign attaches, officers, and journalists to witness the Unspeakable's discomfiture and collapse.

He who pens these lines—then a lad of eighteen—was a lieutenant in the Turkish infantry, and had command of his company, whose captain had been disabled in the second battle. He himself had been slightly wounded in this action by a sword-cut across the face, and had recovered after a week's sojourn in an ambulance. He was stationed in one of the redoubts which protected the north-front of the camp of Plevna.

In the night of the 6th to the 7th of September the Russian-Roumanian Army, completed its march of concentration on Plevna, and with the next dawn commenced the great cannonade which was to usher in a general assault on the Ottoman lines. The shelling lasted four days, during which period some 30,000 projectiles were hurled into the Turkish camp, the effect of which, material and moral, was practically *nil*. The Turkish gunners returned the fire much more deliberately and slowly, but with far greater truth of aim and force of moral impression upon the foe, as the Russian historians themselves admit. In the course of these four days there was some sharp fighting south of Plevna, where the dashing Skobeleff took possession of the two ridges in front of the Turkish redoubts, which the Russian writers have styled the "Green Hills."

The weather, which up to the 6th September had been splendid, had suddenly changed: rain had set in, the atmosphere was raw and moisture-laden, the sky a uniform grey, the nights were chilly. The actual battle, on September 11th and 12th, was fought in an almost uninterrupted downpour of the heaviest and most demoralising description.

Vividly impressed on my mind is the burning of the large village of Radischevo, which the Turkish shells set aflame in the afternoon of the 10th, and which blazed for twelve hours, lighting up the midnight sky in a superb and terrible manner.

It would take too long to describe in detail our many excellent arrangements for battle. To mention only one feature: each redoubt

OSMAN PASHA

had its own cooking, firewood, water, ambulance, and workmen's parties. Particularly in the north front, which contained our first division (of fourteen battalions, including that of the writer), and was commanded by Adil Pasha—one of the best generals Turkey has ever had, and Osman's factotum—our preparations were of the most extensive and elaborate description, and we were all quite disgusted that they were not called into play, for our wing was not attacked; in fact, my redoubt did not receive the honour of a single hostile shell, an absence of courtesy on the enemy's part which quite perturbed the equanimity of my men in the beginning, but which was subsequently compensated for in an unlooked-for manner by my battalion being withdrawn from its redoubt proper and sent to the south to confront that burning soldier Skobeleff.

At dawn on Tuesday, the 11th September, the cannonade was renewed in a way that shook the ground, as if this globe were quivering in the throes of terrific fever-heat. It rained hard, and fog hung heavily over the landscape. About an hour after noon the shelling suddenly ceased, and then commenced the great assault which was meant to end the war with one decisive and tremendous blow, which was to beat the record as regards the storming of entrenched camps, hitherto claimed for the seizure of the Düppel redoubts in the Danish campaign of 1864; but the unexpected result of which was for the assailants a disastrous failure, for the defenders a brilliant success—one that procured their commander that title by which he will be known amongst his own people for all time to come: "Ghazi"—the victorious.

The Russian programme was this. The Turkish camp was to be attacked on three points: the north-east corner—the famous Grivitza redoubts, which the Turks called respectively *Bash Tabiya, i.e.* Head Battery (No. 2), and *Kanli Tabiya, i.e.* the Bloody Battery (No. 1)—by the Russian right wing, consisting of a Roumanian division and two Russian divisions, under the command of General Krüdener, the man who had suffered such a disastrous defeat in the second battle; the south-east corner—the redoubt called *Omer Tabiya*—by the Russian centre, composed of two divisions, under General Krylow; the south front—six redoubts, of which the two northern ones, close to Plevna town, were called *Kavanlik Tabiya* and *Issa Tabiya*—by the Russian left wing, of Prince Imeretinski's detachment of twenty battalions, the real leader of which was General Skobeleff, the prince's adjutant.

The two remaining Roumanian divisions were to keep the formidable Turkish north front engaged by their mere presence, and two cavalry divisions, mustering a total of sixty squadrons, were to cut off Osman's western line of retreat. The appointed hour of attack was 3 p.m., but fog and deficient arrangements wrecked the programme, and in the Russian centre, through misadventure or blundering, two regiments broke up two hours too early.

At 1 p.m., then, these two regiments—Ugla and Yaroslav— started on their assault against *Omer Tabiya*, defended by three battalions and two guns, and came to utter grief. Again and again they charged, but the stubborn resistance of the Turks was not to be denied. In the end 2,300 men out of 5,000 paid with life and limb the penalty of premature attack, and two splendid regiments were, for campaigning purposes, wiped out. The commander of this division, General Schnitnikoff stuck literally to the text of his order, and despatched no aid until after 3 p.m. Can the foolish fellow possibly have imagined that two regiments could have taken a fortified camp twenty square miles in area?

After Ugla and Yaroslav had been utterly ruined, five more regiments were hurled against the death-dealing little enclosure, only to be wrecked, battalion by battalion, until at 5 p.m. Sotow, in despair and horror, ordered the cessation of the assault. The *Czar* had been an eyewitness of this stupendous struggle. How the famous gipsy warning, "*Beware of Plevna!*"—uttered months before Plevna had been heard of—must have come home to the proud autocrat as in his agony he watched his troops nicking onslaught after onslaught, one more futile and disastrous than the other!

The attack on *Omer Tabiya* had failed, with a loss of 6,000 men. The Turkish casualties amounted only to a few hundred. Twenty-one battalions had been practically destroyed by three. Such is the value of fighting from covered positions, however roughly made, granted that they are held by troops like the Turkish infantry, which, when on the defensive, is the most formidable in Europe. The man who commanded the little mud-bank on which seven regiments encountered their doom was Colonel Omer Bey, who was wounded in the last despairing rush of the brave Moskoflus. Not long afterwards I had a lengthy consultation with this officer—an incident of my life to which I shall always look back with the greatest pleasure.

A day after the termination of this battle, on September 13th, I was sent on burial duty to the devastated maize-fields in front of *Omer Tabiya*, which had been the scene of the rush and the downfall of the

Five more regiments were hurled against the death-dealing little enclosure.

enemy's brigades. The sights which I encountered, and the task which I had to perform, have remained with me in their ghastly intensity during all these years. In the high corn maimed men were left undiscovered for three or four days to rot in a living body. May the reader never witness such horrors even in his dreams, much less in their awful reality.

The slopes of *Omer Tabiya* saw also the only cavalry attack of the Plevna campaign. It was the fine regiment of mounted auxiliaries of Saloniki (ten squadrons, each eighty men strong), which charged here into the already retreating Russian columns in a brilliant and successful manner.

Our narrative must now turn to the attack on the Russian right wing. Here the two square-shaped redoubts which I have named, defended together by three battalions and six guns, and separated from each other only by a stretch of meadow-land 300 yards broad, were assailed for the first time punctually at three o'clock. The attack failed after some fighting of the most desperate and ferocious description. At 5 p.m. the encounter was renewed, the assault being directed against the southern work alone—the world-famed Grivitza redoubt, No. 1. Once more the eager young soldiers of the embryo kingdom were hurled back. A third attack had a like result. But at seven in the evening, in the darkness and during a terrific deluge, the work was once more stormed by the Roumanians coming from one side and the Russians from the other, and was carried after a hand-to-hand conflict of the most ferocious description. The Bloody Battery was lost to the Turks forever, and the price paid for the glory of this encounter was 2,600 Roumanians, 1,300 Russians, and 500 Turks, dead and disabled.

Before I shall invite the reader to follow me to the "Green Hills" south of Plevna I may perhaps add a few words as to my personal experiences and impressions during these sanguinary encounters. I had been roused in the early morning by the growl of cannon, and for ten hours my comrades and I were condemned to watch idly the furious fighting on our right and, behind us, and to be drenched in the merciless rain. No enemy was visible in front of my redoubt, and our battery did not discharge a single shot, since there was no one to fire at. Again and again I climbed our signal pole, and searched the misty battlefield through my glasses. How those hours of dead inaction weighed on us as we listened rapturously to the crashes of our Krupp guns in the Grivitza redoubts, to the thunder of the Russian heavy ordnance, to the clatter of company fire!

Around us men were playing for their lives, and all we could do was to sniff the air, which, in lazy, curling vapours of fog and mist, carried with it the smell of powder. At last, past four in the afternoon, my battalion was withdrawn from its redoubt, and formed in march column in the rear. A smoke-begrimed Circassian brought an order, and we started, filing past our divisional general and his staff, who bade us God-speed. We tramped for two and a half miles across sloppy meadows, through ankle-deep slush, in a drizzling rain, and presently we came to the hill on which Osman Pasha had his headquarters. There was a brief delay, and then we passed before our leader. I drew my sword, and joined lustily in the cries of *"Allah!"* with which my men greeted their, grand chief. He pointed to the south-west, where Skobeleff and Yunuz Bey were wrestling with all the ferocity which this well-matched couple had already exhibited in the second battle, and shouted, "That is your way. Go on, in the name of God the merciful, the compassionate!"

We passed through Plevna, which was in a state of indescribable confusion, and left town by the Ternina road; and half an hour later we took part in the futile attempt to recover the two redoubts which had been conceded to the skill and impetuosity of Skobeleff.

This brings us to the attack of the Russian left wing. Skobeleff's task had been to conquer the four southern redoubts, which were commanded by Colonel Yunuz Bey, one of the ablest officers in Osman's army, both in bravery and in readiness of resource, and a match even for Skobeleff. The works were his own construction; one—*Yunuz Tabiya*—had been named after him. This last-mentioned redoubt has been accepted as a model by Russian and German writers, and is planned, pictured, measured, and described in every book bearing upon the subject of improvised fortification. The Russian general, mounted on his white horse and followed by his standard-bearer (an apparition familiar not only to his own ranks but also to the Turks owing to the frequency with which he exposed himself in the very front of the fighting-line), headed a series of desperate assaults, all of which were wrecked on the stubborn resistance of mere handfuls of Osmanlis.

Finally, Skobeleff conceived the audacious plan of pushing past these works, conquering the two redoubts on the southern margin of Plevna, and thus separating Yunuz and his force from the main body of the army. He surmised rightly that Yunuz, whom in this wise he had unbeaten on his left flank, was not strong enough to seize the offensive. The fighting was terrible, the losses enormous. Whole battalions of the Turkish forces sent to Yunuz Bey's assistance were wiped off the face of the earth; but the daring project succeeded. *Issa* and *Kavanlik Tabiyas* fell to the white-capped, white-mounted, heavily-whiskered Muscovite. He very nearly battled his way into Plevna; but, although he did not succeed in entering the town, the latter was so gravely compromised by his proximity that immediate and decisive measures had to be taken.

To recover the lost redoubts, to ensure the safety of the town, to relieve the heavily-pressed Yunuz, and to connect the two now disjointed sections of the Turkish Army, the general of brigade, Rifa'at Pasha, organised a scratch detachment of 2,000 men, mostly disbanded troops. My battalion arrived just in the nick of time (5.30 p.m.) to be incorporated with Rifa'at's little force. With this an attack was undertaken on *Kavanlik Tabiya*, which came to utter grief after furious fighting. It was only with the greatest difficulty that a group of 150 men, which included myself, was enabled to save my battalion colours from the rush of pursuing *chasseurs* and Cossacks. Rifa'at was disabled. In the dusk of the waning day we scampered back to *Baghlarbashi Tabiya* (*i.e.* Battery on the Summit of the Vineyards), the most northerly of Yunuz Bey's redoubts. The fighting was over for the day.

In a wet ditch, forming part of Yunuz Bey's system of trenches, with the drizzling sky as a roof, and the slush—pink-coloured by the rivers of human blood which had flown here—for a bed, I spent a night of unmentionable horrors. How the wounded in the adjoining fields groaned throughout those never-ending hours! and how the fierce blaze burst forth from the haystacks and grain-stores in Plevna which the treacherous Bulgarians had set alight! A tall spire of flame rose literally right up into the clouds, and disclosed all the atrocious sights left by the turmoil and devilry of battle. No food, no water—except the pool-slush—no medicine or bandages for the maimed, no hope of victory, cut off from the main body of the army, and before us another day of slaughter! Little wonder that I heard men praying for deliverance from these terrors.

But every suspense has an end, and Wednesday, the 12th September, opened with a hideous grey dawn and a cold wind like the chill of death. Soon it commenced to rain, and the downpour never left off till nightfall.

In the Russian right wing there was again heavy fighting on this day; but all efforts of the dashing Roumanians to capture also the

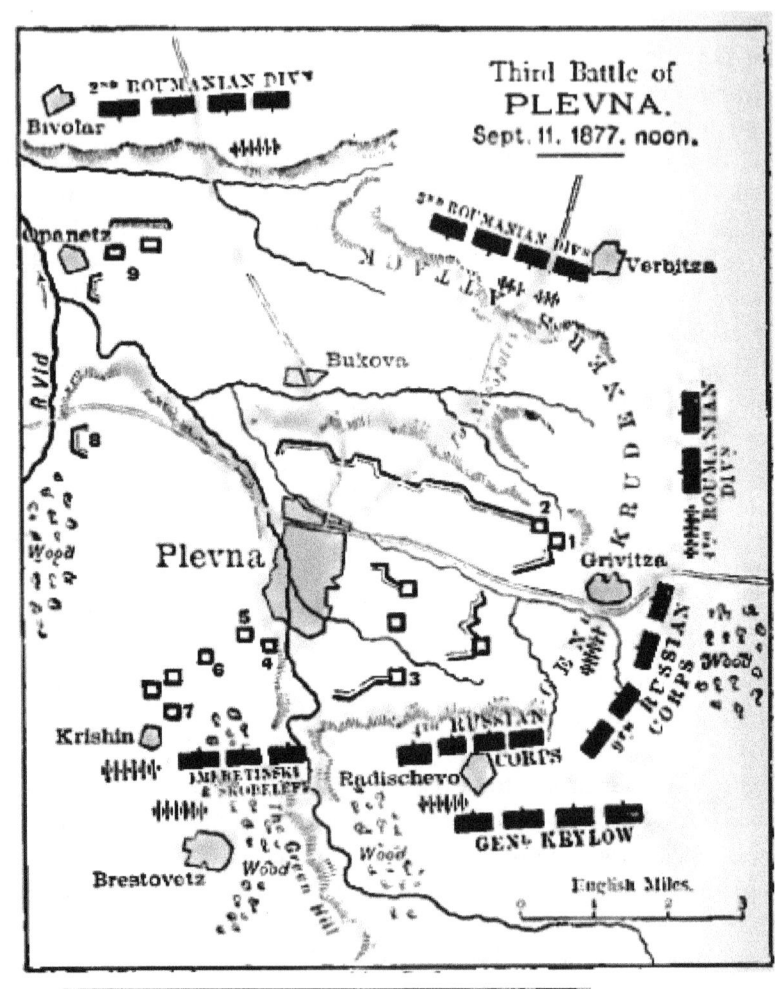

Turkish Defences.
1 Kanli Tabiya or Grivitza Redoubt No. 1.
2. Bash " " " No. 2.
3. Omer " " 6 Baglarbashi Tabiya.
4. Issa " 7. Yunuz "
5. Kavanlik Tabiya. 8 Vid Bridge Redoubt.
9. Opanetz Redoubts.

other Grivitza redoubt were unavailing. In the evening Adil Pasha made a brave but futile attempt to recover the lost work.

In the Russian centre there was no engagement on the 12th. Small wonder; for the few troops left here had become demoralised by the crushing defeat of the previous day, of which they had been either participators or eyewitnesses. General Sotow, also, considered the battle as lost—had, in fact, come to that conclusion already at five on the previous afternoon. Neither the capture of the Grivitza redoubt nor Skobeleff's brilliant and so far successful venture could induce him to modify his opinion. We have it on the authority of the Russian historians that, when Skobeleff urgently asked—nay, implored—for help during the 12th, Sotow responded: "I can send no troops, because I have none to spare: the battle is lost, and you must retreat."

Thus Skobeleff was left to fight out the action alone and to the bitter end. All the time Sotow had seventy-one battalions standing idle, half as much again as the entire Turkish force, but was so utterly cowed as to be unable to dispose of them. The situation is absolutely unique. Let the reader ponder over this: When Osman, in the afternoon of the 12th, staked the very last two battalions of his forty-six, for life and death, and won the game, Sotow had seventy-one battalions idle, forty-one of which had not fired a shot yet, and suffered one of the most disastrous and bloody reverses ever incurred by any general. These things are not surmises by one of the opposite side, but are facts and figures taken from the historical work of the eyewitness and Russian author, Kuropatkin, then a captain in Skobeleff's staff, now, (as at time of first publication), a general. This is the man to whom, next to Skobeleff himself, the Russians owe the splendid defence of *Kavanlik Tabiya* against the Turkish onslaughts.

In the Russian left wing alone the action was fought out to its termination by either victory or defeat. The battle turned now solely and entirely upon the recovery of *Issa* and *Kavanlik Tabiyas* by Osman's forces. At half-past seven in the morning the Turks, reinforced by seven battalions despatched by Osman Pasha from other parts of the camp to the scene of conflict, attacked *Kavanlik Tabiya*, led by the chief of Osman's staff, Tahir Pasha. I had again the honour to participate in the fighting, and my men had already reached the last trench in front of the redoubt when the whole attacking column—eleven and a half battalions, 5,000 men approximately—was stopped and ordered back by Tahir's express command. The reason for this sudden check upon a promising assault has never been made known. Osman was

Russian camp outside Plevna.

furious, deprived Tahir of his command, sent his last available two battalions, and entrusted Colonel Tewfik Bey with the herculean task of recovering the lost redoubts and thus winning the battle. It is but right to mention that Tahir evidently vindicated his character, for he was reinstalled the next day, and retained the post of chief-of-staff until the end of the campaign.

At 3.30 in the afternoon the Turks played their last stake in the great game by undertaking, with every available man, a desperate assault on *Kavanlik Tabiya*. The attacking force numbered thirteen and a half battalions, mustering, after the losses incurred, no more than 5,500 men, instead of the nominal 10,800. The onslaught was delivered with the utmost precision and vigour, and at 4 o'clock the lost redoubt fell into the hands of the jubilant Osmanlis. My battalion was again in the foremost line, and my men were among the first to scale the parapet. Then *Issa Tabiya* was abandoned by the Russians, and at 5 o'clock, as dusk was setting in, the greatest battle of the Russo-Turkish war had been fought and won.

The sight which greeted me as I climbed into *Kavanlik Tabiya* utterly surpasses my powers of description. There were walls and parapets built of dead bodies, erected by the Russians to close the rear entrances of the work; there were piles of corpses and maimed men; there were brooks and rivers of blood. Skobeleff had lost 40 *per cent*, of his force (or 8,000 men), and his division had to be broken up. Of the Turkish casualties in the battle, four-fifths (or 4,000 men) fall upon this wing.

As soon as Skobeleff had been driven out of his position, the Russian Army commenced a general retreat, on all points except the north-east corner, where the Roumanians retained the conquered Grivitza redoubt. Every other section of the huge semi-circle retired to a distance of six to ten miles from the Turkish front. In fact, Sotow contemplated a total withdrawal of his army beyond the Osma, and it was only the grand duke's peremptory order which compelled him to abandon this idea.

During the battle the Russian-Roumanian cavalry had quietly taken possession of the western approaches to Plevna, which they held until the 24th September, when they were driven out of their positions by a reinforcement column coming from Orkanye. Then for exactly one month the roads were open and were utilised almost daily for bringing in stores. On the 24th October the circle of investment was once more completed, and this time for good.

Russian attack upon a Turkish Redoubt

The Russian losses in this battle of giants, which lasted twenty-eight hours, amounted to 18,600 men (inclusive of 5,000 Roumanians); the Turkish losses to 5,000, in killed and *hors de combat*. The Turks had 2,000 Russian-Roumanian prisoners, mostly wounded, but had themselves hardly any "missing" men to record. On both sides the casualties included an exceptionally large share of officers of high rank. Of the twenty-four Turkish redoubt commanders, nine had been killed or disabled. Nine redoubts had been assailed; eight others had participated in the artillery combat; seven had remained unengaged.

The man to whom—next to the indomitable leader, Osman Pasha—the Turks owe their victory is Tewfik, who recovered the two redoubts to which Skobeleff had clung with such wonderful tenacity. He was promoted to brigadier's rank, was publicly thanked in a general order read out during parade, and was ever afterwards popular with the troops. The Turkish army was in a state of indescribable confusion. It took days to restore order and cohesion. To give only one instance of the straits to which the Turks had been reduced by draining their resources towards the south to face Skobeleff: the north front, seven miles long, garrisoned originally by fourteen battalions, was held by four on the evening of the 12th. It was a providential thing for us that the enemy did not attack us here. And to mention but one of the after-horrors of battle: the negotiations between the Turks and Roumanians to establish a line of demarcation in the space dividing the two Grivitza redoubts failed, and as a consequence the 2,000 corpses on this spot remained unburied, and were, under the eyes of the men in the trenches, devoured by carrion crows, vultures, and vagrant dogs.

My company had lost twenty-five in killed and disabled out of a total of 145; but on the evening after the battle quite sixty men more were missing, including the entire squad of my friend Lieutenant Seymour, a young Englishman who subsequently gave his life for Plevna. These had all merely gone astray, and turned up the same night or next day. To make up for this temporary loss I had forty or fifty strangers in my ranks.

Seymour and his men had somehow found their way into Plevna, and had assisted in hunting down and punishing the miscreants who had fired the haystacks—a most dangerous task, since the town contained thousands of traitors. My friend and forty men had to face and charge an infuriated Bulgarian rabble of several hundred men, women, and children.

The fact that the Roumanians conquered and held one Grivitza redoubt is sometimes taken as a proof that the *Czar's* army was not defeated in this battle. An action is a success if the purpose for which it is fought is achieved; if this is not the case, the action must be held to be a failure. The Russians had engaged their enemy with the avowed intent of storming and taking the entrenched camp of Plevna, and they had conquered one small redoubt out of twenty-four, large and small, and that one, as all critics and historians admit, of no tactical importance, the possession of which did them subsequently more harm than good; the loss of which proved to be of no injurious consequences to the Turks. Add also that on all points but one the assailants retreated beyond fighting-range and left the defenders in possession of the vast battlefield, even to bury their slain, and the Turks will be deemed fully justified in boasting of the third Battle of Plevna as one of the most brilliant victories ever won by the armies of the Crescent.

It is somewhat remarkable that not one of the Russian generals who had been defeated by the Turks received, apparently, as much as a reprimand for his misfortune. Schilder-Schuldner, who was beaten on the 20th July; Krüdener and Prince Schachowskoy, who were so utterly routed on the 30th July; Krylow and Schnitnikoff, whose forces were well-nigh annihilated on the 11th and 12th September, and their chief, Sotow, all retained their commands, and, to outward appearances, the full confidence of their superiors.

One feature distinguishes the third Battle of Plevna from many world-stirring actions—the enormous numerical superiority of the defeated. The Russians outnumbered the Turks by three to one in men, and six to one in guns. And yet nobody will deny the wonderful stubbornness of the Russian soldiery, whilst the dash of the Roumanian infantry was the admiration of all who saw the army of the young kingdom in the field. For the display of abstruse tactical science there was neither opportunity nor inducement. The great September battle was won by the superior *morale* of the Turkish leader, by the indomitable will of one individual against which hordes and numbers counted as naught.

The immediate effects of the battle were momentous, the ultimate result was *nil*. The Russians had come to the conclusion that Plevna was impregnable. Dazed and faint with slaughter, they had reeled back, all fight knocked out of them, and for many weeks Sotow's army was utterly demoralised. It was only when the engineer's skill was summoned that the troops recovered their *morale*. It fell to the lot of the veteran defender of Sebastopol to starve the victorious *pasha* into submission. The Turkish spade had won two big battles (not counting the first battle of Plevna, which was fought in the open); the Russian counterspade procured the fall of the best-defended town of modern times. But this was not accomplished until three months later, and not until after Osman had struck a last and stupendous blow for liberty. Todleben's calculating genius succeeded where Skobeleff's and Gourko's audacity had failed. The patient skill of the mathematician and engineer achieved that for which 50,000 soldier-heroes had sacrificed life and limb in vain.

Russian wounded leaving Plevna

ALSO FROM LEONAUR
AVAILABLE IN SOFTCOVER OR HARDCOVER WITH DUST JACKET

AT THEM WITH THE BAYONET *by Donald F. Featherstone*—The first Anglo-Sikh War 1845-1846.

STEPHEN CRANE'S BATTLES *by Stephen Crane*—Nine Decisive Battles Recounted by the Author of 'The Red Badge of Courage'.

THE GURKHA WAR *by H. T. Prinsep*—The Anglo-Nepalese Conflict in North East India 1814-1816.

FIRE & BLOOD *by G. R. Gleig*—The burning of Washington & the battle of New Orleans, 1814, through the eyes of a young British soldier.

SOUND ADVANCE! *by Joseph Anderson*—Experiences of an officer of HM 50th regiment in Australia, Burma & the Gwalior war.

THE CAMPAIGN OF THE INDUS *by Thomas Holdsworth*—Experiences of a British Officer of the 2nd (Queen's Royal) Regiment in the Campaign to Place Shah Shuja on the Throne of Afghanistan 1838 - 1840.

WITH THE MADRAS EUROPEAN REGIMENT IN BURMA *by John Butler*—The Experiences of an Officer of the Honourable East India Company's Army During the First Anglo-Burmese War 1824 - 1826.

IN ZULULAND WITH THE BRITISH ARMY *by Charles L. Norris-Newman*—The Anglo-Zulu war of 1879 through the first-hand experiences of a special correspondent.

BESIEGED IN LUCKNOW *by Martin Richard Gubbins*—The first Anglo-Sikh War 1845-1846.

A TIGER ON HORSEBACK *by L. March Phillips*—The Experiences of a Trooper & Officer of Rimington's Guides - The Tigers - during the Anglo-Boer war 1899 - 1902.

SEPOYS, SIEGE & STORM *by Charles John Griffiths*—The Experiences of a young officer of H.M.'s 61st Regiment at Ferozepore, Delhi ridge and at the fall of Delhi during the Indian mutiny 1857.

CAMPAIGNING IN ZULULAND *by W. E. Montague*—Experiences on campaign during the Zulu war of 1879 with the 94th Regiment.

THE STORY OF THE GUIDES *by G.J. Younghusband*—The Exploits of the Soldiers of the famous Indian Army Regiment from the northwest frontier 1847 - 1900.

AVAILABLE ONLINE AT **www.leonaur.com**
AND FROM ALL GOOD BOOK STORES

ALSO FROM LEONAUR
AVAILABLE IN SOFTCOVER OR HARDCOVER WITH DUST JACKET

ZULU: 1879 *by D.C.F. Moodie & the Leonaur Editors*—The Anglo-Zulu War of 1879 from contemporary sources: First Hand Accounts, Interviews, Dispatches, Official Documents & Newspaper Reports.

THE RED DRAGOON *by W.J. Adams*—With the 7th Dragoon Guards in the Cape of Good Hope against the Boers & the Kaffir tribes during the 'war of the axe' 1843-48'.

THE RECOLLECTIONS OF SKINNER OF SKINNER'S HORSE *by James Skinner*—James Skinner and his 'Yellow Boys' Irregular cavalry in the wars of India between the British, Mahratta, Rajput, Mogul, Sikh & Pindarree Forces.

A CAVALRY OFFICER DURING THE SEPOY REVOLT *by A. R. D. Mackenzie*—Experiences with the 3rd Bengal Light Cavalry, the Guides and Sikh Irregular Cavalry from the outbreak to Delhi and Lucknow.

A NORFOLK SOLDIER IN THE FIRST SIKH WAR *by J W Baldwin*—Experiences of a private of H.M. 9th Regiment of Foot in the battles for the Punjab, India 1845-6.

TOMMY ATKINS' WAR STORIES: 14 FIRST HAND ACCOUNTS—Fourteen first hand accounts from the ranks of the British Army during Queen Victoria's Empire.

THE WATERLOO LETTERS *by H. T. Siborne*—Accounts of the Battle by British Officers for its Foremost Historian.

NEY: GENERAL OF CAVALRY VOLUME 1—1769-1799 *by Antoine Bulos*—The Early Career of a Marshal of the First Empire.

NEY: MARSHAL OF FRANCE VOLUME 2—1799-1805 *by Antoine Bulos*—The Early Career of a Marshal of the First Empire.

AIDE-DE-CAMP TO NAPOLEON *by Philippe-Paul de Ségur*—For anyone interested in the Napoleonic Wars this book, written by one who was intimate with the strategies and machinations of the Emperor, will be essential reading.

TWILIGHT OF EMPIRE *by Sir Thomas Ussher & Sir George Cockburn*—Two accounts of Napoleon's Journeys in Exile to Elba and St. Helena: Narrative of Events by Sir Thomas Ussher & Napoleon's Last Voyage: Extract of a diary by Sir George Cockburn.

PRIVATE WHEELER *by William Wheeler*—The letters of a soldier of the 51st Light Infantry during the Peninsular War & at Waterloo.

AVAILABLE ONLINE AT **www.leonaur.com**
AND FROM ALL GOOD BOOK STORES

www.ingramcontent.com/pod-product-compliance
Lightning Source LLC
Chambersburg PA
CBHW031624160426
43196CB00006B/275